Civil Leadership as the Future of Leadership

Civil Leadership
as the Future
of Leadership

Harnessing the disruptive power
of citizens

STEVEN DE WAAL

Warden Press

© 2018 Steven de Waal, Utrecht

ISBN:
Paperback: 978-94-92004-71-0
E-book (Epub): 978-94-92004-72-7
E-book (Kindle): 978-94-92004-73-4

Translated from the Dutch by Erwin Postma, Malaga
Cover and interior design: Sander Pinkse Boekproductie, Amsterdam
Photo author: Renee Klein, Amsterdam

This edition published by Warden Press, Amsterdam

wardenpress.com

Contents

Preface

Disruption has been a crucial strategic concept and a fundamental challenge for companies for some time now. The term 'disruption' accurately captures the unsettling, threatening, and undermining impact that the arrival of a total newcomer has on existing players in a market, a newcomer that they did not see coming. This kind of disruptive emergence of a new player also brings revolutionary changes to the total playing field in their market segment. By now, everyone is fully aware of the technological factors that are causing market disruption. These include websites with a multitude of options and review features for users, online peer-to-peer bartering platforms that match supply and demand, often supported by Artificial Intelligence that remembers a user's earlier preferences and suggests products a user might like, and social media that compile and share news and views on products and services. Disruption is triggered by a total newcomer penetrating a market segment without using traditional and well-known tactics such as undercutting or taking over existing players, but rather by using new technology to target customers directly, steal customers away from existing players, bind customers, and ultimately take over consumer buying power and influence on buying decisions.

None of this will come as news to a strategic market observer or market trend watcher. Still, from my perspective, which is that of strategic management in the public sector and its two primary private-sector drivers (active citizenship and social entrepreneurship[1]), it is incomprehensible why we take such a restricted view of the impact of such technologies, considering it solely a cause of disruption that is affecting only the market. I am seeing equally large-scale and revolutionary impact on the public domain, coming from the same technologies that are greatly facilitating and stimulating active citizenship, which is having far-reaching consequences for politics, democracy, and public services. This impact is not merely of a technological nature (such as more and faster data sharing, more cameras and sensors in the public space, the use of algorithms and big data in political campaigns, and the use of wearables to track fitness, monitor health care interventions, and record educational progress) or a commercial nature (such as new platforms with different services), but it changes mainly the mindset of and bonds between citizens, also in their mutual relationships and collaboration. These new technologies are thus, in my opinion, having a revolutionary impact on our human existence, on our society, and on our citizenship, meaning that they have the capacity to, as we can already see now in our everyday lives, lead to major and fundamental disruptions in politics, in democracy, and in the approach to and functioning of public services such as health care, education, energy, and security.

This essay intends to describe and analyze the impact itself, as well as the underlying trends and technologies. Loosely paraphrasing a well-known remark by Bill Clinton, my slogan in doing so is: '*It is not the technology, stupid, it is the mindset and power of citizens*'.[2] Needless to say, the nature, pace, impact, and extent of the disruption of politics, democracy, and public services are not the same as when we talk about market disruption. I will detail all these aspects of the disruption, as few seem to realize that this disruption is already ongoing and that its impact, also globally, is already visible in certain areas.

This essay follows from and is based on numerous lectures I have given about these subjects in the Netherlands and Europe over the past months. My lectures were attended by executives and non-executives from many different fields, ranging from health care, energy, and public housing to education, politics, and business. Given my personal background as a strategic organizational consultant, entrepreneur, and former CEO of Boer&Croon (a leading European management consultancy firm), and as the chairman of several non-executive boards (in areas such as professional soccer and the culture sector), I always seek out audiences made up of peers to test out whether my insights are adequate and usable in today's executive governance practices. Their responses to and comments on my lectures provided some of the questions and lessons from governance practices that I addressed in the research on which this book is based. On top of that, I organized several think tank sessions with citizens and executives to go over draft versions of this essay, the results of which I subsequently incorporated into the essay.

My entire professional life, I have worked on conceptual development and theory building, so I have always operated between executive practices at organizations in the private and public sectors on the one hand and academic and philosophical analysis on the other. This has led to me publishing a considerable number of books, mainly in Dutch, set up a private-sector think tank called Public SPACE (see www.publicspace. nl), and earn a PhD with a dissertation about civil leadership in 2014, which was later published as *The Value(s) of Civil Leaders* (Eleven, 2014). I have actively contributed to the debate about civil leadership through a large number of lectures I gave and debates I moderated, also internationally, for similar audiences of elected officials, executives, and others with administrative responsibility. Experiences and insights acquired through such exchanges have been incorporated into this essay.

What I hope to achieve with this book above all is for one end of the spectrum of people who are actively involved in the subject, namely that of *elected officials and those with administrative responsibility in the public sector*, not to be taken by surprise by the disruption and impact of new technologies like many CEOs in the private sector were several years back. Many of these CEOs who failed to see the changes coming, or who simply denied or ignored them, have meanwhile seen their companies topple, go bankrupt, or be taken over. We simply cannot afford to let the same happen to all the great institutions of democracy and public services. We cannot afford to allow the same kind of disruption, or even destruction, to happen in the public sector. Market disruption has, however, taught us that a fundamental and drastic rethink and overhaul of organizational structures or institutions is needed to prevent that we lose sight of the principles on which these institutions are based, to prevent them from disappearing from the visible fabric of the public sector and from people's everyday lives. Only a timely strategic response will prevent that from happening. However, unfortunately, I am still seeing the same psychological phenomenon of denial and disregard in public sector and semi-public sector circles, the same mindset that led to the lack of strategic insight that has done so much damage in the private sector. That said, I am also seeing, and this is the good news, when I give my lectures and moderate debates (in 2018), that this is changing in many areas: the fierce denial and subconscious or conscious ignoring are starting to wane.

Given the mission of my think tank Public SPACE, which I pioneered in 2001, there is naturally also an entirely different end of the spectrum that I feel is slightly more important than that of the officials with governance responsibility I referred to above, and that is the end of the *citizens* who (want to) *actively engage* with their communities, with society as a whole, and with public issues. This is the basis of civil leadership. And that is where both ends of the spectrum actually overlap: citizenship can also be exercised from executive positions, which, in my dissertation, I referred to as 'citizenship in the boardroom.' I hope, and I am actively trying to make this happen through this book, that active citizens and their civil leaders will realize that new technologies will increase their power, scope, and organizational capacity to get things done together as citizens, anywhere in the public space and in response to any social issue! The days that we, as citizens and voters, delegated this to or passively let governments and executives take care of that for us, or were equally passive in our relationships with companies, seem to be well and truly behind us.

The major revolution that has been unleashed by these issues and new possibilities, which has meanwhile caught steam and reached a strategically crucial point, is in my view one that hits very close to home for our human existence and society, so much so that I have chosen to refer to it as the **Digital Civil Revolution**. It is time we took a close, open-minded, and courageous look at this revolution and got you strategically prepared and involved at this strategic point in time and, hopefully, trigger your own civil leadership.

I
Introduction

Today's new technologies that have disrupted markets are now triggering a third revolution, after the agricultural revolution and the industrial revolution. This third revolution is fundamentally changing our human existence, our communities, and our citizenship, and I am calling it the Digital Civil Revolution. This is not good news for everyone. Those in power will resist, authoritarian governments will try to block change, new technologies can and will also be abused, and citizens are not used to their new responsibilities. (Civil) leadership is needed to be able to seize the potential benefits of this new technology-driven revolution for us all.

The Digital Civil Revolution

The technological revolution that is currently changing our lives has not yet petered out. Quite the opposite. The continued development of the Internet and the associated global availability and shareability of just about everything, from data to images to experiences, which reached maturity in the 1990s, could even be classed as old news. This would, in fact, be an observation based on that typically modern sense of time and of the rapid alternation and availability of data and media caused by the Internet and the communication overload that comes with it. However, this is only one of many interrelated technological changes that are ongoing simultaneously. The current situation is therefore sometimes referred to as the next phase of the industrial revolution.[3] I, however, believe this is based too much on an assumption of continuity, while it is simply contradictory to define a revolution as a continuation of a previous revolution. As if we are currently merely seeing the next step of industrialization, and nothing more than the next phase in the process of technology revolutionizing human processes surrounding production, the economy, and wealth. True, this is indeed going on to some extent, but there is much more to it. The impact is much broader and affects, if not changes, the most fundamental foundations of our being: our human existence and communities. This is why I prefer to call it the **third revolution following the industrial revolution**. We are currently in the middle of a revolution of people's information-processing, communication, and intellectual skills, which are partly taken over by machines. As a result, the revolution is drastically changing humanity itself, its communities, and society. Our speech and communication, our intelligence, our brains, the images on our retina and in our minds, how we gather and process knowledge, it is all being automated, or at least supported by numerous, often intelligent or self-learning robots. In addition to the data and communication explosion triggered by the Internet and its platforms and websites, such automation comes in the form of artificial intelligence, *the Internet of Things,* and mobile (IT and media) technology through satellites.[4] This revolution therefore goes to the core of our human existence and how we view and think about ourselves as humans. Previous revolutions, both the agricultural revolution and the various stages of the industrial revolution, can, with hindsight, still be seen as focused on specific aspects of our survival as humans (food production and manual labor), and did indeed have major and revolutionary impact on our lives and survival (the parceling out of agricultural land, increasing wealth and influence of feudal landowners, the shift from rural to urban residency, and the shift from working the land to working in factories and offices). But the current revolution, which I will refer to as the **Digital Civil Revolution**, goes to the core of our existence as humans and our society. It brings sweeping technological changes that not only support and strengthen our uniquely human capabilities in a revolutionary way, but also directly and profoundly change our humanness, partly through their impact on how we live together and interact as humans.

The impact that this revolution is having is meanwhile most evident in the market, and rightfully referred to as disruption. Besides the market, the other two areas of the institutional triangle, the state and civil society,[5] are now also facing fundamental changes. However, the impact of technological developments on their functioning or even continued existence is not yet as severe and instantly undermining as the impact felt in the market. Still, the first signs of impact on the state and civil society are already visible, especially to an objective outsider. Most stakeholders are still refusing to face up to the disruption in the public sector and civil society (much in the same way as markets responded when they were on the receiving end of it), thinking that the disruption will remain limited to the market domain. But the impact is already felt, especially in politics, largely because of the market-style mechanisms in politics, and the impact will only increase across the public domain. Stakeholders in these circles have been lulled into a false sense of security by the fact that, in comparison to the market, there are factors at work in the civil service and public services that are delaying and cushioning the impact. Such buffers and sluggishness are absent or at least less prevalent in politics. Professional politicians operate to a clear market mechanism, even though they will be the first to deny that. In the political marketplace, politicians compete to get people to vote for them, and this market has meanwhile been disrupted to the same extent as the commercial market. This is shown by the sudden emergence of new politicians (Trump) who are making better and smarter use of new technology than their more established competitors, by the success of movements (Macron) that manage to get voters to join new platforms away from traditional political parties in an unprecedented short time span that can only be explained by the use of new technologies, and by increasing swarm behavior by voters and the resulting more extreme election results[6]. For an example of such swarm behavior by voters, just look at Emmanuel Macron's victory in France. The party, La République en Marche!, he founded in 2016, five months before the elections, won an absolute majority at the elections in 2017. Macron's movement won 308 of the 577 seats in France's Assemblée Nationale. Later in this book, I will explain how Macron's victory was produced by a kind of synchronized swarm of potential voters, who realized that their vote for Macron would, despite him being an outsider in the political landscape at the time, and despite widespread warnings from traditional parties not to vote for Macron, not be a wasted vote.

Disruption in the market concerns mainly how we communicate, stay informed, and share information, and, therefore, how we organize. Work changes, connections change, markets as transaction mechanisms change, the purpose of *middlemen* (such as brokers, banks, travel agencies) no longer goes without saying, and organizations are therefore changing as the vehicle for human labor. The hierarchy, management, identity, and recognizability of organizations, in particular, are no longer clear or the most important strategic factors to lean on.

The technological revolution, therefore, affects the core of our human existence and our evolutionary advantage over other species, which is based on cooperation and communication. The latest theories[7] about this no longer claim that our brains have grown in proportion to the rest of our body, more so than seen in any other species, as a result of random mutations. And they no longer claim that this random growth of our brains led to us developing language and starting to join forces on an increasing scale. And that this explains our organizational capabilities, as if it were a kind of physical fluke that has been preserved in the gene pool on a typically evolutionary but mainly biological basis, because it brought success in the struggle for survival and adaptation (*survival of the fittest*) within physical contexts and in our competition with other species. According to these latest insights, it all happened the other way round: our ancestors discovered the major evolutionary benefits of collaboration and organization in increasingly large groups, partly because humans were good at developing and using tools and teaching others to use them (education is one of the mainstays of our human existence). These human capabilities of calculation, estimation, tool development and use, education, and working together in general can even be seen as the basis of strategic thinking and behavior.[8] This is how humans developed language, arithmetic, and the ability to structure. The evolutionary edge that these new skills and behaviors gave us over other species subsequently propelled, in a genetic and a Darwinist sense, the growth and further use in an evolutionarily advantageous way, of our brains. This is how having big brains gave humans a major evolutionary edge over other species, allowing humans to further build on the skills they had discovered, which compensated for the fact that such big brains came with a greater need for energy and caused physical difficulties during childbirth. Certain scientists, most notably archaeologists and anthropologists, have branded this the *human revolution*, the development and importance of symbols and symbolic order as the basis of homo sapiens. In short, communication and organization are fundamental for the nature and success of the human being as a social animal. This is why the current disruptive revolution is having such a massive impact, as it touches on our humanity, our continued existence, and how we operate as humans, as well as our way of being in the world. The disruptive revolution therefore not only impacts on our human functioning, but also on our view of humanity. Who do we, humans, think we are and what makes us human, what makes us unique, what binds us together or sets us apart? Every truly strategic and mainly also philosophical response to this disruptive revolution will therefore have to address these fundamental elements while simultaneously bringing the people concerned on board. And that is where *leadership* comes in.

The definition and practices of leadership have given rise to numerous misconceptions and myths that, as they are being challenged by this third revolution, need to be revised. I am talking about myths such as the idea that your formal position is an indication of your leadership, which suggests that managers always show and must show leadership, even attributing special qualities to them, ranging from visionary and charismatic to almost saintlike in their good intentions and idealism.[9] Hereafter, I will argue that the Digital Civil Revolution not only calls for *more* leadership, as always under exceptional and challenging conditions, but also for a *different kind* of leadership. Technological disruption not only changes the market and politics, but also changes our view of humanity, our human existence, thus creating a need for a different kind of leadership.

The basic idea of the analysis and argument of this essay is that disruptive technologies will create an entirely new philosophical and strategic context for all our actions, our humanity, and communities, on all geographical scales (neighborhoods and districts, cities, countries, globally) and in all areas in which we operate (politics, market, and civil society). It is now fundamentally changing how we organize and lead in general. I will go into this in Part II. This is so fundamental that it directly affects how we interact and organize ourselves, how we view humanity, and our social, economic, and political interrelations. In much of the literature, as well as in many analyses, the technological innovations that are currently ongoing, and their impact, are viewed only in the context of the market sector and the disruption they create there. This is too narrow a perspective. After all, the impact touches directly on our human existence and our communities, as becomes apparent, albeit certainly not only there, in how we organize ourselves for production purposes. It is therefore not only about this being the next phase of the industrial revolution, but also about an entirely new, subsequent revolution, which I refer to as the Digital Civil Revolution. Picking up on this misconception, I will further go into the massive and already visible impact on our public communal lives and organizations, (democratic) politics, and civil service (which will be covered in Part III). In the interlude, I will recap, because I expect we are going to need strategic intelligence and new leadership to make it through this revolution in a way that inspires confidence and hope, while preserving our democratic institutions, good public services, and an active civil society. Both steering this human revolution (which is triggered by the last technological revolutions) and shaping the resulting new human connections require a new kind of leadership from inspiring and reassuring leaders for this fundamentally new future. I have previously referred to this as civil leadership. It requires a fundamental overhaul of our leadership views, philosophy, and practices. This is what Part IV will be about. Part IV will conclude with clear and specific tips and recommendations drawn from civil leadership practices that I have observed. Despite the intense revolution that we find ourselves in at the moment, with all the uncertainties, insecurities, and concerns it entails, I will close with a hope-inspiring outlook for the future, assuming that we realize on time what needs to be done now, and assuming we get the new brand of leaders we need (Part V). This is why the need for and nature of strategic intelligence, and the lack thereof, is a recurring theme in this essay: we need our decision-makers and leaders to see this revolution coming and timely and adequately respond to it. One objective of this book is to encourage exactly that, even though I realize that rational analyses on paper cannot actually do that. The notes at the end of the book are sometimes no more than references to works cited, while others are more detailed suggestions for further reading on a specific subject and yet others will point out in which areas further discussion is still ongoing and which theories are still the subject of debate and philosophical and conceptual quests.

II
Disruptive Technologies
Empower Citizens

The new technologies triggering the Digital Civil Revolution are causing a shift in the triangle of state, market, and civil society that exists in all Western nations and economies. Civil society is becoming more empowered, more autonomous, better informed, and better organized. This will take a lot of getting used to for the state and the market. Executives and active citizens therefore need strategic intelligence to be able to see the disruption of (democratic) politics and public institutions and services coming and take the right steps on time. After all, the Digital Civil Revolution will also change the way we organize ourselves, what our organizations look like, and how our organizations operate. Competition in the platform economy and the internal applications of the same technologies are increasingly turning organizations themselves into platforms as well. This disrupts the role and purpose of managers, which will further propel the shift toward more leadership. It is ultimately about achieving a new blend of management, leadership, and strategic choices, which must also be aligned with the paradoxical phenomenon that the advent of virtual technologies is now actually showing us how important physical, emotional, and direct communication is for us humans. The greatest advance, which is already materializing in some areas, but which has by no means picked up the kind of momentum yet that it has in many market segments, is that of the rise of citizenship platforms. These are platforms that allow citizens with certain ideas and intentions in terms of getting involved and doing their bit to engage with social or democratic issues and policy plans, empowering them to be part of the solution. We still have a long way to go. Although the technology is already available and there are pioneering examples of such platforms and their impact and influence, these innovations are slow to take root due to the ongoing power struggle surrounding them and the lack of civil leadership.

1

Market Disruption: Phenomenon and Technological Explanation

Disruption in the market caused by the new technological revolution has been going on for over ten years now. Companies such as Airbnb and Uber came out of nothing and managed to lure customers away from traditional hotels and taxi companies through direct online communication on their platforms. These platforms allowed them to offer those consumers better and faster service, facilitating peer-to-peer bartering for things such as unused rooms and cars. In addition, the extensive customer reviews of homes and services written by fellow platform users helped consumers make their choices. Information provided in such reviews was the kind of information that traditional providers never wanted to publish, at least not without extensive filtering, censorship, and littered with advertising. People the world over had the same direct and faster services available to them through the same technology on their smartphones.

The new market entrants conquered the market by pulling in customers, their spending power, and their product and provider selection mechanisms through the better, faster communication and service they were able to offer. This is how platforms take over a market, which often leads to disruption of that market for the traditional players. Markets are seized from the customer side, through direct access to customers, and not in the traditional way by taking over an existing company along with their existing product offering, expertise, and equipment. These existing companies are basically sucked dry, as their customers and their influence on customers' purchase decisions are taken away from them, and there is nothing they can do about it. Without customers, and direct access to them to understand their purchase decisions, it is difficult to do business, and some companies therefore topple, primarily because they see their revenue drop or face increasing revenue uncertainty while they still have to service their assets and pay their wage bills. The new platforms, on the other hand, barely have overheads for assets or staff, and their great scope, both on the supply and the demand side of the market, ultimately gives them great revenue certainty.

Disruption in and of the market is therefore called disruption for a reason: it is about the undermining of the market position of traditional market players by unknown emerging competitors from outside the market in a way that they did not see coming. There has been some theoretical debate about market disruption, about the phenomenon itself and how to define it. In 1995, Clayton Christensen came up with the concept of disruptive innovation.[10] Since then, the definition has shifted greatly, partly due to the major underlying technological changes and their impact on the economy, leading to the platform economy, as well as on the back of new insights into growing business practices in response to disruption. In this book, I am going by what I think is the most adequate and modern definition: 'the rise of new and unexpected competitors from outside the current market, innovative in and through their direct access to and exchange with customers.'

Disruption was able to occur because newcomers entered an existing market with a technological advantage. They made their innovative product offering available on a technological platform that was so sophisticated that customers could be served much better and quicker. As a result, these newcomers basically took over traditional players' customers without having to take over an existing company, effectively devouring those companies on the customer side. As a peer-to-peer service that matches supply to demand between consumers, or by making the existing products of traditional providers more accessible and more attractive to buy on the platform thanks to clearer comparative information about quality and price, these newcomers did not have to invest in equipment (such as vehicles) or real estate (such as hotels). Aside from investments in a new website or platform and online advertising, the whole enterprise of entering the market required little investment. It was an 'only-win-no-lose' option. By now, the technological edge of these platforms has become so strategically decisive that successful platform facilitators such as Apple and Google are making their first moves as new entrants in existing markets such as retail, the pharmaceutical industry, and the automotive industry.

The massive capital they have acquired allows them to invest in many different markets and options. A decade ago, this was unthinkable, as all newcomers had to overcome barriers (in the market and toward consumers) in the form of the investments they had to make, the exceptional professional expertise they had to acquire, and the reputation of the existing competitors. But when a newcomer is able to provide a faster, direct, and global service to your customers, and is able to build closer relationships with customers through online platforms and smartphones than your loyalty programs will ever achieve, the barriers to entry are all but eliminated.

In one respect, disruption is about the emergence of platforms (such as Booking.com) that take over your customers, their spending power, and your influence on their purchase decisions or that enable peer-to-peer transactions (such as Uber and Airbnb) without the involvement of existing companies. This can ultimately lead to a situation where the old companies and business models become redundant. There is a real possibility of this happening to, for example, banks. Cash transactions are declining, as digital transactions are at least as easy to process and more secure. One prime example is that of Alipay, which emerged in China and is smartphone-based. This platform gives users a personal wallet on an entirely digital and mobile system. Alipay has meanwhile amassed 520 million user globally, and they expect this figure to grow to 2 billion by 2025. They handle huge transaction volumes. On one of China's most popular shopping days in 2017, Singles' Day on November 11, this platform processed purchase transactions totaling 25 billion dollars, 90% of which through cellphones.[11]

In a market, disruption is immediately visible and perceptible. We are all familiar with the platforms and the services they offer, and we all use them. We have no qualms about ditching any loyalty to traditional brands and brand awareness that has grown over the years, except only perhaps for our most favorite shop, hotel, or clothing brand. But the new technology and options also make us more alert to possible competing offerings, even against our favorite brand. Even our brand loyalty has therefore become transient and more rational.

In the platform economy, the market is still the market, albeit that it is no longer a market of competing companies that offer products and services, but a market of competing platforms[12] that are looking to maximize their customer reach and influence on customers' choice processes on the one hand, as well as their reach in their links to existing product and service offerings. Platforms basically compete on network reach, the nature and scope of their hub function between supply and demand. Such competition is still based on customers' legitimate considerations: am I getting good service from this provider, do they understand me, are the peer reviews of services and products relevant and insightful, am I empowered to make good and quick choices, do I have control over what I am actually provided with, is it aligned with my modern lifestyle, can I use my phone or other mobile device? Aside from that, there is another feature to this kind of competition, one that we know from network and complexity theory: winner takes all. The success of a platform is made by great customer reach on the one hand and by a vast product and/or service offering on the other: the larger the platform on both the supply side and the demand side, the more attractive it is for customers and companies to join. Due to this self-reinforcing effect, platforms that are less successful than the winner on either side soon disappear. We are all familiar with market players, including platforms, that have come and gone in this way, either because they were taken over or because they went out of business. Platforms disappearing as a result of competition between platforms, is something we are likely to see happen more and more, as newcomers will actively compete with other platforms and start-ups will increasingly try to establish their own platforms.

But this immediately visible and great direct effect on the market clouds our view of how that same disruptive technology is also and already having an impact outside the market, on our public behavior, on our political mentality, on our approach to democracy, and on our interactions as good citizens. It is, in fact, quite conceivable that this was also brought on by the disruption in the market. Customers have meanwhile been conditioned by the functioning and services of the platforms in their market transactions, and they have therefore gotten used to (or have even been spoiled by) the competition factors I referred to earlier. Quick service, for example, including the ability to track and trace deliveries, 24/7 customer service, transportation, etc., is something that customers get used to, also in peer-to-peer bartering for surplus car capacity, residential space, and DIY jobs. As the technology develops further, photos and video will increasingly be used in that respect, allowing users to visually track their orders, making the whole process and necessary tests and checks even more transparent. Consumers have grown accustomed to being able to draw on the quality assessments of previous customers in their purchase decisions. Many customers suspect that providers' official reputation and quality assessments of products and services may be manipulated by the providers themselves. There is therefore great demand for more objective additional quality assessments by peers. And finally: customers appreciate and have meanwhile gotten used to the option of real-time choices and real-time availability checks.

As a result of their empowerment in the market, consumers' mindsets, expectations, and behavior are changing in other areas as well, such as in health care, community management, and education. We are therefore no longer dealing with a purely technological revolution, because it directly influences our core as human beings in our society. It is primarily a social revolution that changes our mindset, our society, our interactions, our expectations in the public domain. This is why it is important to clearly define the underlying technology, without focusing only on its impact on market transactions and consumer behavior, but also on the impact on mindset, collaboration, and organizational power. I therefore consider it a new revolution that, like previous industrial revolutions, has been triggered by a technological revolution. But this revolution is not set in the industrial domain, as it impacts on all uniquely human capabilities, leading to a revolution in our human existence, humanity, and communities.

For the purposes of this book, I consider the disruptive technologies at the heart of the Digital Civil Revolution to be a combination of the Internet, social medial, and platforms. The basis for these technologies and their impact and workings is global, effective, and guaranteed operational IT infrastructure (hardware and software) that enables global access to communication and data sharing through platforms that can be accessed by masses of individuals at the same time (which is sometimes referred to as 'mass individualization') through mobile devices, which have also become increasingly available and usable globally. This is the technical side of the story. The greatest power and the social impact naturally lies in the enormous, exponentially accumulating and mutually reinforcing applications in the *use* of the technology, in the sharing of data and information, communication and networking for, by, and between people on all geographical scales, from local to global.

The following are particularly striking features of the new technology from this more psychological and social perspective:

- We all have a small, hand-held computer with greater processing capacity than the huge machines that filled entire rooms only a decade ago.
- Their small size, great ease of use, and numerous information and communication applications make smartphones and tablets highly personal devices, as we literally keep them close to us at all time, even close to our body, close to our lives, close to our physical functioning (also through all kinds of wearables that track our physical activity and health), and close to our experiences and perceptions. These mobile devices are with us in everything we do and experience, mentally and physically.
- This instant availability has meanwhile gone global, there are barely countries or areas left where you cannot get cellphone signal. At this moment, half of the global population has cellphone service and this reach is still growing. In fact: we count on being connected everywhere we go! We simply assume that the global network works wherever we go, even in the most remote or poorest parts of the world, including those we have never physically visited. When one of our children goes on a trip around the world, we want them, wherever they go, to text us their location, let us know the name of their hotel, hostel or campsite, and regularly video chat with us on WhatsApp or Skype.
- Besides data and verbal or text-based communication (such as the traditional telephone), we are now also sharing images to an increasing extent. And the same expectation applies to images as well. We expect the technology and communication platforms and all the data, ranging from information to images and videos, to be available and accessible at all times, reliably, and globally.

This new technological foundation of the way we function in the world (also closer to home: in our communities, families, groups of friends, sports clubs) has caused disruption in the marketplace. At the same time (albeit not as immediately visible initially, mainly because there are more attenuating and delaying mechanisms at work outside the market), the technological foundation is also already having major impact on other aspects of our personal lives. On our mindset, for example, our sense of being in control and being part of lively communities, locally and worldwide; on our perception, knowledge, and idea of the world around us, which we can even openly verify thanks to the immediate availability of knowledge, news, tips, suggestions, and opinions of others. Thanks to disruptive technology, we now have a new direct channel for information and communication between citizens and communities worldwide, without the traditional reframing, selection, and censorship by those who controlled the previous mainstream information channels. Needless to say, this new channel is also subject to manipulation, prompted by commercial interests, through all kinds of selections based on algorithms, personal data mining, and microtargeting, but the difference with earlier channels, such as radio, TV, and the written press, is that much of the content is now produced, published, and shared by citizens directly. The impact this has will only grow and have unexpected effects. We personally, society as a whole, and politics are also disrupted, albeit partly through patterns and mechanisms that differ from those in the market. The new technology makes that we live in a different world, one in which we all interact differently, and we will ultimately become different humans in a different society. We will not only change as consumers, but also as voters, citizens, local residents, patients, students, etc.

2
New Balance in the Triangle of Market, State, and Civil Society

All developed Western nations are, as pointed out earlier, structured according to the triangle of (nation) state, market, and civil society. This was not always, especially not in the 1990s, clear to the dominant parties: government and business. The privatization debates of the 1990s looked only at two legs of the triangle: government could and had to become smaller, as market forces would ensure that the private sector would do a much better job at providing many of the state-provided services, more efficiently and with more innovation. Citizens only ever featured in these debates as (passive) consumers, including of what were, at the time, still publicly provided services. On some occasions, when privatization only led to worse or more expensive services, because the idea of letting market forces do their thing had not been properly thought through or privatization had effectively led to a monopoly, but now a privately run one, citizens would not only protest as consumers (by boycotting a product or complaining to industry regulators), but also as voters (as passive consumers of politics by voting for other parties or politicians).

As I pointed out (in Note 5), I introduced the triangle in my lectures in the 1990s as the basis for a more comprehensive and consistent analysis of the institutional structure of Western nations. One core concept of that institutional structure of Western nations is that of civil society.[13] The public and political debate at the time was largely reduced to a choice between market and state. To begin with, this choice in itself was already conceptually wrong. The choice would either have to be between business and state (which would be about the form of organization) or between market forces and (party) politics (which would be about the mechanisms of the system).

In the book (2000) that resulted from these lectures, I addressed the role of civil society organizations, NGOs, and NPOs and used the term 'societal enterprise' to describe the Netherlands' unique public-private model that hinges partly on the involvement of such organizations (and for that reason the concept is different than the normal use of 'social enterprise').

My analysis covered the following core features of this Dutch-style social enterprise:

- the social mission comes first (ultimately making it a values-driven enterprise)
- the enterprise is customer-driven and not client-driven, meaning that it does not involve the kind of clientelism we often see in politics, as politicians ultimately want to be re-elected
- the enterprise actively looks for all possible sources of revenue, from commercial, state, or philanthropic actors, albeit that the financial side is always subject to the overriding non-profit objective and subordinate to the realization of the enterprise's social mission
- the mixture of revenue from different types of sources is also an effective and stable guarantee of intellectual and mission-driven independence, which would be undermined by excessive dependence on the state or an overly commercial focus

As I explained in the note, I therefore analyzed the unique Dutch model in areas such as health care, education, housing, but also in the public broadcasting system and at pension funds, as a privatized model, but with the caveat that the providers in these areas are non-profit organizations that are clearly rooted in society and have a social mission. In all these areas, there were private-sector organizations active in the Netherlands that were not the product of the political trend of the time, which consisted in privatizing services out of political and ideological preferences. Instead, these organizations had emerged from citizens' initiatives that dated back to around 1900, well before the government realized that there were social needs that public services could fulfill. As expected, my concept met with great resistance and ignorance among the true believers in the dominant opposite ends of the scale at the time, the market and the state, because I was basically embracing the hybrid nature of this historically formed model that was situated between citizens' initiative, commercial revenue, and public services, heralding it as the model of the future and as highly enterprising and socially innovative.

As the debate and the accompanying framing are often dictated by the dominant parties (the state and business), which also dominated public communications, the third leg of the triangle, civil society, long remained under-regarded, under-analyzed, and under-comprehended. Civil society is the whole of citizens who are linked and committed to each other on a basis of voluntariness, solidarity, and spontaneity, simply because interaction and living together in communities is considered important for the quality of life. Alexis de Tocqueville defined civil society as the intermediary interconnections between people, in a domain that exists between that of the individual and that of the state, providing a civil foundation for democracy and citizen power against an overly dominant state. Plato and Aristotle defined it as follows: true happiness, *eudaimonia*, is the building of a good life, not only for yourself, but also for others, good communal life with others. Civil society encompasses areas such as philanthropy (in the broadest sense, ranging from small donations to crowdfunding and entrepreneurial or venture philanthropy, as is now a growing trend), volunteering (such as at sports clubs, community centers, and unpaid and voluntary work in areas such as health care, culture, and education), but also spontaneous political pressure through, for example, nongovernmental organizations (such as Greenpeace) and modern media (such as the #MeToo movement).

Maybe the best way to characterize civil society as a separate force and a separate domain of mechanisms and drives is through the concept of 'social capital'. Social capital broadly refers to such things as interpersonal relationships, a shared sense of identity, shared values, mutual understanding, cooperation, trust and reciprocity. What I am calling the Digital Civil Revolution will see new technology affect, and potentially increase, our humanity and human existence in terms of our social capital, which, in turn, defines the current use of the concept of 'civil society'. Philosophical and sociological users of this concept in combination with democracy, institutional structure, and society range from Alexis de Tocqueville to Robert Putnam to Pierre Bourdieu. In linking this concept and philosophy of 'social capital' to the position and drives and self-organization of citizens, we certainly are close to an understanding of the importance and independent institutional position of 'civil society'.

> *Some particularly inspiring examples of the use of new technology that is based on the concept of social capital are set in the context of the influx of immigrants in Western nations. One such example is Copenhagen-based Refunite, a web-based platform that helps refugees reconnect with family and friends they have left behind. An even better example is the Welcome App that helps them connect with residents in their new country, so as to find housing, work, and get in touch with people who can open doors for them, as well as with people who are willing to vouch for them and give them a positive reference.*

Private-sector non-profit organizations that provide services to citizens who need them are often also part of a country's civil society, while they generally also operate on the interface between civil society and the state and/or market. Their position is, in terms of the historical institutional triangle, therefore a hybrid one. On the one hand, they are close to the citizens they serve and depend on these citizens' voluntary commitment or donations. On the other hand they often also depend on government subsidies and are subject to guidelines governing the design and organization of their services, to whom they are allowed to provide their services, and the extent to which they can bid for public contracts. Public procurement is traditionally how governments around the world contract private-sector parties, regardless of whether they are non-profit or for-profit, to work on government projects or manage public facilities.

The new technologies that have disrupted the market are also having great impact on both other legs of the triangle, as well as on the balance within the triangle.

The impact first became apparent in the market, as disruption takes its toll much quicker and more directly in the marketplace. Market forces are more direct and harder to manage for all parties, making the market ultimately more ruthless. Still, competition is equally fierce in democratic politics (of course not in absolute monarchies and dictatorships), where similar ruthless forces are at work, which cannot be controlled by the incumbent. As such, you could speak of democratic politics as a 'political marketplace,' which even uses well-known tools and concepts from the world of business, such as branding, start-ups, and reputation management. However, the market is a lot more ruthless in case of failure. Without customers and their spending power, companies will simply go out of business. This does not work in the same way for a politician or political party.

In much of what is to follow, I will begin with an as open and objective description as possible of the huge revolutionary impact of new technologies on the one hand, i.e. the Digital Civil Revolution, while at the same time embracing these technologies in their (potential) impact on thoroughly positive things such as citizenship, civil society, and new relations and alliances between state, market, and civil society. This openness with respect to the disruptions that are already visible, while embracing the positive effects of those same technologies, is needed to call upon everyone to take the right strategic steps to prevent that we are ultimately only left with a disrupted democracy and public services, and forgetting to harness the positive effects for citizenship. However, this may very well be at odds with the dominant sentiment among many people today who feel that they are right in the middle of these disruptions that are jeopardizing valuable past achievements. I am hesitant to go into these possibly negative effects of new technologies, as I do not want to fall into the conservative and not very strategic tendency to issue warnings or blow threats out of proportion. If you give in to that tendency, you are only empathizing with incumbents who feel threatened in their position. And yet, it does seem appropriate here to briefly take stock of and assess possible negative effects, albeit not to give you something to hide behind or a seemingly objective reason to dismiss the technology and its possibilities, but rather to be prepared for whatever could go wrong. Only a timely and realistic strategic response will give us the chance to, amid the disruptions, capitalize on the positive effects of the technology on citizenship, civil society, and realize new relations between citizens, and the state and public services.

Helbing offers a convenient rundown of the negatives:

- mass surveillance of citizens, and misuse of surveillance data by dishonest political leaders
- everyone is treated as a potential suspect
- witch hunts
- spyware on digital devices
- misuse of personal data for targeted offering of products or services
- espionage of sensitive trade secrets
- cyberattacks
- industrial espionage
- cyberwar
- politicians vulnerable to blackmail or publication of past personal issues
- manipulation of discussions or information on the Internet

This seems like enough for now.

3

Disruption of Standard Organizational Form and Management

The technological revolution has yet another, more profound effect than the above changes in the balance between the market and civil society or the state and civil society. It is changing the way we organize ourselves. All our formal structures and institutions, that is to say the set structures of old values and routines that have crept in, have come under debate or have started to fade. There is so much uncertainty that some will feel we have entered a situation of chaos, where all the security offered by human bonds and confidence in historical institutions has been shaken. This is noticeable in many areas.

One example, but by no means the only example, is what is happening in the domain of *employment*. Permanent jobs, fixed job descriptions, formal organizational structures and hierarchies are – also on the back of the success of the platform economy, which is managing to match demand to supply faster than ever and with greater ease and in real time – increasingly replaced by new flexible forms of work, varying associations in professional networks, task-based and project-based operations, and all kinds of independent work and self-employment.[14]

Only now, are we experiencing and seeing that offices were no more than the next step in the industrial revolution, and that they are to professionals with a higher level of education what the old factories were to blue-collar workers during the industrial revolution. These factories emerged out of an economic need to build a sufficiently large workforce to be able to make the expensive new industrial technology profitable, with the added benefit that having these workers in factories meant you could monitor attendance and productivity. From the factory owner's perspective, there was also a major downside to amassing this workforce, as it enabled workers who found themselves in similar positions to share their concerns, resistance, complaints, poverty, and other problems. They were able to organize collectively as a group, which ultimately led to the creation of unions. These unions subsequently started to organize strikes and protests, including protests demanding institutional and legal changes that were not raised by employers in negotiations with the government, such as the right to vote for all citizens, collective unemployment and disability insurance, the right to strike, and the prohibition of child labor.

With the arrival of new technology, physical concentration of work (which is non-manual in most cases) in offices is no longer necessary. In fact, what we are seeing now is a physical spread of 'workers' who increasingly work out of cafés, hotels, train stations, and flexible workplaces at highway rest areas, enabled by modern communication and data tools. The traditional power that workers had by uniting in unions is, regardless of what it has already achieved in legal terms in many Western nations, therefore currently undermined by these new dispersed ways of working. We now get teams of non-manual workers physically together in one single space for entirely different reasons, with the aim to improve communications, make them trust each other, challenge each other, and come up with creative solutions through interaction. In the platform economy, organizations become platform organizations. They are more horizontal and there is more two-way communication and more mutual alignment without the intervention of managers, more networking, more direct communication with customers on the front lines.

This same development of the economy in the nineteenth and twentieth century is what led to a new practice called 'management'. Factories had gradually started to implement production lines, based on a division of labor that was in sync with the available machines and level of mechanization. This created an increasing need for staff tasked with supervising the production process, monitoring and improving the efficiency of working methods, intervening whenever productivity and production quality were below par or in case of failures in this interconnected but subdivided process. Blue-collar workers working in the factory were not considered competent enough to fulfill this supervisory role (as it required greater intellectual capacity than manual labor). Plus, factory owners did not like the idea of workers taking on such a supervisory role alongside their regular work, fearing they would primarily look after their own or their former co-workers' interests. They thought such promoted workers would mostly side with their former peers, the blue-collar workers they would now have to supervise. This was a conflict of interest that had to be bridged. And so 'management' became a new organizational level at factories for two main reasons. On the one hand, management came from a distinction between execution of the work on the factory floor on one side and planning and coordination on the other side. And their main focus was on the second. This is still the basis for management practices today, as Peter Drucker pointed out: 'Most of what we call management consists of making it difficult for people to get their work done'. On the other hand, management was a way to maintain power relations and protect different interests. 'Managers' were appointed by the top brass, who were very much in charge of the manager's fate. When the boss was not happy with a manager's performance, the manager would simply be demoted to their former job in the factory. Initially, managers were therefore proxies for the owners/shareholders whose rules and output requirements they followed obediently.

This management based on these principles endured for a long time, even though the grounds for it in settings other than a factory soon became outdated. Take highly professional environments, such as hospitals and law and accounting firms, for example, where those doing the actual work know a lot more about the profession, the primary process, and the client than the manager does. Or take start-ups that are jointly owned by their staff, meaning that there are no or hardly any internal economic conflicts of interest. Or take office environments where workers perform mainly non-manual labor and organize their own work processes in consultation with others, without the intervention of a separate management echelon. The division between management and workers has survived for many years, even though there are barely any sound economic grounds for it today.

The most obvious explanation for this is that managers simply did not want to give up the benefits of a managerial role, such as the greater knowledge of what is going on at the company, a position close to the owner/owners, a hierarchical position from which they can tell others what to do, and of course the higher pay. As Max Weber predicted: '[…] each man becomes a little cog in the machine, and aware of this, his one preoccupation is to become a bigger cog.'

In preserving the managerial role, managers were greatly helped by the fact that it became a profession in its own right (although the scientific or practical evidence that management is indeed a profession has not remained unchallenged). This claim of professionalism has helped create a thriving extensive management industry propped up by business schools (the first of which was Wharton, founded in 1881), headhunters, management consultants, and interim managers. For 25 years, I was personally active in the management industry in different roles and I have also run a high-end consultancy company, so I have helped propagate the management profession and seen the industry develop around me.

So, what were the combined principles or unsubstantiated claims or myths that managers and the management industry hung on to because it suited their interests? (1) Management is a profession you can learn in school, (2) it is both complex and decisive for the success of companies, and therefore scarce (only talented people make good managers), and the higher pay is therefore justified, and (3) it is such a stand-alone profession that it can be deployed in any industry, meaning that managers can move between organizations with different primary processes and target groups/markets (based on the assumption that management is the same and can be executed everywhere, leading to the erroneous view that systematic management rotation is possible and a sound method of management development), including the possibility of having a management career across different industries, which means that a career in management does not require knowledge of the primary process and primary customers in an industry. The combination of specific access to (through accredited and globally ranked management programs at business schools and universities) and upward mobility within the group led to the creation of a *caste*: a closed group that is hard to get into and that takes very good care of itself.

However, there was first and foremost a conceptual error in this development: professionalization led to an approach to 'management' that saw it as a more technical, more unsympathetic, more calculating, more traditionally economic role than the original managerial role of 'supervisor,' 'foreman,' or 'boss.'[15]

On top of that, a relatively recent development in Western countries was that of increasing social criticism of the administrative elite, its culture, and its attitude. Managers were increasingly also put in that bracket. This was quite clearly a consequence of their successful claim that management is a profession in its own right that justifies their higher pay, as good managers are scarcer and more crucial for the company than the efforts of their official bosses, which were the shareholders in the world of business and political administrators in the civil service and public services. Managers themselves never saw this criticism coming (as, of course, in their view their profession was a purely technical one, and they were simply the best for the job), and they had not been taught how to deal with it, as it was well before subjects such as social communication, reputation management and personal integrity featured prominently in the curriculum of business schools and management programs.[16] The fact that they, as managers, had a social responsibility was often overlooked, so it came as a bit of a surprise to them when society started to challenge their position, pay, and responsibilities because that same society had started to label managers, in a growing political debate, as part of the 'elite'. As a result, the emphasis for many managers, management programs, and recruiters has shifted to leadership. This basically marks the return to the personal, values-driven side of managing that had been eliminated by the so-called professionalization of management that was intended to legitimize certain power and position.

The new technologies will further undermine the already feeble rationale behind the profession of management and perhaps lead to the complete disappearance of this kind of management, in the same way as the emphasis in theories about what makes for good management and the practices of many management development programs have shifted to leadership, ethics, and character. After all, the information you need to manage a company or department in this old way, such as budget and productivity details, reports about production and customers, inventories, lead times, insourcing of and arrangements with others or staff departments, can now be consulted directly, easily, and in real time by everyone across the organization. Provided that the required information is shared and updated in an adequate and timely manner, the modern worker's ability to self-organize, in coordination with colleagues and aligned with set objectives and agreements, has increased immensely thanks to modern technology. In this running and coordinating of things, a manager is no longer needed. It is for the first time that we are seeing a split arise between '*management*' as an indispensable organizational function for supervision, control, and intervention, and '*managers*' as stand-alone officers who (so far) have a monopoly on fulfilling such supervisory, control, and intervention tasks and holding the accompanying powers. This is because 'management' can and should now be handled by a lot more workers, alongside their actual work. As always, those in power, in this case the managers, will be the ones who will struggle with the revolutionary change the most. While managers as stand-alone officers will gradually disappear, management as a separate function in the structure of organizations will certainly not[17] – unless the people in official management positions know how to successfully ward off the new technologies and associated culture of modern workers. The latter is not as unlikely as it seems, as the management role has managed to endure for decades amid important economic changes and has been applied in economic circumstances that are entirely unsuited to it. I can already hear young people, who know no different than the new technological age and its tools and their application, complain that information sharing, mutual alignment, and communication are outmoded and a lot less flexible within organizations than they are used to on the open Internet with its numerous platforms. This is not due to the available technology, but rather to a conflict of interest. On platforms, the commercial and competition motives of the market rule. The faster and more targeted the relevant information is truly shared for the benefit of (potential) users, the better. Within organizations, however, personal interests and positions (of power) come into play. Information gives you an edge and influence, and therefore legitimizes your position, such as that of manager.

Management believes in management, in its value added in terms of control and planning. In the early 1990s, I conducted a large study into the economic and financial impact of mergers in the home care sector in the Netherlands. I designed two models and worked out the costs involved. A traditional merger model, with lots of centralized management and a large number of manage-ment and staff positions in a divisional structure, and a much more decentralized, community-oriented model with professional teams that take care of their operations, budget, and care needs assess-ments themselves. I was able to show that the second model was both more cost-effective and more efficient, which I have been asked to explain to many executives and managers over the years. However, decision-makers and administrators across the sector opted for the first model, as it fit their comfort zone with its exten-sive management level and centralized control. Thankfully, new initiatives ultimately emerged that did draw on the second model, and which ended up validating it as a successful model. These initiatives have meanwhile become the mainstream and are often the biggest providers in the Dutch home care sector.[18]

As shown above in relation to collaboration, the management function is also changing as a result of the introduction of modern technology that is making information and communication functions a lot faster, simpler, and 'flatter' (no hierarchy).[19] New technologies are having a fundamental impact on organizational forms and consequently also on the management functions within them. Like the economy as a whole, organizations are also switching to platforms. Hierarchy and formal structure are losing their importance, because internal information and communication functions are becoming faster and flatter. This is often referred to using the term 'agile', a way of working that is flexible, organized in tasks and projects, where workers switch between tasks with great ease and ad hoc teams are assembled and reassembled with new members quicker than before. As a result, the traditional manager figure is increasingly replaced by new roles such as that of project manager, scrum leader, coordinator at team level, often ad hoc, project-based, task-based, and on a temporary basis, as was already common practice at the consultancy business I ran with others some 25 years ago.

This does, however, make it all the more apparent that there is an important physical and human component to '*leadership*.' Leadership turns out to be necessary for far more reasons than only information, coordination, planning, and alignment, or even worse monitoring and budget control. This is because these functions can be automated and shared in real time with anyone through modern IT infrastructure. It is much more about the human factor, such as solving or addressing conflicts on the team. Getting going again following a period of stagnation by eliminating uncertainty about what is and what is not allowed within the organization, or clearing up differences of opinion about what would be the best approach. Dealing decisively with a lack of inspiration or team members hiding in routines, or with miscommunication between generations. And perhaps most importantly, offering vision for the future and the course to steer, which will be more credible and reassuring when it comes from the boss himself or herself.

Again, virtualization and digitalization are necessitating a comprehensive strategic response here. Although the direct, automated channel must be taken seriously and embraced, physical meetings and interactions between people remain equally important. No matter how contradictory it may seem, the growth of modern technology actually makes the human and physical aspect on top of the virtual aspect more important. People do not want to be locked away behind PC screens, tablets, and smartphones, they want to continue to meet others, look them in the eye, and organize things together.

This trend is also happening in management. For some time now, management has been evolving towards leadership as the more personal and values-driven next step of the current standard in management. This is a timely and anticipatory response to what ongoing disruptions have only been making clearer and more urgent. New technology has a fundamental effect on what our world looks like and how we live in it. Work and workplaces look different now, traditional hierarchy-based and rigidly structured organizations are becoming part of flexible networks, and even the traditional boundary between workers and management is being replaced by a working relationship that is based on personal leadership.

Contemporary analyses often define management and leadership as opposites, arguing that the management layer simply has to go, as there is no place for it anymore between (more and better) leadership on the one hand and (smart, well-designed) strategy on the other. The idea is that if you get both ends of the scale right, you no longer need the traditional way of managing, only self-management, organizational agility, and agile project coordination and staffing. This kind of horizontal coordination and self-management would then see the organization 'automatically' realize the agreed upon strategy, also toward markets and customers. Aside from the 'autonomous' development towards more personality, closer group cohesion, processes of sensemaking, and the need to guide people through the newly-forming uncertainties that explain the shift from management to (more) leadership, organizations themselves and the management function at organizations are also changing. Many organizations are going through a real and visible transformation, as they now have to be successful in the platform economy, which is turning a lot of organizations into platforms themselves, both in their internal and external operations. This is partly the result of the same effects on information and communication that new technologies are also having in the greater economy, partly a strategic response intended to keep up with modern employees and what they have seen happening in the market, and finally there is also an economic rationale behind it, as the costs of the new technology you introduce to replace the management layer will soon be recouped because you are cutting management overheads. These shifts (the need for more leadership on the one hand and the disappearance of traditional organizational structures at platform organizations on the other) are thus creating the illusion that management is no longer needed. The shift in accent thus turns into an empty quandary. The way out of this line of thought, which would see management disappear altogether, is a concept called operational excellence management, which is the practice of optimizing quality-driven and customer-driven operations through a clear set of rules, guidance and steering.[20]

The distinction between management and leadership in management theory is increasingly profound, compared to initial rather precipitate and trendy analyses that even went so far as to claim that management would disappear altogether. One particularly good example of a more sophisticated approach to management and leadership dates as far back as 2001 and comes from John Kotter,[21] who argues that 'Management is about coping with complexity. Leadership, by contrast, is about coping with change.' I would add 'coping with uncertainty' to the latter point about leadership (both the 'strategic' uncertainty about external circumstances and the company's own position within that context and the best response to it, and the 'emotional' uncertainty this produces within the organization). Kotter later adds the following: 'To executives who are overeducated in management and undereducated in leadership, the idea of getting people moving in the same direction appears to be an organizational problem. What executives need to do, however, is not organize people but align them.'

4

New Balance between the Virtual and the Physical Approaches

The current technological revolution may have us paralyzed as we are caught in its headlights. Perhaps we are so startled by the bright lights and so overwhelmed that we do not realize that the impact will not be equally revolutionary everywhere. The demarcation point where new technology has a revolutionary, disrupting impact and where it has a really powerful yet controllable and manageable effect is often the central focus of the public debate about disruption of politics, public services, and civil society, which I am proposing here as the core questions of the new technological era. Needless to say, this essay focuses on the fundamental impact on the survival of institutes, fundamental relationships, organizations, and middlemen. That alone is more than enough for an *Umwertung aller Werte, a revaluation of all values*. It is so fundamental because it relates to humanity's most important evolution mechanism, the combination of cooperation and communication, which has given us humans a position, scale, and impact that is unlike that of any other species on Earth. That said, any of our competencies in this area can also be found in other species,[22] especially when focusing on the individual or small group level, like for us on an intimate scale, such as that of our family, community and village. But the sum of our competencies and the subsequent exchange and collaboration on larger scales such as regions, cities and nationally, but also worldwide and even extraterrestrially, and while preserving this connection, exchange, communication, and organization, are unique. This explains why language and communication, especially on the global scale provided by the Internet, are so important and have brought us so far in our evolution. The mere invention, realization, and intensive use of this global communication chain, which strongly depends on equipment that we have shot into space to orbit the Earth, shows how far ahead and unique we are in our evolution compared to other species. And again: not on a purely individual level, like the biological or physical level, but in our organization depending on our communication as humans together. And on that level, the disruptive technologies are now having their biggest revolutionary impact.

The nuance that has to be added to the aforementioned enormous impact of new information and communication technologies lies mainly on the other end of the spectrum, the physical end. This is the end where our lives and survival, in terms of food, energy, and health, are determined to a great degree. The early successful developments of our capacity to organize came in this physical domain, focused as it was on what we needed from our physical environment to survive as humans, like the agricultural and industrial revolutions. Examples of organizations in this domain include those that extract and process resources, such as the oil industry and mining. But it also includes the army, which needs the right equipment at the right time and the right place to be able to win wars. This is all very physical, sometimes even related to the most physical aspects of our existence, life and death. In this context, we can, therefore, not overlook our oldest industry, agriculture. That, too, is ultimately a highly physical process, involving soil, machines, as well as physical harvesting and processing of physical products. And finally, it certainly also applies to hospitals, where we undergo physical examinations and are operated on and healed, which also involves all kinds of costly and scarce equipment. Our body is, of course, the most important connection between our personal being and the physical world around us. In short, while all these industries and organizations, as vehicles of organization and communication, will be faced with fundamentally different technology and a correspondingly different approach from citizens and politics. As a consequence, they will also have to completely overhaul their internal organization. But their physical basis, i.e. the primary importance of their physical products and services and the associated knowledge and handling, cannot be argued away in a new kind of mentalism or postmodernism. Sure, this is often a risk in looming revolutions. The risk that we become so fixated on the new technological possibilities and effects, and feel so fundamentally threatened in our evolutionary survival, that we go over the top mentally and tell ourselves that the new will be our new reality for the full 100%. We therefore need the abovementioned industries to keep doing their jobs as well as before, even though citizens, the state, and the market are seeing the environment around them change along the lines of the revolution. Here, too, we must not be deceived by the IT and media revolution. And we must realize that although it has major consequences for our human existence, our citizenship, and our relationship with politics and the market, there is no need for the abovementioned processes to radically change as well, albeit that communications concerning these processes will change radically.

5
The Need for Strategic Intelligence

Competitors from outside the existing market playing field, sometimes even parties from elsewhere in the world that were entirely unknown entities on a domestic level, instantly shook the foundations of the playing field and jeopardized the viability of established players. What is particularly striking is the weak, denying, or passive response of the executives of these established companies in the face of the imminent disruption in their market segment. For quite some time, this lack of an adequate response was referred to as 'CEOs see it last.' The first stage of many CEOs' response was mostly denial, looking away, defensiveness, sometimes seemingly rational (but taking time they did not have) or to enter into debate about this trend and its signs. The most commonly heard explanation for this was, you guessed it, a psychological one. A CEO is someone who, after a long career, has finally reached the highest level in their business, and who has started to believe in the power, strength, and unquestionability of his or her company and his or her business model. Full-blown disruption of this reality simply does not fit into his or her self-image, it leads to retrospective doubts about his or her own intelligence and career choices, and it unsettles the image of the company that he or she runs.

An underlying explanation is that many of the top brass in business had begun to believe the myths and illusions of strategic planning. That you could estimate the future, that you could see the impact of future developments on your company and operations coming, and that all you had to do was chart a long-term course, split it up into clear-cut steps, and get down to managing the process. There has been fundamental criticism of this school of thought on strategic planning as a manifestation of belief in the myths of predictability and plannability.[23] Later in this book, I will delve deeper into the flawed underlying predictability assumption, which in times of revolution is challenged most fiercely by the fact that the impact of the revolution is completely unknown and unpredictable. The crux of the matter is the difference between strategic planning (which assumes that there is a systematic, rational, and quantitative basis to predicting the future and defining a strategy accordingly) and genuine strategic intelligence and strategic actions (which enable you to, faced with an uncertain and unpredictable future, without knowing how other parties will respond to that future, still achieve your strategic objectives). Genuine strategic intelligence is, in my view, more of a *cybernetic* nature (the ability to extrapolate different possible futures from different interdependent complex factors and variables), consisting of an ability to approach the future with uncertainty, imagination, and dreams, while also keeping your eyes open to unwelcome or subversive scenarios (which is often referred to as '*futuring*') and, more than anything else, an ability to be *smart and cunning* in seizing the opportunities that will bring realization of your objectives closer, sometimes even in a contradictory way by taking seemingly erroneous steps in the short term that pay off in the long term. A recent summary of the key building blocks of strategic intelligence lists similar elements: game theory (to be wise to the games played by parties and people, playing and knowing how to win), cognitive psychology (to be mindful of your own perceptions and put them into perspective, as well as those of others), and systems thinking (which is similar to the capacity for cybernetic thinking).[24] The managerial mindset that embraces old-fashioned strategic planning is caught in an illusion, relying on a false sense of stability and false rationality. History's great strategists, ranging from Sun Tzu (*The Art of War*) and Carl von Clausewitz (*On War*)[25] to ancient Athens and Odysseus in Greek mythology, put greater emphasis on opportunism, smelling your chances and seizing them, tactical nous, cunning and good judgment, especially of the strategic intelligence, character traits, and peculiarities of the 'adversary'. One obvious flaw in this approach of strategy as strategic planning is that it is never a good idea to publicize this plan and so define your strategy and the steps involved, as that would allow competitors and financiers to adjust their own strategies accordingly! The good news is that few companies make this mistake, not even those who are firm believers in strategic planning, so luckily CEOs do have this minimum level of strategic acumen. Strategic plans should therefore at best be considered PR tools for the believers who consider them proof of strategic insight and strategic choices by the organization communicating the plans. CEOs are, of course, more than happy to provide that proof!

It thus seems that politicians are wiser to what actual strategic thinking and action entails than many CEOs, who have become overly invested in their own technocratic strategic planning. The paradox is, however, that an academic discipline to study and develop 'strategic thinking & action in politics' never materialized. Even studies of 'strategic intelligence' go no further than reviewing cases and insights from everyday business practices. We must return to ancient or historic studies of politicians and to the start of strategic literature, namely of the military, to get a grip on and understanding of strategic intelligence of politicians.

The Politician's Split: Strategic Intelligence on Two Fronts

When it comes to strategic thinking and action, it is important to distinguish between direct political strategies, the ones concerning a politician's or political party's own political continuity, political losses or gains in election campaigns, and the ultimate political positions acquired on the one hand. And the government strategies, once you as a politician are elected and have gained an administrative position, aimed at achieving objectives for the countries, its citizens, and the public causes on the other. The latter kind of strategies could be referred to as political programming, which is both intended to curry favor with voters and communicate intentions as an administrator in government, also during election season. So, although there is certainly overlap between both these strategic fronts, it is still an important distinction in the analysis of political behavior. My previous description and analysis of strategic thinking in a political context was about the first type of strategy, but the second is ultimately more crucial for the execution and effect of political leadership for society. What is particularly fascinating in light of the previous analysis of the pitfalls of strategic planning for executives is that many members of government do rely on rational, scientifically substantiated strategic planning for the second type of strategies. This is consistent with my doubts as to whether strategic planning does indeed contribute to successful strategic management at all (maybe the first front of political survival is ultimately the only one for professional politicians, the other one not being important enough to be creative and personally ambitious about it), as well as with my conclusion before that it is primarily a handy tool to get stakeholders and voters on board, because and as long as they seem to sufficiently believe in it. Strategic planning thus becomes a handy tactical tool, as a symbol and sometimes also a rhetorical trick by strategically thinking administrators, also in politics.

Some governments have, perhaps also due to a longing for (the wrong kind of) efficiency or because it seems handy from an administrative point of view to be able to outsource the development of visions for the future to 'experts,' taken the illusions of strategic planning as truth. In the Netherlands, for example, there is an institutional structure of so-called planning offices, which are government agencies that perform analyses in different fields as input for the government's strategic planning efforts. In fact, these agencies have a formal procedural role in the government's decision-making process and sometimes have actual political influence. The formal role and methods of these planning offices, of which the Bureau for Economic Policy Analysis is the most prominent, is based on the same illusion of strategic planning that says that future trends can be analyzed quantitatively and objectively, and that such analyses provide an adequate basis for objective advice about the desirability, suitability, and effectiveness of possible government interventions. The Netherlands Bureau for Economic Policy Analysis and related planning offices focus heavily on complex models that are supposed to map the future, define the various variables for the future, and calculate the costs involved in the possible scenarios. No matter how quantitative this process has been designed to be, and no matter how much they keep adjusting economic models to changing circumstances, which create an illusion of objective data and comprehensive figures, these models are still built on the same quicksand as oracles and fortune tellers from antiquity that predicted the future by looking at intestines or birds' flight patterns. In this case, blind faith in this so-called objectivity is basically nourished by the huge volumes of data and the complex formulas and calculations propping up the data. The damage, however, is done on the side of the elected officials that commission these planning officers to produce reports and take them (overly) seriously. Essentially, this way the government is using third-party experts to reduce or even eliminate altogether the uncertainty and unpredictability of the effect of their decisions, but too much so. There is nothing wrong with wanting solid scientific and mathematical bases for the likelihood and effects of certain future scenarios. And neither is there anything wrong with studying the nature and scope of certain phenomena through clear quantitative analyses and observations, as is common practice at most government planning offices. But when politicians subsequently unquestioningly follow these planning offices' advice, they are simply not doing their jobs well. Today, these flawed political routines are not only being challenged by the enormous turbulence stirred up by the Digital Civil Revolution, and with that the growing belief that predictions based on insights and models from the past will not help or contain only a beginning of truth, but they are facing an even more fundamental challenge. By operating in this technocratic and obedient manner in the past and hiding behind so-called science and methodology, politics has squandered its authority as a visionary of that turbulent future, right when citizens need such a visionary more than ever before. The basic question is where citizens will turn for that vision, now that it has become so clear that politics has always been hiding behind the false certainty of 'predictive' science, even in a world that, with hindsight, seems a lot more stable and predictable than today's world. When we dig deeper, we stumble on another, purely political illusion that is rooted in the myth that these kinds of civil servant planning offices are apolitical, that the reasoning behind their recommendations is not based on the different interests at stake, but rather a rational kind of reasoning as per Jeremy Bentham's utilitarian definition: 'The greatest happiness of the greatest number is the foundation of morals and legislation.' This is part of the public rhetoric that planning offices use, with the support of a political sector that surrenders to their 'scientific' insights,' to defend their undeniable political influence as apolitically as possible.[26]

Needless to say, this belief in an all-encompassing, rational, and systematic analysis of social phenomena, including the subsequent advice and vision for the future, was always naive and the result of a kind of engineering-based approach to the social domain. Due to the increasing connectivity and variability in the platform economy, this thinking gradually has to make way for complexity and swarm theories.

Cybernetics and complexity theory[27] study and map out the interconnections between variables, bursting the bubble of the illusion of simple predictability. Citizens are increasingly showing swarm behavior. The connection between citizens is becoming more instrumental than the possible influence of formal leaders or a predefined goal through a well-calculated plan. Modern management happens through insight into cybernetic functioning, into the way in which variables interact and positively relate to each other, rather than through rational targeted action. In a more general sense, the philosophy of control in any position is shifting from a hierarchical vertical perspective (someone who knows best and sets targets is in charge) to a much more horizontal, interconnected perspective (we will determine together in mutual consultation what we want to work out and achieve). This is the most fundamental change in politicians' management role (or the pretense thereof), in case of lack of foresight or defensive action, even the disruption of that position.

6

Alternative: Citizenship Platforms

New technology is not only changing consumers' behavior in the market, but also citizens' perception of the market and its players, as well as the way in which citizens want to influence them. This change is brought on by more than merely the consumer perspectives and interests, as consumers are starting to ask the following questions: is the market acting in my best interest as a partner in society, as a parent to my children, as a resident of a city or a member of a local community? Again, the bartering and contacts between citizens, which are becoming more intensive thanks to new technology, will lead to more and more public pressure on companies. It has already been clear for some time now that consumers who collectively protest against a company out of their own interests and from their own perspective, such as when companies cause environmental damage, are thought to use child labor, engage in fraudulent practices, or pay top executives exorbitant salaries, can cause considerable reputation damage. Such public pressure will only increase as consumers are more enabled to share rumors and facts and become a growing and more and more prominent public force on social media, as became clear in the sex scandals involving Anthony Weiner and Harvey Weinstein and the subsequent #MeToo movement.

In a structural sense, one of the main effects is that new online platforms facilitate and thus stimulate bartering, direct communication, and direct group formation between individual citizens. On the one hand, new technology individualizes, while on the other it groups people together and creates masses. Large groups of independent individual citizens can choose freely, but people with similar opinions are also rallied more and on a larger scale. This is a trend that all three legs of the triangle of state, market, and civil society will face, and each leg will have to find its own response. At its core, this development basically boils down to the middleman and woman disappearing. The reasons for having and the value added by all filters, intermediaries, go-betweens, and indirect structures will be fundamentally challenged. In the market, examples of go-betweens include realtors (between supply and demand of houses) and retailers (between wholesaler and individual consumers). In the current old news and information media, the intermediaries are the critics, for example, who mediate between cultural product and the general public with respect to the quality of the product offered. Or journalists, who are the interface between news data and opinion, and pundits or public opinion makers, who explain or frame the basic data of the news or politics. In public services, the intermediaries include teachers (between knowledge and students) and doctors (between medical knowledge and customized treatment of individual patients). The intermediaries in politics are all politicians who make decisions and policy on voters' behalf. In organizations, managers are the middlemen and women (between data and information on one side and planned action and collaboration on the other).

It will be patently obvious that when the market and the information and communication tools used by citizens, not only as consumers in that market but also as citizens who are committed to the public cause and the common good, change fundamentally, so will politics, especially in democratic systems. Professional politicians themselves will undoubtedly be the first to deny and at least keep quiet about this link between the commercial market and the political market, as their positions are most under threat from the new developments. Incumbents tend to be the last to become aware of revolutions. It should be noted that in dictatorships or absolute monarchies, the political system does not work like a market, because citizens have no say, let alone a vote. In such political systems, platforms will not soon lead to any kind of change, unless engaged citizens have access through the back door of an international connection. Possibly also through social media, provided these are allowed to operate uncensored, without government control, and with respect for users' privacy, which is not the case in any dictatorship in the world. We can therefore see that new technologies and democracy mutually presuppose each other. The direct channel of, by, and for citizens needs to exist in a democratic system to be able to function adequately, securely, and reliably. As Bellamy already argued: 'citizenship is the right to have rights,' in this case to privacy and freedom.

III
Disruption of Politics and the Public Sector

New technologies are having major impact on the public sector. First of all on democratic politics, of course, because it functions like a market, with politicians vying for votes like companies vie for customers. The greatest and most visible disruption here is that of the position and function of political parties, which is threatening to undermine representative democracy and replace it with permanent direct democracy. Let's hope professional politicians are strategically intelligent enough to shape a new blend of traditional and direct democracy before it is too late. Significant public effects are also caused by citizens' increased and more extreme swarm behavior coupled with the radically changed media landscape. The latter has added a media channel for, by and with citizens directly and this includes self-production by these citizens. This generates influence by publicly sharing information and opinions and showing the public support, sometimes even in quantitative terms, that is prominent, sharable, and quotable in other media channels and in the public debate about formal decisions, such as legislation and appointments. The civil service and public services will also feel the severe consequences and must steer toward adaptation and respond in time, creatively and strategically by setting up new channels and, like the market has already learned to do, changing their culture and attitude towards the new citizen power and adopting new working methods.

7
Disruption of Politics

The term 'disruption' is a very apt one from the perspective and sensation of current parties in markets. Although the political 'marketplace' has seen the same phenomenon that has been plaguing the commercial marketplace, it is not referred to as such, neither by political parties themselves, nor by the hordes of political commentators and pundits. This is due to various reasons.

Politics refers to itself not as operating in a 'marketplace' where voters have to be won over through promises, an attractive candidate, and a modern campaign. They naturally do not want to publicly link their practices to what is often perceived and politically framed as the especially selfish motives to operate in the market: personal financial gain, making (loads of) money, preferably getting rich and securing the continuity of those financial gains so as to continue making financial profits for eternity. After all, you officially go into politics for more socially engaged or even altruistic reasons, such as the common good or to serve society. Politics is then presented as working on good things for 'the people up and down the country.'

The idea that their political success in the market for votes is subject to developments and backgrounds that are similar to those in a commercial market is one that politicians deny most emphatically by referring to this message of their ideological commitment. Market behavior and market success are considered egotistical, and any association with this kind of self-centeredness must therefore be avoided at all cost. And it must be said that many companies and their 'experts', i.e. economists,[28] have been feeding this framing for a long time and have even been openly propagating it by their lobbying and behavior.

The transparency of an explicit strategic plan that factors in the disruptive technologies and builds in a timely response in politicians' own political behavior, is, in electoral terms, not expedient. If the plan in question fails, sounds inadequate, or seems vague, voters will punish you for it. And they will be particularly likely to do so when it concerns truly large-scale and therefore complex problems. You run the risk of voters not buying into your strategic assessments and answers. But if these plans turn out to be successful, you cannot claim the success as your own, as others will simply, after a few minor adjustments, present the ideas as theirs. Aside from that, overly explicitly claiming success can work against you as a politician, because you also need other parties to do their bit and you have to include them in your praise and gratitude after such a success. This is the paradox of political leadership. On the one hand you claim that you want and can handle the responsibility personally, but on the other you have to be able to blame others when your plan or your execution of the plan fails and, paradoxically, also allow others to share the spotlight when the plan is a success to increase your status as a 'statesman.'

On top of that, politicians were already used to the highly uncertain and unpredictable existence in the 'market' of votes that comes around generally once every four years. They were never allowed to settle into a position of strategic stability or predictability. Current affairs, incidents big and small, damage to one's reputation, and gaffes had always been around in the world of politics, and not only during election season, albeit that the impact on election results was always great. Politicians never enjoyed the commercial market's false stability and rationality of systematic and well thought-out strategic management in the first place. Their success hinges more on their tactical nous and capacity for opportunism, as well as the associated intellectual flexibility and cunning, which basically boils down to their strategic intelligence. The foundation underneath explicit strategic plans, that is the strategic considerations, doubts, and appraisals, is often not welcomed by voters and fellow party members, because they have greater faith in the traditional 'good leader' who 'can see everything coming,' is never caught off guard, and will therefore never see future developments as problematic or open to debate. Explicit strategic planning in this culture will be seen as weak leadership.

The shock effect of an intruding newcomer who suddenly lures your voters and their votes away from you is nothing new to experienced politicians and political strategists, and it can even be factored in, but it never leads to the full disappearance of the 'beaten' political party. At most, such a defeat will be classed as 'too bad' in political parties' own strategic analyses, blamed on 'fear' or voter 'volatility,' (a term that is also used in the market) or put down to 'not having managed to get the message across.' The most common mechanism that kicks in after the first shock has died down is that of '*naming, blaming, and shaming,*' which has been a trusted way of publicly punishing bad performances since ancient times. The unreliability of voters and their lack of direct loyalty to one political party has always been a (political) given. New technologies have now added to this phenomenon, producing more extreme election results (swarm behavior), as apparent from the rapid rise and extensive reach of fresh-faced newcomers (such as Macron), or not so fresh-faced candidates (such as Trump), who are able to swiftly mobilize mass support from outside the political establishment.

Failure is also dealt with entirely differently in the political marketplace than in the commercial market. A political party does not go out of business, not financially and not factually, although a major defeat does always trigger internal debate about a party's relevance and purpose. Thanks to voter volatility and the constantly changing circumstances and issues that 'politics' has to respond to with a new answer every time, there is always the possibility of voters giving a party a second chance. What a party has to offer in the form of candidates and policy ideas is much more flexible than a company's proposition. Still, the core campaign message must at the same time be that nothing has changed fundamentally and ideologically and that the party still 'represents the same values.' 'All new' is an effective marketing cry in the commercial market, but is often the opposite in the political marketplace, especially when referring to a party's vision and priorities. In fact, it is considered an admission of weakness, a form of flip-flopping, or lack of backbone. Things are different, however, where it concerns the front man or woman, the candidates, after an election defeat. Changing the political leader after a defeat is sure to lead to renewed support from disappointed voters, as such a change at the top marks genuine renewal for them. It makes evident that the pain of the defeat is suffered by those who were at least partly responsible for it, and this personal pain is something voters recognize. Again, the differentiating feature of the modern public arena in the new media landscape clearly comes to the fore here, as now emotion trumps content, and character is the message. It also allows for more flexible and at the same time structural responses to voters changing preferences, so that a political party can still change radically over the years, also in terms of its message (as long as the party does not too openly admit it). The lack of brand loyalty among voters thus meets with a lack of identity on the side of the party. The risk is, of course, that a political party becomes nothing more than a marketing machine for its politicians, who are primarily out to hang on to their jobs and positions of power, leaving only a wafer-thin dividing line between politicians' practices and the so-called self-centered motives of companies in the commercial market.

All of this goes a long way toward explaining why the term disruption is not used to refer to the meanwhile highly notable revolutionary transformations of political mechanisms. This is partly due to the fact that politics attaches much less value to explicit strategic planning for its own functioning and its direct political survival strategies and never believed in the myth that strategic planning could predict, rationalize and plan the future. So, they are not so overawed and caught off guard by the new strategic environment as many market parties were. Also in the public positioning of a company, strategic planning has much more strategic value than for a political party or leader. Strategic openness, thoroughness, and methodology, including explicit publication of inevitable uncertainties, contributes to companies' economic position, both toward major clients and toward key staff and shareholders. In the assessment of a company, and the board in particular, bluffing in plans or suggestions of full manageability and having the future under control is primarily considered to be ridiculous, and therefore undermines the authority of the board and will later, as soon as the board has indeed failed to deliver on the plans, be used against them. This is exactly how it doesn't work in the political marketplace. In politics, it pays to pretend that you know what is coming, and that you will respond in a timely and controlled manner. Politics is much more the business of inspiring hope and bluffing about being right and about your vision for the future. The trick is to make sure that, when things do go differently or wrong, there are others you can blame, so as to preserve the illusion of your great statesmanship and strategy skills. Politics takes place in the domain of the future, peddling hope, and especially the hope for reliable and good leadership toward that future, more so than in the domain of assessment of administration by comparing actual results to promised results.

The Power of the Swarm

As I pointed out above, swarm behavior[29] has increased enormously in recent years.[30] Swarms move primarily based on the mutual bond and distance between its participants, which explains the rapid and exceptional movements the swarm makes collectively as if it were a single entity. This is due to the fact that the all-dominating factor that explains swarm behavior is that of permanent direct maneuvering based on mutual distances within the swarm, as shown when, for example, a fish or bird on the outer edge of the swarm suddenly veers to try to evade danger (and the interconnection of the members of the swarm and their mutual steering based on distances from their neighbors subsequently makes that the rest of the swarm also responds collectively and rapidly), but also when the swarm follows the leader or takes one member of the group as its leader.

New technologies are leading to closer and more information-rich ties between (much) larger groups of citizens than ever before. Such groups subsequently show large-scale and more volatile swarm behavior without losing the ties between its members. In that greater whole, they remain engaged and able to more intensively coordinate their movements based on interrelations in terms of information, position, and opinion. The most important control mechanism between humans thus starts to resemble that of a swarm of birds. As long as the members of the swarm experience the interrelations and connections, the swarm can collectively swerve far more extremely than each insecure individual used to be able and wanted to on their own, unsure as they were of the larger group's judgment.

The recent fidget spinner craze provides a great example of how technology can intensify traditional social behavior, which a craze ultimately is. Originally invented as a toy that helps children focus, fidget spinners were soon picked up by other children as just a fun toy. The craze started in the U.S. in February 2017. Three months later, it was the best-selling toy on Amazon. And three weeks after that, the hype went global, even reaching deep into Africa and Asia. Estimations have it that between 19 and 50 million fidget spinners were sold across the globe. Toy crazes have come and gone, we all remember them from our school days, but the huge scale and global reach of the fidget spinner craze, as well as the great speed with which it spread, and the self-managing and copycat behavior of children themselves, albeit using this new technological channel, were completely new aspects in this case. The school playground can now sometimes be seen on a global scale, with children still able to initiate their own crazes and pass on toys. Again, new technology is accelerating social behavior that has been around forever, greatly amplifying the impact of the behavior. This is an example of genuine swarm behavior. In terms of the business side of it, it is interesting to note that what was actually preventing the craze from spreading even faster was the sluggishness of toy stores, who did not see it coming and therefore had not stocked up on spinners.

Donald Trump's victory in the 2016 U.S. presidential election can, at least partly, be attributed to his successful use of social media (well before newspapers and even the Republican party itself had cottoned on to how much steam his candidacy was picking up). His success partly came from the fact that he managed to carry his celebrity status earned as a TV personality and the camera skills he developed working as a TV presenter over to the new channel offered by social media, which saw him outscore his rivals on the more visually oriented modern (social) media. On top of that, the greatest publicity is generated by the cumulative combined exposure on all media channels. When they pick up items that first emerged on modern social media as a trend or issue that was on the collective mind of 'the people', TV channels and newspapers increase exposure and even lend a certain authority to the item. So, the informal world of the new direct media channel gets 'official' attention and recognition and this increases its influence. This also seems to have been the sequence of Trump's rise to political stardom. First, he became a prominent figure on a mainstream public medium, TV, building up traditional celebrity status, which he subsequently capitalized on during the election campaign, stressing his deal-making skills and how he would drain the political swamp (his words) in Washington, D.C., while constantly reinforcing this image on social media through the tone and nature of his tweets. Next, he became big in mainstream media (again), because these had to report on his massive reach and following on the new channel, and because mainstream media (such as newspapers and Fox News) wanted to use him as they competed with social media for the public's attention. And finally, so much for their strategic intelligence, he became big in the Republican party, which, albeit reluctantly and after much internal resistance, simply had to accept his candidacy. Trump's public power and ensuing political power grew thanks to his great public reach, which was accelerated and increased as he was able to reach so many people directly without the traditional media, but with the new media channel, creating a direct following for him personally (and not the party). This is one of the most impactful strategic changes in politics: a person can garner personal support and attention from voters directly, independent of political parties. Ultimately, this empowers this person to call the shots in the party, or in even stronger terms, the person comes to embody the political party, as has happened in Trump's case after his election. The great thing about modern media is that the scope of the support can be measured and tracked instantly and openly at all times. In the traditional televised debates with his rival Hillary Clinton, Trump also turned out to have better camera skills and come across as more personable and authentic, including the usual – highly consistent with his Twitter persona – intimidating behavior and belligerence. The swarm behavior of his supporters came from the fact that people who liked and retweeted his tweets and became Trump followers (which made his reach grow exponentially), subsequently also started to convince each other that Trump was a good political choice, a candidate who was a lot like them, and who also happened to be very consistent in his attitude and behavior. In the traditional channels, such as political parties and the news and information channels they dominate, such as TV, radio, and the written press, each newcomer always has to break through internal barriers, cultures, and routines first. With the advent of the new direct channel, any newcomer can build up a public following first and then use this public support to pressurize the traditional channels into accepting him or her as the candidate. Next, swarm behavior on the new channel would be needed to quickly grow the candidate's reach and see him or her acquire massive and visible public support, whereby the swarm maintains unity and coherence via its internal communication that is facilitated by new technologies.

Swarm behavior was also at the basis of Emmanuel Macron's election victory in the 2017 presidential election in France. Winning a vast parliamentary majority out of the blue, representing a political party that had been founded five months before the election, is possible only by using a direct channel of, for, and among citizens moving as a swarm that is capable of sudden collective deflections. French voters were fed up with traditional politics, and modern media and platforms empowered them to share these feelings with each other and realize that they were not alone in feeling that way. They saw that a political revolution was achievable, and that a vote for a non-traditional freshly founded party would not be a wasted vote, prompting many to try to convince others to change their vote as well. During the previous elections in the old media landscape, all voters could do was listen to the official presentations and promises of established parties. They had to assume that those politicians were aware of the general public mood and knew what they were talking about, but of course those politicians were not very objective in their analyses and predictions, in the end they wanted to protect the status and position of the political parties they represented. The main thing that voters in parliamentary democracies have to worry about before casting their vote is not to vote too differently from others so as not to waste their vote on the election loser. Thanks to new platforms, this pre-election assessment is now far easier to make, even when a voter intends to vote for an entirely new party and candidate. Voters have their own, direct, and non-politically-colored information channel, where they can talk to each other, gauge the mood, exchange arguments, and weigh up each other's arguments. This also shows another political effect of new technology: the emergence and growth of the importance and possibilities of the *wisdom of the crowd*.

Swarm behavior is not a new phenomenon when it comes to public opinion. This was always politically relevant, as it enabled polling and election result predictions, no matter how precarious. Analysis and, more importantly, influencing of swarm behavior has therefore always been an important political skill, which had to be used in the messages to get across, the formulation of those messages, their underlying rhetoric, and most of all in political parties' selection of the persons who had to convey those messages. But new technologies are adding two extra dimensions to this swarm behavior. First, they give the swarm a greater ability to self-manage through mutual influencing within the realm of public opinion, detaching the swarm from official political leaders and their official, party-politically colored messages. Second, it leads to much larger swarms, which sometimes even extend beyond borders. The swarm of citizens is therefore increasingly autonomous in charting its course and defining its opinion, also when it comes to political issues and party political preferences. But an even more important effect is that swarm behavior with respect to opinions on the common good will even arise outside official or representative democracy and will touch on all issues that citizens themselves find important or even want to tackle themselves, away from the domain of official politics or government. Their autonomous agenda-setting power increases, as does their independent capacity to organize to tackle public issues. When faced with this kind of swarm behavior, politics follows instead of leads. This will take some getting used to for many politicians and their lobbyists. Still, this is not really that revolutionary. It is still about public opinion and its influence on politics and government in a traditional sense. As said, all politicians are trained to meet this challenge. The underlying technological revolution is leading to an acceleration, increased autonomy, and a growing scale of the direct mutual cohesion of citizens within this process.

What is the most revolutionary aspect, however, is that the increased speed and intensity of the swarm's collective capacity to react can lead to a far quicker and more intense tackling of public issues. Especially when it no longer needs to be routed through the traditional democratic process (voters called to the ballot box every so often), but when direct collaboration by citizens is needed or possible. Citizens will then not only swing into action themselves and collectively, but also do so quicker than would ever be possible under the central management of the government (which is partly slowed down by lobbyists, capital, and the weight of institutional interests).

> One example is Germany's approach to wind energy, as compared to policy in other European countries. Germany has made it possible for villages and neighborhoods to adopt wind turbines. Not only to foster sustainability, but also to allow communities to benefit economically. Across Germany, citizens have a direct stake in the transition to cleaner energy through ownership of renewable energy systems. This was part of the first Renewable Energy Act of 2000.[31] The initiative also led to the creation of numerous energy cooperatives across Germany to pool individual citizens together so that they could afford the green energy systems. Unlike in many other countries, such as the U.S., municipalities and companies can also be members of these cooperatives. Over the period from 2006 to 2013, over 700 cooperatives with over 200,000 individual members were created. Germany is looking to tap into the potential underlying values of citizenship: a positive mindset with respect to the public cause (the greening of energy), combined with a sound understanding of one's own interests and the possibility of exerting direct influence on one's own and others' collective actions. By 2012, as much as 50% of Germany's wind energy production capacity was owned by citizens and local communities. And by 2015, Germany was producing nearly half of all wind energy produced in the European Union. This just goes to show how fast things can go when official government management and planning is replaced by a different kind of arrangement (based on the alternative mechanism of citizenship). Again, the power of the swarm is harnessed in this example: large numbers of citizens are in favor of sustainable energy production and want to do their bit in making it happen, but they also want to see the direct benefits for their personal households, also to offset the equally direct negative impact of visual and noise pollution caused by wind turbines. This arrangement they could wholeheartedly promote to each other in the modern swarms.

The German initiative makes maximum use of citizens' swarm behavior. Personal and economic calculations that each individual could make about this important issue, instead of adopting a passive wait-and-see attitude and see what politicians, bureaucracy and lobbies come up with, are shared between citizens quicker and on a large scale, which leads to a shared attitude and approach. This truly moves masses, and far more so than the traditional top-down government approach, no matter how well-intended (the official rhetoric of paternalism). This 'normal' traditional government-controlled way is also a lot less attractive, as it basically boils down to a top-down government intervention in your immediate environment, which comes with a visible negative effect on the surrounding landscape and with doubtful benefits through a 'promised' tax break that still remains to be seen, or an even more indirect 'promise' of 'national' greening of all energy consumption. What is happening here is that the status of the legitimacy and authority of the formal democracy among modern, self-organizing citizens has dropped compared to their own bold and committed citizens' initiatives. Actions by the government are considered more unreliable than citizens' effective joint self-management, especially when it comes to 'promises' that are at odds with the 'natural' drive towards expansion of government, such as 'promises' of tax cuts. Few still believe in the reliability of those kinds of promises by governments. Citizens feel that they themselves are doing an equally good job for the common good, and have greater trust, perhaps also based on prior experiences, in their own motives for commitment to social objectives (*eudaimonia*), justified by reliable and transparent canny behavior, more so than in those of politicians or civil services working on behalf of 'the government.' This is why Germany is currently the most productive country in the European Union when it comes to wind energy. Tellingly, politicians in very few other countries are even considering adopting, let alone copying, this best practice – ignorant to the fact that they are only further confirming mistrust of politics and politically-imposed objectives!

> *A case in point is Denmark, which has meanwhile copied this better and more effective approach to the energy transformation. On the Danish island of Thy, for example, nearly all wind turbines are owned by local residents. In fact, you will be hard-pressed to find*

a spot on the island without a wind turbine. The fact that revenue generated by the wind turbines largely remains on the island makes that the nearly 3,000 residents do not get worked up about the visual pollution. Meanwhile, nearly 44 percent of Denmark's nationwide power production comes from wind turbines.

8

The Battle between the Media for Dominance as Public Channels

The disruptive technologies are creating an entirely new direct channel for consumers, and, as shown above, for citizens. On this platform, data, opinions, and analyses are compiled and shared by consumers and citizens. They produce the content themselves, respond themselves, sometimes publicly, sometimes in private communities, to each other and are thus able to gauge what people support and to what degree. This is therefore a direct data and news channel for citizens themselves.

This is proven by the fact, which also happens to be the effect of it, that social media are creating their own village culture with their own rules and etiquette. Social media have social standards, just like a grandstand at a stadium or a village square. But users are still looking for balance between etiquette rules (What is appropriate language? What should interpersonal conduct be like? How do you deal with adversaries?), while also wanting attention and influence, whereby this cry for attention could be at odds with the etiquette rules and actually be off-putting for some.

You could even go so far as to say that public opinion is now, for the first time ever, truly in the hands of the public. All the filters that exist in traditional channels, such as pundits, journalists, critics, commentators, as well as politicians who like to 'interpret' the world for us, are still there, also in the new channel, but now explicitly so, as the filters they are.

My analysis should, however, not lead to the conclusion that the new media, where citizens publish news and scandals on their own platforms, are as clean as a whistle and completely transparent in how they work. Still, I have noticed that the addition of this more direct channel gives citizens greater control over and insight into data and news, and leads to healthy competition with traditional media as they compete for scoops and double-check news posted on the new media platforms. Journalists are becoming more critical and are starting, often triggered by news published on new channels, to look more for hidden or forgotten scandals and negative news, spurred on by their editors, because they are also seeing that competition across the media landscape is now primarily for the scarce attention of the general public. The personal networks built by a small group of professional politicians and journalists that served or fed traditional media, and also could lead to self-censorship or the sweeping under the rug of sensitive issues, are exposed and opened up as all media, including these new ones, must compete with each other. Competition, here too, generates belief in one's own strengths and dedication to transparency and innovation. In this same way, opposition parties in politics are gathering more ammunition to fire at the incumbent government, with better substantiation and undeniable facts. This further breaks open the political agenda and public debate.

The battle between traditional, new media, and information channels ultimately revolves around establishing the truth, about finding data and facts, and publishing them, and about framing. Framing is about how we interpret these facts and news, and about how we get our interpretation accepted as the best or only correct one? The battle for the underlying frames through which facts are viewed and which steer our interpretation of the facts is now also fought much more out in the open than in the past. In philosophical and underlying terms, the battle is about whether there is 'objectivity' in data gathering and interpretation. This more open battle of information and opinions and subsequently of frames, triggers doubts about the old frames, the old news selection and the old interpretations. Doubts about 'objectivity' explain why all kinds of pundits and professors are no longer instantly believed as objective commentators (although there was always this subtle difference between a scientifically substantiated opinion and the opinion of an interested and intelligent citizen, which is yet another difference that is now being exposed and accentuated in the battle of the media) or have lost the natural foundation of this objectivity under their public authority. The seeming objectivity of the old filters is therefore criticized more fiercely because their filtering has been exposed for all to see, thanks to the open and direct gathering and sharing of information by the 'crowd'.

The direct channel has exposed the manipulations by the traditional channels, even allowing citizens to contrast these with their own interpretations, their own knowledge, and even their own experts. Key elements of the manipulation tactics of traditional media, which are now increasingly being challenged on the larger platform, were:

- individualization of an opinion: 'yes, that's your opinion, but others…'
- brushing aside possible complaints: 'we're already working on it, just wait and see', or: 'it's a very minor problem, you're the only one with this complaint'
- challenging the complainer personally: 'are you not just being difficult?'
- brushing aside information: critical and real news is countered with fake news
- denying facts that were gathered in a bottom-up manner: 'no, we really have not seen that in our much larger day-to-day practices'

This explains why the term 'fake news' is so widely used these days and has even become a dominant theme in the public debate and in journalists' professional day-to-day! On the new direct channel, all those traditional experts with public status will have to re-establish their authority. Their filtering is no longer hidden behind rhetorical skills, good intentions or blind authority based on their position as a recognized 'expert'. The battle of facts, truth, and framing is basically fought more out in the open and has become fiercer, without the old reassuring rooting in 'objectivity' and 'expert status'. This will take a lot of getting used to, especially for those who had some kind of public authority in the old media. They simply cannot escape the fact that they are going to have to re-establish their authority, and that they are going to have to add modern rhetorical skills to their public appearances. In the modern public arena, those who think they can continue to rely on their old expert status will only be dismissed as arrogant, elitist, and pretentious.

It should also be noted that, since the new public arena and the underlying technologies are enabling swarm behavior with increasingly extreme synchronized movements of larger groups of citizens, many typically human phenomena will be intensified. Voter volatility and lack of loyalty, for example, have always been around in political markets, but they are now becoming more extreme, as already seen in the most recent election results.

We have always known that images hit home extremely fast and directly, more so than spoken and written content, while also having the power to make and break a reputation. One example is that infamous photo of President George W. Bush peering out of a window on Air Force 1 as it flew over Katrina-hit New Orleans. The negative impact of this image of the president, watching the great misery of so many of his fellow Americans safely from a distance, surrounded by his personal security team, is one that Bush never managed to shake. These physical images, including photos, videos, and vlogs, are now appearing on the direct channel, further amplifying their impact. New technologies have been showing common human behavior in a magnified and more extreme form for some time now. The social impact of these technologies is amplified by the feedback loops and swarm behavior. Their effect on public opinion is also heightened as their content is copied or referenced by the traditional channels of politics, TV, radio, and the written press. In this sense, there is a cumulative and self-amplifying effect across the entire new media landscape, an effect that is ultimately based on the fierce competition for eyeballs.

Elsewhere, this development has been called a quest for and possibility of a *digital agora* enabled by social media,[32] referring back to the home of the direct democracy of ancient Athens: the Agora. It should be noted that my assessment of a new direct channel and of the ensuing competition across the new media landscape does not mean that the traditional channels and the new channel are completely separate channels in terms of usage and production. Precisely the competition fueled by and on the new channel has made that virtually all traditional media, such as TV and written press, are anxiously using all kinds of online applications to (try to) join in and be visible and relevant on the new channel. All in all, the digital agora has substantially improved civic participation in democracy, even besides the fact that it has lifted the lid on much of the manipulation that the old channels engaged in. The public that is now reached (and partly getting involved) is more diverse, broader both in terms of being a reflection of society and in terms of its interests (not only political junkies), more coherent thanks to mutual community building and interconnection in networks. And then there is my earlier point: in terms of content, the messages on the new channel and in the agora are more personal, more relevant, more transparent, less selective, and more inclusive in terms of interests and even emotions. The digital agora is a public forum, a public grandstand that is always 'on'. This does, however, sometimes lead to loud, negative, foul-mouthed behavior.

This is the other side of the same revolution in social relations; not only politicians and executives have to make major cultural changes, citizens do too. Over the past few decades, citizens have been conditioned to protest, rather too much so. The louder and fiercer the protest, the more effective it was in getting elected officials and corporate executives to listen. And this protest was also fueled by the frustration left by previous experiences of being completely ignored and having no influence whatsoever. If the new media channels end up leading to citizens visibly getting involved in the public domain, having influence, being heard, being able to take part in the decision-making process, citizens will have to adopt a different style in the public forum to match this more serious and more powerful role. Cultural behavior always results from earlier assessments and experiences, emotional gains, and status; if these swing the other way, citizens' public behavior will also swing the other way.

New technology is not only focused on data and information, but also on images and other types of media. As a result, a politician's personality and sincere and seemingly authentic communication and the associated rhetoric skills in the public debate, and consequently the political debate itself as well, have become decisive. Nowadays, every citizen feels empowered to, through new technology, judge politicians on these human factors behind the facade of the 'professional politician.' In fact, in the modern perception of authenticity, politicians are seen as more authentic when they come across as unprofessional and do not have a background as a professional politician. Aristotle's rhetoric had already taught us that one's authority is based on one's position and life story, and the more personal the match between person and message, the more effective one will be in playing to the grandstand.[33] This explains the success of Emmanuel Macron and Trump's victory over Clinton. It is clear that Hillary Clinton excelled on each of Aristotle's Logos elements, as she had solid knowledge and understanding of current affairs, good arguments, and good plans, but she fell short on both other elements. It should be noted, however, that in Trump's case, Aristotle's Ethos does, quite confusingly, not stand for his ethical caliber or ethical principles, but instead refers to the authority awarded to the speaker by an inherent and immediately visible connection between his message and his personality and life story. This particular component of rhetoric is far more important nowadays in a public arena that is changing through the use of new technology. Although the trend of the growing importance of politicians' appeal, charisma, and how they get their message across dates back to before the emergence of new technologies, the new public arena and greater visibility are making this trend even stronger. Every voter feels empowered to directly, almost physically close, as if it were in the flesh and in real time, judge the personal nature, character, honesty, and appeal of any politician on their smartphone through videos of interviews, reruns of debates and rallies, and 'scores' in the public debate. In Trump's case, his style and biographical background made his message of draining the Washington, D.C. swamp instantly recognizable and credible for many people. Anyone with some knowledge of the world of real estate, from which Trump hailed, could suspect that his relationship with lobbyists and politicians would in fact turn out to be a lot less disruptive than he suggested it would be. Also in terms of Aristotle's Kairos (see also note 33), Trump probably outdid Hillary. Although this has been a well-known and well-managed factor in political campaigns for some time already, and both camps will have focused on it heavily, expertly, and based on traditional polling, assessing what message and slogan can best capture the political mood at this time.

The unexpected success of Jeremy Corbyn's campaign compared to that of Theresa May in the 2017 UK parliamentary election can also be attributed to the greater perceived authenticity in how he presented himself, which was a good fit with his personal biographical background. Much more so than in May's case, whose campaign was found to be overly controlled, mechanical, distant, and laden with vague statements. 'While the Tories are doing their best to keep the Prime Minister away from real people and tough questions, the Labour leader is happiest on the campaign trail.'[34] Most media referred to May's campaign as a 'managed public appearance.'

So, the new media landscape has a fundamentally different structure, as an extra direct channel has been added to it. This leads to entirely different competition factors between all channels:

- in the battle for the public's scarce attention
- in the battle between 'self-production' and 'professional' production
- in the battle for public power and influence (like in public framing) and therefore between all manipulations, by old and new media

The new direct channel is primarily a media channel (aside from, for example, a bartering and organization platform), because it is focused mainly on sharing increasingly self-produced images, data, information, and opinions. The old dichotomy of 'professional' and 'personal' has completely ceased to apply. When I refer to the old channels as the written press (newspapers and magazines) and TV/radio, I am referring to the old, traditional media channels, to be defined as channel no. 1 (press) and channel no. 2 (TV/radio). This makes the new direct channel of, for, and by citizens channel no. 3. The dividing line between these channels has meanwhile started to fade, as traditional media join the third channel with their own websites, apps, and online accounts and archives. My designation of the new media channel as 'direct' could lead to the misconception that I have failed to acknowledge that there are also new manipulations that erode the 'directness' of the channel, such as the use of algorithms and big data, both by the owners of the channels and by the platforms' technology suppliers. Classing the new media channel as 'direct' can also lead to confusion as elected officials and politicians will join the new channel as citizens. Again, this shows how the traditional distinction between 'professional' and 'personal' is slowly disappearing. Trump himself is a great example of this, as he, throughout his presidency so far, has been communicating more,

more directly, and more autonomously on Twitter than through official spokespersons, press releases, or cabinet members. I expect the third channel to dominate the other two in democracies, because the public forum is always 'on' and, more importantly, is (still?) harder to manipulate by professional parties (admittedly, manipulations rely on secrecy, so perhaps manipulations are already rife in new media beyond our knowledge at this moment).

One important indicator of the increasing dominance of the third channel is that formal democratic politics is increasingly taking its lead from the third channel when it comes to sounding out public opinion, setting the agenda, and formulating positions. In my analysis of the media landscape, I therefore often refer to the democratic political system as the fourth channel (even though parliamentary politics has a lot wider scope than the other media), because politicians are increasingly taking their lead from the people as their traditional manipulations in the form of information management, systems of leaking, rhetorical tactics and framing are gradually losing their effectiveness. In the old days, before the technological revolution, there was certainly some kind of balance of power, and consequently a lot of two-way manipulation between the political channel and both mainstream media channels, nos. 1 and 2. In the modern age, with growing competition for readers', voters', and citizens' attention, which is increasingly in short supply, the fourth channel will become more reactive, primarily taking its lead from the now dominant third channel, but also from both the mainstream channels, because these will copy the flows and messages and polling on the direct channel and therefore increase its strength.

One particularly clear example happened in Germany in July 2018. It came following German professional soccer player Mesut Özil's announcement that he would no longer be available to play for 'Die Mannschaft,' the German national team, citing racial discrimination as the reason behind his decision. Özil's move triggered a massive Twitter campaign with the hashtag #metwo, raising awareness of the fact that there are millions of Germans, like Özil, who have two identities, and sometimes also two passports. Many took to Twitter to share revelations and feelings of

similar discrimination. But the most striking thing about this
particular Twitterstorm was that people increasingly started to
express indignation at the fact that the widespread raising of this
issue on Twitter was not getting it onto the agenda for political
debate. Apparently, the crowd has become so used to influencing
the political agenda that they criticize politics when they fail to
put their issue on the agenda and are shying away from engag-
ing on the issue the crowd has raised! The political tactics of
ignoring, keeping a lid on, and denying an issue are increasingly
made impossible.

The position of the old information and framing intermediaries, such
as journalists, political commentators, columnists, and pundits, has
been weakened tremendously, as new technologies allow citizens
to poll each other directly on certain news or check the accuracy of
scandals. The traditional 'filters' (of which we only became aware
because we now have a direct citizen-to-citizen channel!) are forced to
re-establish their authority. As was to be expected, they are trying to
do so by focusing on their core business of seeking out and comment-
ing on unpleasant news and scandals outside the official channels of
politics and governance. In the old days, professional politicians and
the independent press could be found to scratch each other's backs,
they often needed each other too much, in the long run, following
and thus reinforcing each other's manipulations of data and news.
This behavior was partly a tacit business arrangement perpetuated by
mutual interests, and partly occasionally unsettled, thankfully, when
the free press had to investigate and report on an issue or scandal. Of
course, the right political culture and the rule of law helped to stimulate this independent information gathering and news production as
free press was institutionally protected and valued. In the new era, a
competing direct channel has emerged, and both politicians and press
have to find their bearings in it. Editorial staff at U.S. newspapers,
for example, have meanwhile cottoned on to the fact that instead of
White House correspondents attending official press conferences by
a fake-news-spreading president, they need journalists out in the real
world, close to citizens and companies, to report current and factual
news, preferably as painfully dissenting from official policy myths as
possible. This was also a cultural revolution in the media. As being a

White House correspondent used to be a high-profile job with lots of status, media would send their most senior journalists to attend press conferences at the White House. But it has now lost much of its status, prompting media to send junior journalists, just to have someone there or even as part of their training, while authoritative and seasoned political journalists are sent out to cover stories and gather news away from the White House in the real world. A drastic reversal of status and the tools of status!

Social media are particularly useful in picking up on the first signs of discontent and unrest, which journalists subsequently report on and amplify in mainstream news media, backed by the authority of reputable newspapers and cable news channels. Politics and traditional media are both feeling the competition from the new direct channel. In response, the independent press can validate and use its independence by seriously investigating news reported on the direct channel and considering it in their prioritization of what is or should be news at any one time. In their battle for the public's and voters' attention and support, both parties also want to strike up alliances with each other, which sees the authority of the direct channel bolstered in and by traditional media. This is the new media landscape for every single party in the public domain.

All of this makes that anyone with a formal institutional position in the representative democracy, such as a political leader, whip, cabinet member, mayor, etc. now has a dual role. Occupying a position of authority may increase or intensify your impact on the direct channel of the citizens, but it is certainly not a given that it will. It may just as well work the other way round. Your high profile and formal importance may make it more likely for you to become the object of people's scorn. So, if yours is a prominent position, you need to realize that your authority is not a given, and that it needs to be based on your personality, on you coming across as authentic, and on a visible attitude of citizenship ('he/she is one of us'). This goes for any kind of formal governance position. For many elected officials, one of the biggest changes that the new public arena has brought is that they can no longer rely on the old professional filters, such as press and PR officers and reputation management firms. They are going to have to get to work with their own tone of voice and personal insights. A prominent position may now well be a burden rather than a privilege, as officials have to work extra hard to come across as personable and authentic. The public debate is informalizing to a great degree, becoming more personal, closer to home, more network-oriented.[35]

In the public debate, the exact division of powers between all existing communication channels (Internet, social media, newspapers, radio, TV) is yet to take shape. All those who have the subconscious (manipulated) belief that the old channels were entirely free of manipulation will now have to face up to a frustrating truth. The new, direct channels are revealing both the lack of transparency of information and opinions and the underlying manipulations by the mainstream media channels from the perspective of citizens.

> So, on the one hand, there is competition between all these media channels, while on the other we are seeing collaboration grow. In Latin America, there are fact-checking websites at work that use the expertise, observations, and knowledge of the crowd, such as Chequeado. A recent survey showed that another such fact-checking site, La Sila Vacia, is currently Colombia's 3rd most influential media channel. Some of these websites have meanwhile earned praise for having lifted the lid on political scandals, including Mexico's Animal Politico, which ran a story on the corrupt governor of the state of Veracruz, who subsequently went on the run, was eventually captured, and is now awaiting trial. Competition also has a positive effect on democracy: the free press in those countries, which never really behaved that freely and independently in the first place, now has to make sure they do, otherwise no one will take any notice of what they publish.

One of the power factors of the new channels is that they enable transparent opinion polling by and among citizens, providing real-time insight into how many people endorse a certain opinion, and recording this instantly and publicly. As a result of the latter aspect, both traditional media and institutional channels, such as politics, end up quoting and using information from the new channels while reporting to their respective target audiences. Again, you can see the influence of the new, direct channels grow, as they are being copied and quoted on traditional channels. It is precisely the resolute, textual, and public nature of new media that makes that no one can afford to ignore the citizens' message.

9
Disruption of Democracy

The massive influence that disruptive technologies are having on the workings of our political system and on our voting also affects democracy as a whole, but that is not all, because democracy itself will also change. The entire institutional order of democracy is being disrupted, not only the selection and influence of politicians as the primary representatives and rulers within the democratic structures. Again, the new direct channel of, by, and for citizens is responsible for this. A non-revolutionary analysis will also show that the direct channel will have different and greater impact on politics, elections, and the competencies we want our key political figures to have. It is undeniable, citizens' influence on the workings and outcomes of democracy is growing.
But as is so often the case with those who fail to see the revolution in human society and relations, this analysis is still based on the impact on the traditional relations between citizen and democracy, while there is a far more revolutionary and disruptive development going on. The biggest threat to our representative democracy is analogous to what happened to market players who have meanwhile gone out of business. If our representative democracy fails to adapt on time and embrace the direct channel and make it its own, it will disappear and be replaced by an uncontrolled and unmanageable permanent direct democracy. The revolutionary and disruptive question, one so fundamental and values-driven that incumbents will be the last to face up to it, is how much representative democracy we still need alongside the abovementioned loud, outspoken and powerful public forum. I am seeing political elites the world over commit the well-known mistakes in response to disruption, as described at length in literature about disruption. They deny, they ignore, and they think they can stop it, such as by abolishing referendums and other forms of public polls. Incumbents are also going on the defensive by blaming and shaming and drawing attention to scandals and new manipulations on the new channels in their struggle to keep their heads above water. That said, there is nothing wrong

with uncovering scandals, highlighting malicious manipulations, and challenging tacitly acquired monopolies, as is also the case on new media and platforms. It should, in fact, be applauded. But still, citizens need to be alerted to any of the incumbents' interest that may be driving their newfound role as moral crusaders. Interventions must not lead to undermining of the power and impact of the new direct channels, as these must continue to be able to take part in the public debate uncensored. The power of the permanent public forum is here to stay. The political routine in democracies that lets otherwise passive voters elect their officials once every four years is a thing of the past. And what is also a thing of the past is citizens' regard for this right to vote, which is not a God-given right, but something people have had to fight for, which in many western countries only became a universal right around a century ago. Citizens' regard for this right has waned because the platform economy has taught modern citizens to be much more active, to make their own choices, to gather and compare their own information, and to make their own decisions. Citizens are now used to voting, choosing and comparing all kinds of issues, services and proposals. For them it is almost incomprehensible that political voting is a scarce right across the globe and that, in most countries, it took long civic struggles for people to gain the right to vote. And now citizens want to extend this emancipation to even more aspects of their lives. A system where mandated politicians only have to ask citizens to renew their faith in them every four years is entirely out of sync with citizens' new-found emancipation. What is also a thing of the past is that a politician's political authority is guaranteed for four years, they are now going to have to fulfill promises and live up to expectations on each and every issue and occasion in front of the permanently open and active direct public forum. In the media landscape of the past that was, of course, already partly the case with comments and muck-raking by traditional free press, but now every politician knows it comes directly from the voting public and their answers will be judged collectively and explicitly on their public forum.

As a result, promising digital democracy experiments are popping up across the globe. The most far-reaching ones seem to be those political parties that are opening up and giving their members more say and even letting them decide who will represent the party in elections, parties such as the Five Star Movement in Italy, Spain's Podemos, and The Pirate Party in Iceland. What we are seeing here is that innovation is accelerated within and by new political parties, which are thus becoming disruptors of the old-fashioned political landscape. They better understand and serve voters than 'incumbent' parties thanks to their embrace of direct democracy in their internal operations and in their approach to statesmanship, they are quicker in becoming citizen platforms themselves. Due to the fact that traditional political analysts, caught up as they are in their own routines, were so naive as to emphasize programmatic aspects and content in their analyses of the difference between political parties to explain their varying levels of success at the ballot box, they are now also tarnishing these emerging parties in a largely programmatic manner as parties of 'extremists' and 'populists'. It could, tying in with my analyses here, very well be that these new parties, like disruptors in the market, are better at dealing with their members and (potential) voters, better at approaching them more directly, and better at serving them faster, also through their policy, arguments, and the positions they take, but also with offering government jobs and career prospects, hence inspiring loyalty, as a result of which, unfortunately, and perhaps even as a side effect, an extremist political course becomes more likely to succeed. Although new technology therefore certainly creates a fiercer and livelier permanent public forum, I do not think it automatically breeds right-wing extremism. In Europe, meanwhile, the populist tide is turning.[36] In line with my call for strategic intelligence, this may be because 'incumbent' political parties are becoming more strategic intelligent and are starting to learn to adjust their strategy and methods, also internally, to stem the rise of populist parties. Still, I am not seeing many good examples of this. What is the most fascinating and, in objective terms, the most valuable aspect to observe in the real-life political experiments that are now going on is whether this analysis that current political success can be explained by a necessary tendency toward direct democracy, political parties becoming citizen platforms, will also affect the internal party organization of the so-called populist parties that had earlier political success and often demand more direct democracy from the state, but are actually far from democratic internally. Geert Wilders' Freedom Party in the Netherlands, for example, only has 1 member: Mr. Wilders himself. The main strategic effect of the disruption among political parties is therefore, like in the market, that they need to turn off their reflex of interpreting and competing on content and rhetorics, and instead learn to fundamentally change their organization, routines, and internal working methods. Here too, disruption leads primarily to numerous increasingly fundamental interventions and breakthroughs in the existing approach to voters, like their hierarchy, their procedures of decision making, selecting representatives, and the routines that were established in the past.

> But there are also experiments emerging from government initiatives, in my observation it seems mainly at the municipal level, such as Decide Madrid, Better Reykjavik, and Better Neighborhoods. Another interesting example to highlight here is 'Madame Mayor, I have an idea,' which is focused on participatory budgeting in Paris and can ultimately award or submit proposals for 100 million euros in funding every year. Amsterdam has an online platform on which inhabitants of a certain part of the city can submit proposals for their local district and join a vote on them. The proposal that gets a majority of the votes is then discussed in the relevant political bodies, in a fine example of cooperation between direct and representative democracy. Civil servants help develop these ideas of citizens to prepare them as an official proposal. This is in line with arrangements where governments give citizens a say in the state's most important legal and political monopoly: taxation and public spending. This was called tax choice, as also considered by the U.S. government in some proposals for bills around 2007. These proposals died in committee. Needless to say, there are also more and more examples of citizens being involved in bills that are to be submitted to the legislature, such as through Estonia's people's assembly and vTaiwan. This latter initiative is a collaborative process that is intended to reach consensus on policy, legislative, and regulatory issues. They also arise out of genuine concern and civic duty in civil society, such as Decide Madrid.[37]

As I have outlined, the direct channel's power over formal democracy is based on:

1. direct self-production and publicity; citizens are now able to produce, show images, and 'post' without the intervention of others
2. transparency, through written text and citable statements and numerical polls, of the level of support among citizens for certain proposals or bills, like a continuously ongoing referendum
3. collective opinion forming through open sharing of opinions and greater and certified group support through transparent swarm behavior
4. and, to ease the minds of those who still value traditional democracy, regardless of how indirect it currently is: the power of the new direct channel is also boosted by its reverberation in the other channels, both other media and political, both in the form of amplification (similar to that of a megaphone) on competing information and media channels and in the form of official political channels copying their message from the new direct channel. Every politician who wants to be re-elected will listen more and more closely to, and try to gain control over, the direct channel by openly supporting what the majority of users there show they support.

The most important powers that this new channel places in the hands of citizens and that is disrupting representative democracy are:

- **power of information**: jointly gathering contrasting data, sourcing other experts and expertise, sounding a counterargument
- **power of opinion and communication**: opinions are formed out in the open, anyone can join the debate, which is also shared with other social groups, thus allowing the argument, the scope, and support for certain views to grow exponentially. This is a theoretic benefit that comes with new technology and the new public arena. In practice, we are also seeing other more negative or restricting effects: the information and opinion overload makes that people lock themselves into new selections of groups that they want to be a part of or of information they consume (bubbles), on top of that there is increasing proof of how manipulating parties are now, using algorithms and other resources, doing the same and basically reinforcing this bubble reflex
- **power of publication**: discussions, debates, and dialogues not only unfold in the public domain, the public can also instantly fact-

check and public support for a certain viewpoint is easy to measure. Finally, this leads to publication of text and images, which can be cited by other, more traditional media channels and the political channel, both more used to working with proposals on paper: it now is not only public, but also becomes a publication

How exactly the power shift between the channels, as outlined above, will play out is impossible to predict. The good news is that parliamentary democracy is still the best form of government when it comes to dealing with empowered citizens who strike up alliances and keep each other informed. Our rulers will not soon, contrary to their Chinese and Russian counterparts, try to censor and manipulate the direct channel (although worldwide some examples have now popped up). But one thing that democratic politics is going to have to get used to is that the direct channel will be where issues are put on the agenda, complaints about current governance practices are voiced, visions on the best approach are formulated, approval ratings tallied, and the place where all these things will generate momentum and garner public support.[38]

While new technology will (threaten to) disrupt representative democracy, there are also positives, as new technology also has the potential to greatly improve, accelerate, and expand democracy among an entire population. Both above and in what follows, I pointed out and will point out several relevant examples, which are currently developing and being applied worldwide, sometimes even initiated by democratic governments themselves. Improving democracy through new technologies ranges from enabling governments to extend their reach to a larger and more diverse part of the population to better exchanges of arguments (than the meanwhile extremely traditional yes/no vote on some pre-cooked proposal in official referendums). What is also interesting is the call for and use of the wisdom of the crowd and the enormously wide-ranging expertise of citizens, who are more than willing to join the thought process about proposals and provide professional input on how to improve them. And finally, innovations relating to the organization of a permanent digital agora are showing that governments are starting to realize that they need to embrace new technology and seriously deploy it to improve democracy, and that to ignore it or see it only as a threat is simply the wrong answer from a strategic point of view.

One excellent example is Government 3.0 in Korea, where the Korean government encourages citizens to get involved and participate, using concepts such as collective intelligence.[39]

Direct democracy is openly visible in terms of its points of view and arguments, and in terms of its quantitative support, purely because of the omnipresence of this new technological channel. This ranges from collective public resistance, such as the global #MeToo movement, to targeted resistance (such as local communities that are getting organized to protest against plans to reroute traffic flows through their local area) to calls for collective public resistance through official political channels (by making people aware of a complaints procedure or public hearing about a legislative amendment). This is why we no longer need legal or constitutional positioning and legitimization for this direct democracy, this public forum or the population that wants to join in, in comparison to and contrast with representative democracy, which is often still the constitutional starting point. From now on, the public forum is always on and is able to wield great power through its massive and open reach among citizens, reinforced by the fact that in a democracy elected officials ultimately want to get re-elected. The manipulations that existed in traditional democracy, such as denial and disinformation, reiterating myths, citing so-called neutral research that was actually guided behind the scenes, and diverting attention from certain problems or information by creating new problems or information, will all be challenged openly by engaged citizens who in certain cases know more about an issue than researchers and experts or than those with administrative responsibility, and who manage to rapidly get their own experts together and deploy them in the public debate.[40]

In addition to the aforementioned massive overhaul of how we elect our officials, the following are further important effects that the disrupting new technologies will have on democracy:

1. Due to modern citizens' notion of time and changing use of information, representative democracy's decision-making process will look ever more sluggish, as it is indirect and without civic involvement, manipulative, and in the view of this modern trained citizen who is used to being active on the permanent public forum, too focused on its own network and interests.

2. 'Behind-the-scenes' and 'backroom' deals as a way of reaching political consensus, subsequently presented to the public as a fait accompli, will increasingly be measured against new requirements in the new public arena. These deals will have to be transparent, fair, well thought-out, consider the impact on citizens and immediate stakeholders, etc. In other words, legitimization of any of these kinds of compromises reached by politicians shifts to convincing, generally accessible, understandable, and most of all public explanation. It is then no longer enough to ensure negotiators keep in close contact with previously elected parliamentary politicians and secure their backing. After all, these politicians may have an entirely different stake in supporting a compromise and will, if it serves their interest, not hesitate to publicly go with 'the swarm' or 'the crowd.'

3. Similar to disruption in the market, the direct information and choices offered by platforms, websites, and social media will also undermine loyalty in the political arena, albeit loyalty to political leanings and parties. Consumers no longer choose their hotel based on loyalty to a certain chain or type, but instead based on an open comparison of all options and peer reviews on Booking.com or Trivago, and also based on their particular need at that specific time. Voters have shown a similar change in behavior, as they have become more and more unpredictable, and guided by specific issues and moods. Contemporary voters' main voting criterion can be summarized as follows: 'What have you done for me lately?'

The impact on politics and elected democracy is huge: voters are now able to view and evaluate politicians' character and rhetorical skills on their personal screens in real time on their own screens. Their judgments and votes are increasingly based on this. They have learned from the market that their own preferences should be dominant and they expect politicians to address them directly. This latter point was indeed heeded by both the Clinton and the Trump campaigns in 2016 when they targeted voters in swing states using messages on Facebook. And it is where Dutch politics and media went wrong during recent coalition talks. Dutch media kept reporting on this absolute non-event, endless coalition talks that seemed to be going nowhere and had no news value at all. So, there was no reason for citizens' actual attention because there were no interim public results or political statements. But neither traditional media nor the politicians involved seemed to realize this, so reporters kept on reporting and politicians kept on giving vacuous interviews. They simply could not say anything substantial about the talks. And what neither professional press nor professional politicians realized was that there was now a new direct channel competing for the eyeballs of the public and that citizens would tune out this 'managed news' that traditional media were churning out.

Of course, this new tool for citizens has some negative features, such as excess gossip, sometimes with a devastating public impact, rash judgments of politicians or celebrities, snippets of information, and abusive language to name a few. Those 'experts' who now accentuate these negatives are partly right, but they are also in danger of being on the side of the incumbent elite. They sound objective and nuanced, but in the end they only support the current public elite's not taking steps towards recognition of this new power. They are more on the side of old political elites than on the side of the people, while I always thought that democracy was invented 'for the people.'[41]

For those who feel strongly about democracy and are able to pierce through the historically grown institutional practices of elected representative democracy, all these developments are good news. This does not include today's professional politicians, though, as they are seeing that their jobs and positions are on the line, they feel threatened, just like all those struggling companies and professionals in the disrupted commercial market. A beneficial effect that all those new technologies will have on democracy is that they will facilitate the rise of deliberative democracy, as the same technologies that created the new public arena and the new public forum are used to enable much more direct dialogue with citizens. By this, I mean an active attitude to engage in dialogue, broader debate across larger groups in society, in other words engaging with the crowd. This goes a lot further than the simple like/dislike dichotomy on social media and the simple yes/no of elections and referendums, as it moves toward an online platform where opinions are shared, which leads to better arguments and viewpoints than could ever be achieved in the backrooms of the political establishment.[42]

This ultimately leads to a totally different concept of how govern-ment works, decides and delivers services, as shown by examples such as Medialab-Prado Madrid and neighborhood initiatives and platforms in Berlin, such as Holzmarkt, Ex-Rotaprint, and Prinz-essingarten. These neighborhood platforms combine citizen input on plans and the decision-making process for issues such as the spatial design of their neighborhood, the solution of traffic bottle-necks. They do that through a combination of votes among citizens, deliberations by the local town council, and the voluntary deploy-ment and harnessing of citizen organization with official services to tackle these issues together. When it comes to setting the agenda, decision making, and implementation, platform technology is used to the fullest and leads to intensive collaboration between politics and the civil service on one side and neighborhoods and citizens on the other. Traditional roles and collaborations suddenly seem very passive, technocratic, and hands-off.

True, these analyses are also alarming or even, in the eyes of many, overly simplistic. Many rightfully feel that the current representative democracy and today's professional independent press are still impor-tant. The thing is, however, to preserve and support them in this revo-lution, and to first admit, from a truly strategic perspective, that this new public arena with more open participation features is here to stay. The new public forum must not be brushed aside or ignored, but must instead be judged based on its value and its pros and cons with respect to the values that ultimately prop up the institutions of democracy and the free and independent professional press. From this acceptance and strategic assessment, current and future politicians will have to learn to live and engage with the new public forum, as well as learn a new or adapt their current rhetoric style, which is a much more imperative need in the public forum.

The possibilities offered by technologies also come with certain risks, as market disruption has taught all those companies that had estab-lished themselves in the market before disruptive technologies hit. This is the reason behind the sting in the earlier disruptive question: how much representative democracy do we still need if the public platform is constantly 'on' and so influential among the people and voters? This is the kind of disruptive question that many CEOs initially failed to ask themselves, just as many politicians and elected officials are failing to do now. The biggest danger that is looming as a result is that of 'populism' (specified here in a programmatic sense: people versus the elites and anti-immigrant. The term 'populism' in a literal sense is, in fact, incorrect, as all political parties need some form of populism in a democracy) no longer having to reach voters through political parties that have always shunned it, but now getting through to the people directly thanks to the public platform, using the platform, and picking up steam. This leads to a link between populist political parties and the kind of direct democracy that new technologies are enabling, as shown by M5S in Italy, which actively campaigns for direct, Internet-based democracy.[43] The good news, however, is that M5S, as far as I know, is the first political party with this program of promoting direct democracy, that actually tries to be consistent in its pursuit, as they have even already implemented it internally by allowing candidates for positions in the party to present their candidacies online and letting members vote for them directly without any selection committees.

In the transformation of democracy, there are two fundamental dimensions: first, representational structures versus participatory decision making and dialogue, and second, majority rule versus consensus-based joint decision making. Needless to say, all kinds of intermediate versions have been developed over the centuries, both in the constitutional order and in actual political behavior, precisely to keep shaping the value added by democracy or to adapt democracy to developments in the views of elected officials or among voters. Along both the above axes, many innovations are bound to pop up in response to the strategic developments I outlined earlier. Pure direct democracy, which many right-wing populist parties are aiming for, is often a continuation of the delegated and mildly deliberative construction in the above dimensions, albeit with the modern different tools. Citizens can get more directly involved, but they still have to let politicians decide what they can vote on and the politicians still run the country for them. What basically comes first is to protect the closed shop that is the party political system, and thus to protect politicians' personal chances of landing government jobs, despite the reproaching rhetoric on this very point against politicians of other parties or the political class in general.

The most notable exception to this rule is Italy's M5S party, which has actually implemented direct democracy internally in how candidates are selected for public office, based on the concept of majority rule. Every party member can put themselves up for an available position in the civil service and all members get to vote on who represents the party in the elections. So, in most political parties there is still a long way to go from professional politicians to directly elected officials who come straight 'from the people.' Just look at the oldest democracy in history, the Athenian democracy of approx. 500 BC, roughly 2,300 years ago, which had very explicit rules when it came to electing officials to prevent corruption and demagogy and to ensure certain expertise for special public offices, such as for the position of treasurer or person in charge of the military. The main reason why populist parties' banging the drum of direct democracy is so successful in the political system is that current representative democracy and the politicians operating within it only manage an approval rating of 50%, while the approval rating for their government practices is even lower, 42%.[44] In the modern public arena, these low ratings are even more visible and openly shared. All of this potentially undermines the authority of many traditional institutions such as elected politicians, judges, independent press, and universities. Admittedly, it is by no means clear exactly how much formal power the new public forum has. For a large part, the public forum's power is still indirect and runs through the traditional powers, such as politicians, reporters, judges, business people, administrators, and executives who anticipate, copy, and listen to opinions expressed in the public forum. Still, the public forum is gaining in importance, especially after recent experiences of the forum being used to meddle in elections, and the strategic need to take the forum into account is growing, also for these formally independent parties and persons.

So, maybe new technology will not directly change the formal power structure surrounding decisions to appoint persons to political or governmental positions, but it will increasingly openly rank these persons, publicly comment on and define their performance, and in the end this will directly influence their authority, their personal influence and so, ultimately, their career.

The Media and Framing Power Struggle

With the institutional order shifting as new technology gives citizens more direct power and knowledge and facilitates self-organization and swarm behavior, the present revolution is not merely a technological revolution, but rather a social, cultural, and anthropological revolution that is shaking our human existence to its core. Such revolutions, which are about real power and power shifts, therefore also require a power struggle, the contours of which we are already starting to see, both in dictatorships and in democracies.

For now, both parties that, in my analysis, stand to lose a lot of their power, the market and the state, would benefit most from denying that we are really dealing with this kind of all-encompassing revolution, painting it as a gradual and predictable transitional phase that they will, of course, still be able to control (with nothing but good will and good intentions).

The businesses that dominate this technology development and have often even become monopolies, such as Facebook and Alphabet, present this transition as a natural process, where the latest technologies are introduced to make all our lives better and their main intention is to contribute to our good life, *eudaimonia*. But what they are trying to hide are the negative effects of this new technology. While doing so, they claim a purely neutral, facilitating role, and attribute the – possible – damage to other parties that basically 'abuse' the new technology and artificial intelligence. You will not hear the dominant technology providers speak about how the power of traditional parties with the most influence and control, such as politics and current businesses (disruption!), is diminishing and how they as the new parties are ultimately making a lot of money, partly thanks to all kinds of manipulations, through data-driven targeting of consumers and advertising (and, as shown by the Cambridge Analytical scandal, political messages) based on data mined from consumers.

None of the parties that are visibly and dominantly involved in the platform economy can turn the other cheek amid calls for transparency, even less so as the major ones have or are seeking a listing on the stock market. Parties that have positioned themselves as mere 'facilitators' and 'providers' are increasingly forced to behave like media parties on the platforms, and are consequently co-responsible for whatever appears on these platforms in terms of information, visual content, and opinions. A case in point is the recent purge by Facebook, Twitter, and Alphabet to rid their platforms of Iranian and Russian users that are deliberately feeding their channels with manipulations, unrest, and misinformation.

This latter example also shows clearly that modern and uninhibited, if not unscrupulous, politicians can also benefit from the strategic use of the direct channel to citizens, using the same targeting technology for the purposes of their direct political strategies to win re-election, run a successful campaign, and influence public opinion. This behavior of the powers that be proves my point of how important and influential the new direct channels are becoming. My main purpose here is to demonstrate that the powers that support real democracy will be first and foremost in using these new technologies.

The state increasingly uses the same technology to monitor and control citizens and combat or prevent tax evasion, crime, and terrorism. This is a continuation of the traditional power of the state, but with new means, using the same technology that citizens have signed up to in droves, because citizens like using it so much and have been led to think by the companies behind it that what they are using is an entirely open, neutral, and non-manipulated channel.

As far as this development is concerned, there is also some hope, as new technology is now leading to the creation of platforms where citizens can inform and support each other, as well as new governments that not so much try to control citizens, but instead want to facilitate them, as in the case of Estonia, with its digital republic.[45] Still, this hope must never lead to gullibility on the actions and intentions of all those parties that are currently involved in the functioning, growth, and use of new disruptive technologies. A recent report published by the Rathenau Institute, a Dutch technology advisory body to the government, spoke of 'rules for the crowd' and highlighted the risk of new technology leading to the 'cultivation and taming' of humans, in reference to the work of German philosopher Peter Sloterdijk.[46] People are already being tamed and trained by politicians, marketing professionals, and public relations officials that are trying to steer or tempt them through targeted communication based on, like with Facebook, big data on citizens and algorithms that steer towards the most important target groups. The technology itself must therefore always also be assessed in terms of how it is used and for what purposes. In a power struggle, there is no neutrality. Even with so-called rationally reasoned government interventions, one must always wonder what possible political strategic goals could be behind it.

As stated earlier, new technology gives citizens the kind of power they never had before, both in the political domain and in the market. But new technology can also lead to greater power *over* those same citizens. In this sense, the focus on citizenship, solidarity between citizens, mutual commitment, and proactivity in tackling issues together, is certainly not a neutral undertaking or without obligations. It would be strange and inconsistent for me to, amid such a fundamental power struggle, want to take up a neutral, seemingly objective and purely rational position. Or have that pretension, because ultimately citizens will also have to join the struggle, fight the power, and fight for their power in the new technology-dominated reality and in the new media landscape. The major battles in this revolution will be a power struggle (who will win or retain power and will wield it over whom?) and a moral struggle (what do we consider good or bad behavior and results of behavior, and what is our view on the best future of mankind?).

Strategic Answer: New Blend of Representative and Direct Democracy

As covered at length, new technologies and their growing applications are having a major, revolutionary impact on politics and democracy. The associated risks are real. However, our previous experience with market disruption has taught us that ignoring, denying, or discrediting the new only shows poor strategic intelligence. So, after having outlined in an open strategic analysis the power of today's new technology and the inevitability of its impact, it is now time to think about how to deal with these technologies and their impact.

The biggest risk involved in the new public forum and arena is that they become our only source of insights, viewpoints, outlooks, and policy choices. This could lead to the following strategic challenges for incumbents in the political domain, as well as for existing democracy:

- Huge dominance of **demagogues**: those who best manage to play on the mood of 'the people' and 'the public forum' and to mobilize them, also for their personal interests. This particular effect has, of course, been visible for some time now whenever elections come around in representative democracies, but it will increase. This is also because public debate on the public forum will explode outside election season. This permanent public forum will become more agenda-setting and its influence will grow tremendously. This forum is permanently 'on,' which will also allow the influence of demagogues to grow.

- The disruption will mostly affect the existence and influence of **political parties**. This applies to the many different ways in which they contribute to democracy: development of ideology, framing of the political discourse, setting the political agenda, selection of candidates, training and stimulation of modern public leadership, and experimentation with direct democracy within the party as a learning process for citizens and governments[47]. At a minimum, this applies to their role in setting the political agenda, including the underlying influence of ideologically driven or well thought-out analyses of public and social issues. This role has already weakened considerably in today's revolutionary and transformational times as old ideologies cease to offer a solid footing and new ideologies are still in their early stages. As pointed out, one way to prevent disruption is to use new technologies to apply more direct democracy internally at political parties. The first initiatives in that area have started popping up. But it also touches on their most crucial role in democracies, the selection of qualified and ideologically consistently positionable politicians for a wide range of representative and governance jobs. At most political parties, this selection process has for some time now been based on a mixture of professional ('Is she/he up to the job?') and ideological ('Does she/he toe the party line?') considerations on the one hand, and outward, oriented toward the larger audience of voters, personal ('Will she/he be able to convince voters?') considerations on the other. This is the formal, objective, and professional outline of the selection process, but at most political parties this procedure is overrun by selection based on internal acceptance, proven loyalty, and friendships with the highest-ranking party members. From a psychological perspective, this culture that has grown is more than understandable. 'Politics' is an open and permanent power struggle. As a professional in the political domain, you want support and reliable loyalty around and behind you in that permanent struggle for power. If you add to that the fact that the new public arena enables candidates to attract and mobilize their own public support, the first two criteria of candidate selection will lose even more of their value, with the party amounting to no more than a passive vehicle for these candidates for further legitimization or, if legally required, for formal access to certain positions. Political parties will then only be founded on their ideological soundness and appeal and select candidates who support that program. This is not a very solid basis, because I have outlined that in the current new public arena personality and personal appeal will be decisive factors. This is aggravated by the fact that many voters do not believe that political parties currently select candidates objectively based on quality and have a sound track record in it.

- A permanent public forum also increases the risk of **erroneous or false information**: fake news, rumors, urban legends, confusion, manipulations by parties that want to steer certain decisions or prevent the debate from going into certain directions, et cetera. The biggest danger is, and this goes with saying, that this kind of misinformation not only affects public opinion, but also enters the decision-making process. This will turn into a permanent public struggle, one we are already seeing. Exposing falsehoods in certain information and news only triggers another public argument, which will take a lot of getting used to for many 'experts'. In the view of many in the public forum, there is often no dividing line between formal institutional resistance based on well thought-out and fact-based analysis and resistance that is based purely on reluctance to change tack or relinquish power. Many of the dissenting opinions coming out of institutions are often a mixture of both forms of resistance.

- The largest underlying risk of a dominant public forum, is that **long-term** considerations and systematic reasoning and measures are overlooked. The public forum has a short memory, needs that it wants met instantly, complaints that it wants resolved immediately, and generally little insight into and regard for systematic correlations, institutional problems, and legal requirements of due care. This is partly the result of institutional relations and behavior that have grown over decades, especially in representative democracies, where formal decision making and governance often takes place in secrecy, out of the view of the public, and without the public having any kind of say in it. So this culture, where the real institutional and long-term weighing and considerations are left out of the public defense of proposals, has reinforced a protest and self-centered culture in citizen opinion and public debate. Those who shouted the loudest, as well as the biggest demagogues, already knew that they played no role whatsoever in such backroom politics and that they could therefore shout whatever they wanted.

Part of the new public dialogue about these truly important issues is, in fact, easier to conduct through modern technology that enables more dialogue, more subtle distinctions, and more objective input than through dumbed-down official government-initiated referendums. New technology unlocks the wisdom of the crowd by creating a digital agora (see the examples in Chapter 9).

The use of new technology also shows that citizenship, as a solidarity- and values-based community and spontaneous value orientation of a large number of citizens, was there all along and has always been in working order. New technology therefore disrupts the old political frame, which was very well aligned with the interests of politicians, painting people as 'commoners' who only think about themselves, are calculating in what they can get out of the government, and only stand up for their own interests (nimbyism). Fine examples are offered by a wide range of local neighborhood apps that are used for security purposes, such as to share information of suspicious persons or burglaries, but also for bartering and volunteering or jobs for freelance professionals who offer their services on the app. One such neighbor-hood app is Nextdoor, which over 100,000 neighborhoods across the globe have meanwhile signed up to. China has meanwhile taken this one step further, using neighborhood apps to enable local volunteers within what are called 'grids' to help monitor security issues in a neigh-borhood, watching out for things such as fire and theft. That said, this system could quite conceivably also be abused by the Chinese govern-ment to monitor those citizens themselves and make sure they are sticking to the government's rules.

We have, however, not yet reached this level of openness, nuance, and dialogue about things that actually matter to the public, not by a long shot. Just as in the case of market disruption, we have to aim for a new and, also in the eyes of the public, serious blend of democracy based on a public forum, public consultation, and dialogue, and at the same time based on formal, legal anchoring of citizens' rights in these areas in representative democracy. All fake adaptations or manipula-tions of the political agenda or issues will be 'jeered off' by the public forum, precisely because trust in politics is at such a low level. A new public arena with a formal voice in representative decision making and debates will require a considerable learning process for citizens. Giving the public access to power, also in legislation, will be a great challenge for incumbents, i.e. the political class that is simply cut from a different cloth.

10
Disruption of Civil Service

The mechanisms of politics are a lot more similar to those of the market and therefore more likely to be affected by the same kind of disruption than the rest of the public sector, i.e. the civil service and public services. There is often still the reassuring belief that the disruption will not affect them, will not alter the workings of the civil service, and will certainly not jeopardize their existence. In these circles, there are indeed delaying mechanisms at work that will keep the disruptive effects of the Digital Civil Revolution at bay for some time to come. Much of their work is laid down in laws and rules that will remain effective until they are formally revoked, which is often a lengthy process. Funding is not subject to market volatilities, because both civil service and public services are funded publicly, often enshrined in law and protected through guarantees or citizens' entitlements and sluggish procedures. And there is underlying political and therefore legislative and legal support. Plus, the public expects public services to simply be available whenever they need them, ranging from waste collection to police, hospitals, and schools. The public can do without disruption of such services like a hole in the head, unless there are clear guarantees or alternatives.

But, in our drastically changing world, these shock-absorbing factors will not keep them safe from disruption forever. If voter volatility were to stretch to a broader and more extreme range of preferences and opinions through swarm behavior, the resulting political impact will also translate to a policy change in civil service and other kinds of public services. This still assumes a traditional pattern where disruption in the political domain leads to a changing of the guard, with new politicians coming in and, therefore, new political arrangements, which will lead to a change in the scope and requirements for the civil service and public services. This is still not very revolutionary and based too much on our knowledge and the routines of existing relations between politics and

the civil service: *So far so good and nothing new.* It is precisely this miti-
gation of the disruption in this domain that creates room to come up
with a timely strategic response to the imminent revolutionary changes
that are about to start taking place and which I will analyze here, first
focusing on the civil service, and then, in the next paragraph, on public
services.

For the civil service, revolutionary changes will come in the form of:

- Growth of the *'wisdom of the crowd'*
Civil servants are deployed as pundits, experts, and authorities on
certain subjects and cases, in which roles they will now face competition from civilians. They will have to learn to share their expert role
with online panels and citizens who know more about something than
they do, who will now be able to express their criticism and comments
online and openly, as well as with counterexperts deployed in the same
public forum by opponents of the policy.

- *Leaks from the policy incubator*
The policy incubator used to often be closed, unless one of the stakeholders stood to benefit from a leak. Still, more often than not, it was
even a secret that a particular issue was being discussed at all or that
policy negotiations were even going on. But stakeholders often spill the
beans, deliberately or by accident, supported by a public opinion that is
always eager to hear from whistleblowers, expose scandals, or identify
mistakes.

- In addition to official lobbyists who come in through the back door
and operate in the shadows, trying to influence civil servant policy
makers, a new brand of lobbyist will emerge, *informal but openly operating, well-organized lobbies of concerned citizens.*
Such citizens' lobbies will find it easier to get organized as new technology gives them the tools they need to openly challenge or even wipe
the floor with the viewpoints of professional lobbyists. For the civil
service, one complicating factor is that citizens will prefer to deal this
blow in the final stages of the public and political debate, such as when
an actual proposal has been submitted to parliament, as that is the
most effective moment. That is when citizens can hold up a mirror to

the civil service to show them that they are not as neutral and expert as they claim to be. And they can show how civil servants have given in to lobbyists too often, even when it (in the eyes of these civil servants) was not in the best interest of the common good. The public and political debate about this is held out in the open, whereby the civil service, which is used to operating out of the public eye and is also more effective that way, is reduced to being a surprised onlooker after the fact instead of the 'silent' director they always used to be. Consequently, the work of civil servants will be appreciated less or even be attacked. Political players will also be less satisfied, because expert and solid official preparation no longer yields sufficient predictability for a politically favorable outcome.

Clearly, new technologies have become an important focus point across civil service organizations at both the local and the national level, as I experienced personally at various of my lectures across Europe. However, the impact of the disruption toward genuine citizen power still needs to be incorporated into the perspective. In a number of ongoing case studies, I have discerned three common phases:

Phase 1: Greater call to residents/citizens to share information, preferences, and expectations.
Citizen panels, citizen polls, and virtual dialogues and debates are popping up everywhere. New technology and the massive adoption of this new technology is used as a tool for a traditionally existing key government and political objective, which is to find out what matters to citizens.

Phase 2: Asking residents/citizens as users of public services to rate service quality.
Like in the world of business, citizens are considered 'customers' and asked, through questionnaires, alerts, and emails, about their experiences with public services provided by local authorities, the national government, and other layers of government. The main problem in this respect has always been the discrepancy between bureaucratic requirements and consumers' requirements for the services. These are often at odds with each other. The government asks more privacy-sensitive questions and uses threats, potential fines, and warnings to

get people to comply with requests for information, while refusing to provide services quickly because they first have to run several checks. In terms of customer service, this is the wrong way to work and not at all in line with what citizens consider good service. And this is sometimes even aggravated by automation of the current bureaucracy. To citizens, this kind of automated bureaucracy is a lot more impenetrable and anonymous than an actual civil servant behind a service desk or on the phone.

Phase 3 (the most disruptive, but as yet rather uncommon): Asking citizens online to join the public and political decision-making process
This is public consultation as disruption of traditional policy-making and decision-making relations between politics and civil service, getting the public involved before backroom negotiations or official political institutions and experts get a chance to churn out a policy or decision. So, the timely and open use of the public and direct channel to get citizens involved in public decision making on an important, high-profile issue, such as a change to the traffic layout, new building projects, energy production, local services, elementary education, etc. Citizens are thus given a role that resembles the role that has traditionally been fulfilled by civil servants, who now suddenly find they have new partners or even competitors in their policy preparation activities. In areas where this has already materialized, the main lesson learned turns out to be that many of the agenda items of our political institutions are hopelessly complex and politically inward looking, while citizens want things addressed in concrete terms and want to have a say in decisions and then after a while see the practical effect, preferably in line with their input and otherwise with a clear explanation of why their input was not followed. I cannot rule out that many governments' hopelessly laborious policy-making process is actually the result of a desire to keep citizens out of it, to not consult citizens on changes to the traffic layout in a certain area, on how to deal with poorly performing schools, or on how to combat littering, keeping up the appearance of public administration being too complex for citizens to get involved in, and that it is best left to elected officials. However, the disruption has changed the criteria for good political performance. Now, if you are unable to openly explain on the direct channel what you are doing and how you will go

about solving citizens' problems, you are simply not doing your job and only displaying your own incompetence.

This, of course, will have major impact on leadership and the organization of the civil service. Civil servants who have to work with citizens directly, visibly, tangibly, and verifiably will be the ones who will feel this impact the most. More than anything, they need greater decision-making power in their interaction with citizens to be able to come up with tailored responses to their input, which is something bureaucracy just happens to be very bad at. The shield of bureaucracy used to make civil servants come across as professional and authoritative toward citizens, but will this still be the case? One potential major internal bottleneck may be the question of who knows best when it comes to citizens' needs, the elected official or the frontline worker? And finally, there is the question (and this is also closely related to the impact on public services in general) of how to deal with good or at least well-intended citizens' initiatives on all kinds of issues, ranging from public security to neighbors helping each other out and reciprocal childcare? Traditionally, governments would respond to such initiatives by launching a bureaucratic and legally sophisticated procedure to subsidize or contract external parties to put such initiatives into practice, but how do you deal with a bottom-up citizens' initiative in a way that matches citizens' preferences, takes their voluntary initiative seriously, how do you assess that, and can the civil service even make that assessment itself?

Strategic Answer: An Independent Citizenship Assessment Body as a Countervailing Power

As set out above, representative democracy will only survive if it embraces the direct channel, direct democracy, and makes it its own. In public services, this will mean that citizens need formal tools to be able to claim or enforce dialogue, partnership, and co-production with the government or providers of public services. Tools such as voucher systems, the right to a second opinion, and the right to challenge. More on this in the interlude.

The democratic government has another tool at its disposal to forge more systematic citizen power: a Citizenship Assessment Body. This would be an independent body with constitutional authority, such as a constitutional court or a legal body that reviews laws. It would have to work based on a constitutional manifest in which state and government solemnly swear to work toward increasing citizen power and agree on how to measure and assess this. All proposals put to parliament would first have to be submitted to this Assessment Body to have the proposal's respect for citizenship and citizen power reviewed, precisely because politics and civil service, including in democracies, have a natural tendency to overlook, deny, or go against citizen power. This makes citizen power a formal countervailing power against (subconscious) manipulations by elected officials and civil servants. The power of bureaucracy, often in combination with lobbies of the industries and social groups involved, is then taken seriously by the house of representatives in openly and explicitly incorporating this formal countervailing power in its considerations. It would not be right and even be counterproductive if only politicians were to have this authority in the new public arena, as that would lead to both politics and civil society continuously being frustrated, caught off guard, or passed over by deals made in backrooms and behind the scenes, as lobbyists and the civil service are used to. It is necessary to break open this policy-making process between civil servants and politics to challenge their proposals openly on their incorporating citizenship and citizenship tools. Thereafter, of course, democratic politics still has the final say on laws and other proposals. Still, the new public arena with its new media will break down these backrooms and bring the shady deal-making out in the open, allowing citizens to instantly challenge or reject such 'surprise' deals. Then government must strategically anticipate this new citizen power by opening this discussion themselves. To facilitate assessments by such a new Citizenship Assessment Body, it would be helpful if top-level civil servants were to be required to appear in formal public hearings before this independent body. It would give them the opportunity to introduce more expertise into the debate, and, perhaps even more importantly, to improve their sometimes suspicious image in the new public arena.

11
Disruption of Public Services

In the preceding text, I mentioned that political disruption slows down when it moves on to public services. Only after some time, does the decelerated disruption manifest itself on the input side of public services, in the design, funding, and supervision of public services. This seems reassuring, as it gives those involved time to come up with an adequate response. In the old days, the clique of politicians and civil servants was an impenetrable bastion for citizens. Lobbies from the health care industry, energy industry, education, and public housing are still extremely well organized and influential, both in the political domain and in the civil service. But, as is the case everywhere in disruptive times, there is now a revolution going on, and the center of gravity of public services has shifted in culture, position, and organization. It has shifted to the citizen-facing side, even more so as political disruption leads to politicians increasingly taking their lead from the swarm of citizens and their more volatile and extreme opinions.

Although the delayed impact on public services provides an opportunity to come up with an adequate strategic response, it also comes with a risk of lulling those involved to sleep: 'That disruption we saw in the market will only affect the market, and it will not happen here.' This is an illusion. Even though public services have more time to prepare for the impact, the impact will be just as severe, albeit in other areas. Politics are disrupted, citizen power increases, and citizens' clamoring for a serious say is here to stay.

The main causers of potentially beneficial delays to protect the continuity of public services are in the political domain, namely parliament and administration. And this while politicians will be the first to start flipflopping, as they have to listen to the swarms on the direct channel, especially because their direct political strategy is geared towards winning re-election.

Other Citizenship-Boosting Technological Innovations

As each public service interfaces with citizens, additional differences may arise as a result of technological innovations other than those highlighted in this book. Here, too, my focus is on the potential effects, some of which have already materialized, on further bolstering of the power and influence of civil society.

When it comes to these other new technologies, there are four features that stand out in terms of their effect on fostering more opportunities for citizens' initiative and better citizen organization in relation to common public services:

1. Small Scale
New technologies in the area of energy production, such as solar panels, heat pumps, and (small) wind turbines, allow previously large-scale services to be reduced to an individual or neighborhood level. This makes it easier for citizens take initiatives to get organized horizontally and engage in collective production. The swarm behavior among the citizens involved subsequently triggers a boom as other citizens and communities follow suit, much more so than government-run projects ever can, as these are a lot less flexible due to their centralized organization or the constant need for political deals and exchange of favors to get things done, such as with existing energy producers.

As we saw earlier, Germany managed to tap into this with its wind energy policy. Top-down interventions, no matter how formally democratically legitimized, often spark off nimbyism (Not In My BackYard) among citizens: 'I will support what's good for society as a whole, but I don't want it here in my backyard, where the solution will cause me great inconvenience, probably more so than the large group of citizens who stand to benefit from the solution.'

Nimbyism is not an innate negative characteristic of citizens, but rather something that is created in the interplay with government behavior. After all, formal democracy uses overly distant procedures, which creates problems in garnering direct support for painful decisions. Also, past experiences of government's direct behavior as unreliable and based mainly on the organization's interests further reinforce the NIMBY response. In the case of small-scale energy production, personal responsibility and a clear link between economic and environmental considerations lead to citizens and communities embracing the initiative in their backyards. This shows that their 'normal' nimbyism was, in fact, a response to an anonymous, technocratic, and pushy government, no matter how democratic it officially was!

2. Self-assessment, self-knowledge, and self-discipline to supplement the traditional dependency on expertise: Quantified Self
The concept of quantified self revolves around personal measurement and control engineering, sometimes literally on a person's body, such as wearables, to gather data on and monitor a person's physical and psychological activity. Such permanent self-tracking creates the possibility of sharing data with disruptive IT (which actually also involves a risk of abuse of personal data). It allows each individual citizen to better track themselves and stay disciplined (such as in terms of fitness and health), while it also paves the way for more tailored therapy and health interventions. This leads to further personalization of what used to be generic, one-size-fits-all interventions. The medical industry has already realized that medical trials and tests are going to have to evolve from evidence-based to personalized. The good news is that we still need doctors for this kind of personalized medicine. Again, increasing digitalization is, paradoxically, encouraging more physical contact, dialogue, and more personal options and expertise. But this is not only going on in the health care industry, but certainly also in education (such as in the tracking and self-management of learning progress).

3. Greater insight into patterns among citizens: Big Data
Increasing availability of all kinds of data on patterns among citizens and the ability to rapidly and selectively analyze these patterns using new technologies will have major impact, first of all in health care. Just consider, for example, the impact this will have on the system of universal health insurance that exists in many countries and covers the entire population. If every major disease and its consequences in terms of prevention, prevalence, treatment, and recovery likelihood can be predicted on the level of individuals or certain groups of the population thanks to the use of Big Data, the foundations of collective health

insurance may be eroded. Knowledge will lead to people reconsidering their commitment to solidarity and their choice of insurance premiums. *Insurance* is basically an agreement to jointly shoulder certain risks. Collective, or group, insurance is based on agreeing, out of a sense of solidarity, to jointly pay for coverage of important but unknown risks of disease, but also unemployment, or disability in an unknown spread over a random group of the population that should preferably be as large as possible. Big data can eliminate much of the unpredictability, because it allows for calculations based on a bigger picture, more measurements, and better calculation methods that ultimately show that the randomness is largely an illusion. As the predictability of risks of disease increases, saving becomes a more effective option than insurance, especially for those who can afford it.

4. Self-management through robotization
We are on the verge of seeing a deluge of individually usable resources that will either make many standard services and products that are organized on a large scale redundant, or require a more tailored approach and at least put greater control in the hands of individual citizens. This ranges from robotization of domestic and home care (to replace the bureaucratic standardization of this kind of care) to public transport in self-driving vehicles (to replace standard timetables, routes, and waiting times).

These developments will amplify the previously described disruptive trend of increasing power and influence of citizens and their citizenship toward public services.

The New Sources of Power of Citizens and Their Impact

In general, I am seeing the following effects of new technology and the subsequent greater power of citizens in virtually all public services, including health care, energy supply, education, security, public hygiene:

- *More data power*: citizens will increasingly get used to having all relevant information instantly available online, including data about themselves. They no longer accept secret files. The concept of 'confidential file' is now often still used to refer to files that are accessible only to authorized employees, and not even to the person involved themselves. Control will shift to citizens themselves, they will get ownership of these data and so will decide who is authorized to access and update these kinds of files. The focus in the data world will shift from privacy (central idea: others cannot access and use your personal data without a valid reason, even though these personal data can be mined and managed behind your back) to ownership (central idea: others need your explicit consent on your terms to access or process your personal data). Professionals such as doctors and nurses, who used to be the primary 'owners' of your data (concerning your health or illness) now have to ask you for consent to access and process your data. We now have hospitals where patients can access data, such as x-rays or lab results, before their doctors can, albeit that the data will come with a disclaimer saying that 'the doctor has not yet reviewed the results.' These hospitals have understood what the future is for data and personal files.

> Since 2008, hospitals in Estonia must keep and share patient data in electronic format, whereby each patient can decide whether doctors get access to all or just part of their electronic patient file. In the Netherlands, an action group called 'Mijn Data Onze Gezondheid' [My Data Our Health] is also fighting to ensure patients have full access to their own data.

■ *More knowledge*: citizens will increasingly go looking in all kinds of databases and knowledge platforms for background information on their queries or needs, and confront the professional with what they found out. When I mentioned this in the health care industry a few years back, medical specialists explained to me that they used the term 'Google patient' to refer to people who come into their consultation room with knowledge sourced online, and that their first aim was always to cast this knowledge aside as soon as possible. Meanwhile, these health care professionals have figured out that not only patients themselves greatly value the results of their googling, and therefore want and expect a serious reply. Also that this knowledge is sometimes more up to date and more adequate than the knowledge they (can) have readily available, and that they had better take that knowledge sourced online seriously in the conversation with a patient. As a matter of fact, I have seen cases where a doctor, after seeing a so-called Google patient, also went online himself to do some more searching (also in medical research databases that are only available to professionals) to check whether his own knowledge was still up to date. First and foremost, citizens want to hear solid arguments and expect doctors to know what they are talking about, instead of a paternalist, dismissive attitude that brushes aside patients' own research.

> *This expectation could actually also be an attitude that citizens have learned due to the automated, online information and knowledge sources to which they have grown so accustomed. Compare it to a satellite navigation system in a car, which keeps recalculating your route without complaining as you keep taking the wrong turn or take an unexpected detour. In the old days, the person in the passenger seat would be the one giving you instructions or helping you find your way on a map. But they were generally quick to get irritated by your stubbornness. In comparison, a navigation robot is a paragon of flexibility and tolerance. Perhaps we expect the same from the formerly unquestionable experts we talk to.*

■ *Open rational dialogue*: Patients, trained by new technology, now consider this kind of dismissive behavior from doctors a way of hiding their ignorance on a certain subject that actively undermines their own authority. Sure, there is a lot of nonsense and false knowledge available online, which a doctor will find easy to refute, but still the doctor should do so in an open rational dialogue about the value of such knowledge found online. Such a rational, well-reasoned dialogue is appreciated by citizens, and will therefore continue to be a central element on the patient-facing side of the medical profession. Also when it comes to choosing the best possible treatment, citizens suddenly have a lot more knowledge available to them and claim a greater say in such choices. Doctors have meanwhile started calling this new brand of patient-doctor interaction shared decision making. Although it sounds like a good description of what they always said they were doing, it is seen as an entirely new relationship with their patients, partly brought on by disruptive technologies. Again, we see how the technology breaks through rhetoric, but also facilitates the old pretenses of this rhetoric.

- *More reputation power and peer review by citizens*: citizens realize that by complaining publicly, protesting publicly, or publicly exchanging experiences, they are able to exert great influence on how they are treated and the quality of public services, even if this influence is not as great as consumer power in the commercial market. New technologies are not only giving citizens greater influence in the public debate and public sharing of information and viewpoints, they have also made the public domain collectively owned by citizens themselves instead of the exclusive playground of politicians, elected officials, lobbyists, journalists, experts, and opinion makers.

- *Greater choice and knowledge of individual providers and professionals*: thanks to new technological possibilities, citizens are already comparing and sharing opinions about providers in the public domain. This includes providers such as schools, hospitals, and universities, as well as individual professionals such as teachers, doctors, etc., who had managed to stave off these kinds of comparisons and reviews and hide – in part – behind their organizations and quality management systems. Their new position resembles that of professionals in pure market environments, where clients already base their choices on the person and reputation of the professional: '*the man, not the organization.*' For professionals with publicly visible products, such as movie producers, stage actors, criminal lawyers, and professors who give public lectures, public reviews were always important and based on a judgment of their performance and products. This change can easily be seen as a disruption of the relationship between organization and professional in public services in relation to citizens as clients of public services. As a result, quality assurance tools such as site visits, certificates, diplomas, and protocols can be disrupted and will at least have to be supplemented with this kind of client and public assessments. Again, ignoring this kind of citizen power will only be counterproductive.

- *More collective opinions as a means of exerting pressure*: this factor follows from citizens' increased power to make and break reputations. Citizens are now empowered to better and collectively express their opinions and hence increase the pressure on politicians, which is the traditional and not revolutionary route along which politics has become the main catalyst and center of the public debate, and they are also increasingly able to put pressure on individual providers of public services. Not only as a voice in a public debate, but also toward the public service itself. New technology is enabling an exceptional form of transparency in this context, as never seen before with public opinions. It is now instantly clear how many citizens back certain criticism of a specific public service provider. While the funding and associated political policy choices always made that the availability and choice (if there was even a choice!) of service providers was driven by a political mechanism rather than a market mechanism. Not citizens' preference for a specific provider, let alone for an individual professional, is what counted, as providers and professionals were selected by those in charge, either politicians or managers. New technology is now amplifying citizens' influence, allowing them to make their choices based on reputation and peer reviews by other citizens with relevant experience and publicly announce and explain this.

> In the Netherlands, there was recently a major public case where questions were asked about the quality of nursing homes. In response to these concerns, the government's health inspectorate launched an investigation. Entirely along outdated lines, they disregarded residents' own assessment of the care they received, ignoring also the views of family members, and chose to tackle this assessment using medical protocols. But in modern public services, thanks to new technology, one single question is all important, and therefore easy to gauge: what is the view of the patients themselves (and perhaps that of their family members as well) on the quality of care and what is the resulting reputation among the general public and, therefore, future clients?

- *More individual or collective self-management*: beyond merely expressing opinions, individually or collectively, citizens are now also increasingly able to self-organize and position such citizen organizations as additions or competitors, and sometimes even partners, to existing public services. Such initiatives have already popped up in the areas of childcare, energy production, and long-term care, where modern technologies are making it easier to match supply to demand, also between initiatives, enabling faster communication and organization of such civil startups. Existing public service providers, including public-facing and state-funded ones, are forced to assess whether such civil organizations can be incorporated into what the public service stands for, based on an approach of partnership and professionalism. An outdated arrogant attitude based on a claim of superiority thanks to professional training will be increasingly ill-chosen and, as pointed out above, actually undermine the service's perceived authority.

When it comes to co-production (which I will go into later), it is important, though, to make a distinction between individuals joining in and committing and groups of citizens getting collectively organized and demanding or claiming partnership of current public services. Citizens particularly get organized collectively when they feel that their input can make a difference and really tackle public issues in a way that differs from what politics, the government, or public services has done so far.[48]

In health care, this will lead to a situation where supply chain planning and alignment between intramural or hospital care and home care, and all intermediate versions and care options, become part of shared decision making and co-planning for effective organization of care. Wearable and home monitoring and tracking systems connected through new IT channels will become very helpful in this context. Patients can just as easily be monitored at home as in hospital, and a possible intervention can be scheduled automatically while the patient receives care at home.

For years, the Dutch energy industry, actively backed by the Dutch government, managed to block the kind of self-organization by citizens in the area of energy production that is now enabled by new small-scale energy production technology, such as solar panels. Recently, after this original resistance became obsolete and was no longer effective, because the citizens' initiatives became too large, the energy industry switched its approach and started to accept certain forms of tailored civil society organization, and even allowed citizens to feed their surplus energy into the general power grid. After I had visited a village in the West-African country of The

Gambia (where residents showed me their very own power produc-
tion facility, which they were forced to build themselves because
the national government never invested properly in energy access
in rural areas), I was able to confront executives from the Dutch
energy industry with the fact that when it came to self-production
by citizens, the Netherlands was lagging behind a country such as
The Gambia, and that this was due to the energy industry's own
powerful lobby in political circles, which was testimony to the fact
that established interests always outweigh innovations or civil
initiatives. It is a typical example of how progress can actually hold
you back, as incumbents, both in business and in the administra-
tion, whose success is based on past performance, realize too late
that times have drastically changed.

The traditional 'greater participation' in the decision-making process
as an administrative answer to social unrest will not cut it anymore.
Thanks to their new (public) power of opinion, citizens have already
gotten used to having a say, often with much greater impact than they
ever had in traditional citizen and employee participation tricks. The
old administrative 'promise' that people would be allowed to have a
say in decisions has therefore long ceased to be sufficient, and will have
to be replaced by true partnership and joint shaping of public services
(co-production with citizens).

Again, we are helped by the technological development on the plat-
forms. These platforms are increasingly fulfilling a different, more
intelligent role through the application of artificial intelligence (AI).
And so all those transactions, bartering options, choices between
demand and supply on these platforms are increasingly pre-
programmed and prepared by AI, which basically remembers your
preferences, your needs, and your previous choices, and applies
these to swap or purchase options that continuously pop up. A
recurring phenomenon in this context, similar to earlier responses
triggered by disruptive technologies, is that the combination of
artificial intelligence and human insight produces the best result.
We are also seeing this in public services such as health care.
One example is the area of radiology, the use of x-rays to detect
diseases or tumors, where AI helps spot irregularities sooner and

better, while it is still up to the radiologist to assess them, define
treatment options, and engage with the patient on what they think
and on their assessment of their options in consultation with their
medical specialist and family members. New technology frees up
valuable time for scarce and busy doctors.[49] The same happens
in medical labs that also look at scans and x-rays, they are also
benefiting from the huge leap forward in terms of quality thanks to
the combination of AI, medical expertise, and human interaction
in assessing medical problems. The classical fear that AI would
make many professions and jobs redundant, which leads to defen-
sive behavior, is proven wrong as AI actually enriches professions
and practices, and as the combination of AI and human expertise
produces better results.

Strategic Answer: Co-Production with Citizens

If public services have to make the switch to co-production, because
citizens have become smarter and increasingly headstrong, are used
to having their own knowledge and choices, and are better organized
with family, network, and local community, there is bound to be some
tension in the current system.[50] Again, the technological revolution, the
Digital Civil Revolution, is making it imperative to be alert to the revolutionary impact on human, political and organizational relations.

To begin with (as covered above in the section about political revolutions), the authority of political management of public services is
subsiding further, as the political, often paternalistic, hierarchy ('we
know best, as long as we keep you clueless and without a say') erodes.
After all, public services will increasingly need to be shaped in a much
more personalized way, as in a partnership, in line with local and
individual conditions. Standardization and bureaucratization used
to be how public services were managed under political control. This
already clashed to some degree with organizational practices based
on professionalism and craftsmanship as a way to ensure excellence
in providing high-quality customized services. This clash is now intensified as co-production and shared decision making are needed to
accommodate a critical and powerful civil society, and shift to a more

personalized public service, that is contrary to standardization and bureaucratization.

This leads now to a very politically relevant phenomenon of 'reversing privatization' and 'reclaiming public services.' This phenomenon is demonstrated by a large global study[51] that found that there were at least 835 examples of what they called re-municipalization, involving more than 1,600 cities in 45 countries. These were all examples of different new models of public ownership. The most striking examples that are perfectly aligned with the line of thought in this book are those of a new combination of public services in new models of joint ownership by municipalities and citizens. The study found examples in areas such as energy (Hamburg and Bristol), water services (in France and Spain), and fully licensed citizen cooperatives on Kauai and in Minnesota. They found the most promising examples of these new combinations, including in the realm of representative democracy, in Catalonia.

This development is confronting public services with three major strategic questions they need to answer in their response to disruptive citizen power.

a. What is the level of public support for our work and our organization in general?
How do we manage our reputation in the new public arena? After all, reputation breeds public support, gives the public the confidence that a specific public service will meet their needs and expectations in the context of the kind of co-production that has meanwhile become the new normal for them. The traditional, politically propped-up buffer against citizens' individual choices used to be scarcity, specifically the scarcity caused by distributing scare resources over locations, regions, or target groups that leads to waiting lists and needs assessments by civil servant allocation bodies. We can already conclude that this new reputation mechanism will also drive citizens' choices, bypassing traditional political mechanisms, precisely because it will also have electoral consequences for politicians. This old formal brake on citizens' freedom of choice and options will be harder to maintain publicly, as the public becomes increasingly aware of the ulterior motives behind it, which will trigger even greater public response to it. Here, too, the communication

and network effect of the modern public space demonstrates its swarm aspect. Especially when your specific organization comes under fierce public criticism, the question is whether you have a fan club that will defend you amid calls for your organization to be axed or doubts about the legitimacy of your policy or practices.

b. What does my co-production in the primary process look like?
Is it professional, high-quality, open, and searching, and do the relevant citizens perceive it that way? Are informal care and care by family members also used for long-term care needs? One example of how not to do it comes from nursing homes that, when family members offered to continue to care for their elderly parents after they had moved into the nursing home, even offering to stay at the nursing home to keep them company, politely but insistently asked them not to. Are family members asked to get involved in certain aspects of their children's education? Do such initiatives take account of each child's individual needs, also in light of whether there is a supportive family and what these family members (or the lack thereof?) can contribute? Is the willing and committed local community asked to get involved in energy production through placement of solar panels on their roofs? This is still primarily about the influence individual citizens (possibly supported by direct stakeholders such as family members) have on the primary process of public services, such as energy, health care, education, or security. It is therefore mainly a management issue that demands a different attitude from professionals. In this sense, the reputation mechanism will also increasingly determine how quality is defined. This definition is no longer made by bureaucrats (whose quality definitions are almost entirely cost-based, where the required quality comes second) or professionals (whose quality definitions are strongly based on their own status, level of education, and routines). This is all about a cultural and mindset revolution, as disruptive technologies not only add to the weight of open and openly supported quality perceptions of citizens, but also eliminate a number of historically grown certainties and habits of those who used to reign supreme, namely politics and professionals.

c. How do I relate to civil society initiatives of a more collective nature?
This goes beyond merely designing the primary process in concert with
an individual citizen. This is about how you deal with collective civil
society organizations such as a neighborhood watch and Amber Alert[52]
(security), community-based care (child or elderly care in the community or sharing of home care services), energy production, DIY services,
et cetera. Such civil society initiatives are basically breaking down the
old monopolies from the bottom up. This also means that the supply
side can no longer call the shots in terms of what services to provide,
because they will have to become more demand-driven and include
individual customization.

It goes without saying that I am also aware of – the sometimes justified – objections to this kind of increased influence for citizens, especially with respect to the sudden indispensability of co-production,
the vulnerability of reputations, and also the increased importance for
underlying choice behavior. The risks include the risk of *amateurism* in
co-production (people thinking their expertise is at the same level as
that of a doctor, artist, or teacher). There is, of course, also the risk of
demagogues who erode reputations with false claims or by complaining merely about how they themselves were sold short (an aggrieved
citizen can try to get others to join him/her in his/her fulminations).
And there is the risk of damage to the *public nature* of a service because
many communities have a tendency to discriminate against those
with different beliefs or those who look different (the anchoring in the
legal reality of the state has led to a combat against such discrimination based on the principle of 'equal treatment under the law'). I by
no means want to evade or hide all the deeper or more philosophical
themes beneath the analysis and discourse given here. But the points
and issues around which the struggle revolves must not obscure our
view of the main line of the strategic analysis. Market disruption has
taught us that many stakeholders failed to see the revolution coming
due to their ignorance or denial. While they sometimes responded to
the imminent revolution with subtle-sounding criticism, they generally
failed to take it seriously and talked it down. Too many people, including so-called experts and college professors, benefit from a resound-
ing, balanced analysis of these developments, precisely because they
do not see or do not want to see the bigger picture. If you look at their

arguments, you will often see that they are refusing to accept ideologically that citizens now, thanks to new technological resources of more direct democracy, have a greater voice in what used to be manipulated news provision. For the first time in history, public opinion is becoming truly public. Needless to say, it is a good thing that modern manipulations in this new direct channel are being highlighted, and that part of the data, information, and communication power is placed directly in the hands of citizens, who are consequently becoming self-producing citizens. This is new, even though there is a different, largely automated, kind of manipulation of the news and communication going on in the background for commercial reasons, as we have known from the beginning. Such manipulations happen through data theft, cunning algorithms, and all kinds of other behind-the-scenes practices of dominant tech firms such as Apple, Facebook, Alphabet and other hardware and software providers. Criticisms of these manipulations and legislation to combat them are good things, albeit that they must not be based on the illusion that traditional media channels were manipulation-free. Whenever such semi-balanced criticism implies that we need to regain control of the information stream, opinion channel, and communication in a way that would see us return to the 'secure, objective, and open' pre-digital-revolution information and news provision, democracies are basically responding in the same way as dictators such as Putin and Xi Jinping. It would be a return to institutional power over citizens and their opinions. Back to the vague, listless citizen involvement of 'being allowed' to elect our officials every four years, and that in today's new age with new IT and communication channels. Back to the illusion of seemingly 'objective' media, which was already difficult to live up to in the past: journalists who endeavored to be objective in their news gathering often met with opposition and obstruction from politicians and civil servants, at least they are now helped in their muck-raking by critical citizens.

Given that I am not among those who want to stop or even ignore the disruptive revolution and who hide their lack of strategic insight behind high-brow presentation of their objections and the potential negative effects, I have chosen to mention these objections in my analysis, albeit without emphasizing them. After all, a future-oriented analysis must start with truly strategic insight into the ongoing revolution. One key property of true strategic intelligence is that you also open your eyes to those trends and developments that are a threat to your position or that might even floor you. This kind of potentially threatening impact is what this book deals with, hence the term disruption. The avoidance of nuance and counterarguments in my analysis and explanations so far, no matter how at odds it may be with my ultimate faith in citizenship and democracy, is certainly also a result of my viewpoint that we are dealing with a power struggle (see above, Chapter 9). In a revolution and a power struggle, there is no room for neutrality. Only after the revolution, you can look back from a position of neutrality. My analysis, on the other hand, tries to identify beforehand what we must and can expect, what signs are already visible, and what kind of response to these initial signs would be the most appropriate, also even the most threatening and disrupting ones. In doing so, I am not taking up a position of neutrality, as I reason based on over twenty years of insights and my firm belief that citizens and their influence and voice matter enormously in Western nations, as shown by all kinds of social initiatives we have seen emerge so far. This is also why I embrace modern technologies, which are in line with my think tank's mission. Thanks to the broad availability and major impact of these technologies, my work to strengthen civil society and boost citizens' influence is not obstructed by the ever changing moods and insights of incumbent politicians. After all, this is also a power struggle that directly, structurally, and culturally undermines their political, influential position and seriously disrupts their existence as professional politicians. As said, incumbents, i.e. established parties with established benefits and positions, often lack the strategic intelligence to see truly undermining developments coming.

The first and most important part of a truly strategic response to the ongoing disruption is now to openly acknowledge its impact on our mindset and interconnections, and then to start a gradual transformation of democracy and public services before it is too late. The objective behind that must be to preserve the good things from the past while creating more room for input from citizens and citizens' initiatives, which in itself in my view is also a good thing. My goal is to trigger, encourage, and stimulate open and deep-seated strategic insight. That is the best response to the inevitable disruption and its presupposed negative effects. In this power struggle and the much-needed changes to the institutional order, such as the rights that go with recognized citizenship, the legal status of citizens' initiatives in existing public services, and allowing more direct democracy in the representative system, the ball is not in the citizens' court, but rather in the court of today's elected officials and politicians. Revolutions put incumbents' leadership to the test.

Interlude:
Overcoming Disruptions
through Strategic Intelligence

It will probably be clear by now that the technology-driven revolution stirred up by new technology will have massive impact on Western nations' institutional order, as it boosts citizen power, influence, and organizational capacity. This is why this book substantiates and defines it as a new and third revolution for mankind, the Digital Civil Revolution, one that will go well beyond industrial, economic or instrumental processes. It will also lead to rediscovery of the importance, value added, and workings of the commons as a basic governance approach of self-managing citizens that together organize the common good. This will also, like with every revolution, lead to a power struggle with traditional, dominant, paternalistic, and regulatory government and political leadership, who will try to hang on to their power. In their rhetoric, representative democracy and the associated bureaucracy will, of course, embrace the democratic principles and act as though they are natural champions of a more active and powerful civil society; their actions will prove otherwise. This attitude and behavior will, however, increasingly be noticed and undermined by the people in the new media landscape. We are going to have to create stronger building blocks for a powerful civil society, which requires more than just technological capabilities and well-meaning citizens.

12

The New Strategic Context: Reinforced Citizen Power and Civil Society

The balance in the triangle of state, market, and civil society is shifting. Citizens are gaining a stronger hold over representative politics, while their increasing swarm behavior is making life for politicians even more uncertain than they rightfully already thought it was. As consumers, citizens disrupt existing markets and unsettle existing market parties by suddenly changing their preferences and loyalty based on new information and new platforms, and demanding different services and the possibility to compare products and services. In fact, the development of the platform economy is already entering the next stage, as platforms that use artificial intelligence and algorithms to make their recommendations and design their services are getting to know their customers better and better, thus acquiring an ever greater ability to advise and serve customers.

> One example in the market today is Stitch Fix, a platform that uses algorithms to advise and help people make fashion choices and offers the clothes that go with the advice, while, of course, also allowing customers to return and not pay for items that they did not like after all. Ultimately, the algorithms come up with suggestions and options, which the fashion advisor goes over first before putting them to the customer. Like Stitch Fix's CEO said in an interview: 'Fit and taste are just a bunch of attributes: waist, material, color, weight, pattern. it's all just data,' but at the same time: 'It's simple: a good person combined with a good algorithm is far superior to the best person or the best algorithm alone.'[53]

Platforms are currently still largely seen as peer-to-peer sharing and bartering platforms that let you choose items from a range that is offered to you in an increasingly transparent manner and in real time, and on which you also sell or swap items that you own, but soon it will become a meta-choice between intelligent and assisting platforms, as you will have to ask yourself which platform to use for advice and support on which choices.

Citizens are also more demanding when it comes to the socially engaged practices of companies that previously, based on economic science, cherished the illusion that consumers only looked at price and a little bit at quality. Such social criticism of companies is now also increasing in volume thanks to the exponential growth of citizens' swarm behavior. Large groups of citizens can now suddenly decide that a certain company is no good, even though its products still offer excellent value for money.

> *This is what happened to United Airlines. Back in April 2017, circumstances required United to remove four randomly selected passengers from a United Express plane that was about to fly from Chicago to Louisville. One of these four passengers refused to get off the plane. He was forcibly removed, which was widely filmed by other passengers on the plane, who subsequently posted their videos on Twitter and Facebook. Two days later, United Airlines stock had lost 255 million dollars in value. The company's reputation was further damaged because of allegations (which were widely shared online) that this particular passenger had been selected because he was Asian.*

Citizens are taking a different approach to public services. They now compare services. They share experiences with and reviews of public services in much the same way as they have learned to do in the travel and hotel industry. They go beyond traditional indirect participation structures and demand to be heard directly. And more than anything, citizens are organizing themselves to collectively tackle issues and get things done in areas such as health care, energy, or community management. This is turning citizens into self-managing, sometimes slightly erratic partners to public services. But this is actually the most favorable scenario for both parties. There are still numerous public service providers that consider citizens' initiatives as competition, which they feel they have to beat or have the government ban, and with which they certainly will not enter into a partnership. However, this defensive attitude is viable only with the support of politicians, which will dwindle when citizens come up with a good and well-reasoned initiative and post it on the direct channel.

13

The Growing Power of Citizens over Market and Public Services

A number of major revolutionary changes will make civil society, or the mutual organization of citizens, stronger, more important, and more powerful, heralding a global shift from passive citizenship and consumerism to active citizenship.

- *Data and information availability will grow*, which will prompt exponential growth in demand for greater transparency, supplementary data, confrontation with information sourced online and from other media sources.

- *Public opinion becomes truly public*: no more formal filters or self-proclaimed experts between opinions of 'the people' and 'institutions' and 'politics'. This does not mean, however, that those experts, administrators, and PR professionals will stop trying to influence public opinion and disappear altogether. It means that they will be reduced to being merely one of a multitude of voices heard in the fully horizontalized public debate. Still, there are certainly new manipulations by commercial parties, such as the owners and IT providers, but these mainly consist in targeting certain groups of citizens and getting certain commercial messages across. As shown by the Facebook/Cambridge Analytica scandal, the biggest threat to the open and horizontal sharing of data and opinions is created by the political manipulations of old that are now powered by algorithms, big data, and commercial targeting techniques. All data, opinions, facts, and scandals can now be shared, including those of experts, but also those of unlikely counterexperts (disruption of expertise). Authority is no longer a given, but has to be conquered in an open public struggle.

My biggest worry is not these 'silent' manipulations, also because they are increasingly happening out in the open and publicly and politically challenged, but rather the public threat of the rise of what the ancient

Greeks already considered a threat to their direct democracy: the power and influence of demagogues. In the ancient Greek definition, a demagogue is someone with great charisma and rhetorical skills who primarily serves his or her own personal interests, is sometimes even a criminal, and unfortunately often manages to appeal to voters' desires and preconceptions. Demagogues are also the main new competitors to the incumbent political class of professional politicians, who are often far inferior in terms of rhetorical skills and charisma, and clueless when it comes to working the crowd. Career politicians generally operate in routine-based, formally regulated meeting rooms, behind closed doors, or in the comfort of their informal personal networks. When they must make a public appearance it is all very standardized, formally managed, not alluring and not even intended to be. They often simply lack the charisma, personality, personal background and personal training that would allow them to forge an emotional bond with the crowd. The public arena has been revolutionized, also for other professionals in the political domain, such as journalists, opinion leaders, and public relations officers.

- *Participation becomes more collective and direct, representational structures are all called into question*: many organizations and legislators have in the past, out of (well-intentioned) paternalistic motives, set up structures or created procedures that seemingly give citizens a say in policy, choices, and administration. The problem with these kinds of arrangements is that even though citizens get a say, a right to be heard, there is no way for them to enforce that they are actually listened to when decisions are actually made. The participatory element is restricted to multiple parties being allowed or invited to express what they think about a certain issue, and their place is therefore clear. They can speak, and sometimes the decision makers are formally obliged to invite and hear them, but they cannot decide. Since it is evident that decision makers ultimately decide what they think is right, these citizens' input is in practice often requested when it no longer matters, when a decision has – secretly – already been made. Citizen participation then only extends to citizens listening to the reasoning behind a certain decision, asking questions about it, and giving some advice for next time. The new Internet chain, however, undermines the position and purpose of middlemen and representational structures such as this

kind of citizen participation. Participation structures are also an intermediary, allowing representatives of citizens, employees, or customers
to join the discussion process. But new technology undermines this
in several ways. Why do we still need representatives when we can all
hear the relevant citizens in their thousands directly thanks to modern
software? This kind of skepticism is increased by the visible workings of
representative democracy. Why do we let all those arguing, petty, and
often clearly clueless councilors or members of parliament make such
important decisions? And why are we not replacing this system with a
well-managed and well-facilitated public forum of all citizens involved,
mobilizing and accountably using the expertise and wisdom of the
crowd in the decision-making process? Besides, these members and
participants in the public forum may not even be experts at all and may
also have a propensity for the kind of bickering and chaotic arguing
that is so common in politics and parliaments the world over. But that
is where modern technology can help improve these new public arenas,
creating order and making sure that everyone can have their say
publicly. Representative democracy does not lead to better and more
knowledgeable decision making or more measured debate, and after
the debate it also lacks legitimacy in our modern times, while the latter
was always a given formality in traditional democracy: 'these people
were elected by you and they therefore make decisions on your behalf.'
In this context, having a larger public forum that organizes the wisdom
of the crowd among truly committed citizens is surely an excellent
development. Unless, of course, we want to protect the jobs of elected
politicians. The fact that new technological capabilities are enabling
citizens to provide input quickly and en masse provokes the question
why citizens are not allowed to do so earlier in the decision-making
process, before the decision is made, when choices and citizen input
still matter. In fact, the question to ask is why we, as committed citizens,
are not allowed to voice our opinion on the arguments, on the estimations and facts that call for a decision in formal procedures, because
now in everyday life citizens are very much getting used to and can do
that personally on every issue they want. It is strange how democratic
governments are lagging behind in giving their citizens a formal and
decisive say in decision-making processes, when citizens are now used
to being treated as adults and powerful clients in their market decisions
and choices. New technology is making it possible to poll opinions and

for very large groups of citizens to exert direct influence on the decision-making process (which is already actually happening in certain areas), including better quantitative insight into approval and disapproval ratings than earlier ways of polling and also using all kinds of methods that ensure no viewpoints go unnoticed and that everyone whose views would otherwise be overlooked has their public say. The public forum is permanently on, allowing citizens to join the conversation at any time, and it can be managed better and more transparently in terms of its accuracy and rational exchanges than the traditional forum.

> In the Netherlands, various local authorities have adopted the Argu digital approach, with crowd-sourced innovations with respect to issues and policy proposals and solution-driven broad debate. This is one of the major democratic benefits of new technology. It allows the authorities to reach a larger number of people than they ever could with traditional means such as surveys or town hall meetings, while the arguments are presented out in the open and come from and are shared between a broader and more diverse range of citizens. One example of the major advantage of new technology is that all arguments out there are shared and that someone who lacks verbal skills or does not fit in cannot be muzzled. At the end of the day, all arguments are ranked in terms of the quantitative backing they have garnered in the consulted group, so that a balanced decision can be made, one that is well-reasoned based on open, diverse, and broad debate. See www.Argu.Co for more information.

> Again, you can see the same underlying phenomena as highlighted earlier in the section about disruption of democracy and public services:
> - the embrace and adequate use of new technological possibilities;
> - consequently building broad and diverse scope, as larger numbers of people find it easier to join in on the new channel than on the old ones;
> - choices made based on a combination of virtual information and intelligence and physical expertise, dialogue, and careful consideration to achieve the best possible result. Here, too, expert democratic officials may not disappear altogether, but their role

*will be redefined as one that is focused on facilitating, listening,
and weighing pros and cons in a much more mature dialogue
with their citizens and voters.*

This shows once again the socially disruptive effect of new technology.
This will first see citizens realize that much of the current 'participation' structures are mere smoke screens and that executives always
end up making the decisions they wanted to make in the first place,
while claiming that stakeholders were involved in the decision-making
process. These practices are entirely at odds with what new technology has taught them. Next, they will not only start criticizing the
smoke screen-based tactics, but also start highlighting the possibilities
offered by the even more far-reaching version of joint and timely decision making. All of this will trigger a rethink of administrative relations
with respect to decision making. Elected officials and executives will
therefore have to come clean on what they really want to achieve with
their so-called 'citizen participation'. The ultimate outcome of all these
revolutionary developments will be that representational bodies (eventually also including local councils and parliaments) will have to adapt
to this new brand of citizenship. People will get accustomed to direct,
real-time choices, to weighing pros and cons, and to looking for relevant
data and knowledge themselves. This will not only translate to a different attitude toward collective citizenship, collective management of
collective assets, or natural resources that are for everyone to use, such
as fishing areas and agricultural land, but also assets like a common
pool of volunteers or energy production system (which I will work out
in detail in the next section about commons as the most suitable form
of administration). It will also lead to greater participation in the public
debate and ultimately to different, more active involvement in decision
making. Incumbents will perceive this as an expression of mistrust or
excessive obstinacy on the part of citizens, as well as a drive among the
population to make their own justice, but soon they will still have to
come up with an adequate response to it. It is already clear that politics and press will have to track and comment on this swarm behavior,
effectively assigning authority to it and admitting it to the corridors of
parliament and backrooms of power that, until recently, were closed to
the public.

- *Bartering as one of the foundations of new citizenship*: In the same way that citizens are learning on online platforms how to review physical items, specify possible applications, and settle payment transactions in real-time in a bartering economy, citizens will start using the same technology to barter for more psychological or political elements, such as opinions, reviews, rumors, scandals, data, and information. Given that these connections meanwhile reach much larger groups of citizens, it will also trigger swarm behavior with respect to such elements. Press and politics already must and want to track this swarm behavior and report on it (so as to let everyone know how in tune they are with 'the people'), thus giving it and increasing its authority. This is clear to see in recent major developments on important, emotive subjects and the associated actions. An obvious example is the #MeToo movement that started in the film industry in response to misconduct in the workplace. A similar movement emerged following the Parkland school shooting in early 2018, the #neveragain movement, which culminated in the massive March for our Lives in Washington, D.C. on March 24, 2018.

- *From passive consumerism to co-production of public services*: on the back of new technology and prompted by the new mindset, citizens will want greater involvement in all kinds of public services, from street cleaning to health care, from the quality of education to healthy food. This goes beyond citizens' passive role as consumers, as they want better explanations of and consultations on what professionals have come up with based on their routines, regulations, protocols, and standard solutions. They also want an active say in the exact individual assistance that they will receive, and want a personal role in it, as permitted by their own respective capabilities and circumstances. We increasingly look beyond our personal needs (and turn to the online knowledge source to find an answer to that question), looking also at what we ourselves, as part of our network and together with our family members, can contribute to meeting our needs. It is important to realize that bureaucracy meets citizenship here, and that this is a grating encounter. The desire for co-production must not lead to bureaucracy starting to dictate such practices as the 'new normal' and reassessing citizens' needs or anticipating these needs based on their own interests, and the expectation that it will produce savings. Co-production must be voluntary, but also highly personal, and therefore needs to be shaped on an individual basis. This is one of the consequences of this new age for public services. On the one hand, they must respond to and antici-pate collective citizenship and the associated politics that takes its lead from the swarm. And on the other hand, they need to learn to operate on a more personal level and not to formulate their response as stand-ard rules and regulations, but instead in flexible and adequate dialogue, based on each individual situation.

■ *Mutual and solidarity-based organization through commons and cooperatives will be the new issue in the administration of public interests and facilities, but also for citizens who want to actively get organized themselves:* as such, increased bartering and swam behavior will not lead to greater influence on, let alone control over, public environment or decision making on collective issues. At most it will lead to identi-fication of and alertness to issues and perhaps to these issues being put on the agenda of official and political bodies. The new tools that many citizens now have at their disposal will, however, as a result of the possibilities they offer and because citizens get better at using them, inspire them to want to make their own decisions, get organized, and collectively put pressure on institutions. They will increasingly assume that they know what is best and perhaps ultimately also decide to just do it themselves. Public sharing of information, opinions, and views will therefore lead to a mindset that says that 'collective issues' are their 'collective problem' and will therefore, perhaps, in the long run, once citizens realize that self-organization is easier now, or when incumbent politicians and public service providers make it clear to them that they will not be listened to, and citizens therefore have no alternative, neces-sitate 'collective action' by citizens themselves. When it comes to this latter point, the old trusted routine of the traditional relation between citizens and government/public services will perhaps remain in use for some time. If so, citizens will initially still consider formal institutions or politicians as their first point of contact, and may therefore send them complaints, angry letters, or calls for action, but I must say that I doubt this will actually happen. The new tools can also encourage citizens to take action themselves, especially when they lack faith in the unselfish-ness and/or effectiveness of these kinds of public-sector entities, which would ultimately see citizens shape their own public services through social entrepreneurship. In this respect, too, the relationship between government and the governed is likely to change drastically, or, in the eyes of the incumbents, be disrupted. Below the surface, this is exactly what this fundamental point is all about, about the relationship between state and (civil) society. As has been pointed out several times in this book, the revolutionary aspect of this new technology-driven phase in history will have to lead to us opening our eyes to the funda-mental change in relations that it will bring, including in this particular one. The institutional system is shifting fundamentally, which also leads to a power struggle, fought either out in the open or behind closed doors.[54]

This shift is, of course, largely a learning process for citizens, who until recently were expected to maintain a passive approach to the public good, and at most to protest now and again and express their opinions only once every four years come election season. Professional politi-cians and public administrators are therefore likely to, with some level of glee, point to the errors of civil society organizations, or to the limits of what these organizations can handle or underlying problems, which undoubtedly exist or will pop up. The great question will therefore be whether the public sector will welcome the ongoing learning process of increasingly active citizens.[55] That said, there are certainly opportuni-ties, as highlighted in a recent study of emerging cooperatives in Latin America[56] that found examples in both urban and rural areas, and in areas such as:

a. Providing services of common interest, such as energy, water and transportation
b. Promoting solidarity, such as in coffee production and start-ups
c. Improving livelihood and breaking isolation, such as through fair trade and with respect to the environment
d. Financial services, such as credit facilities

14

Commons: Future Governance Mode of the People, by the People, for the People

The commons model and the associated literature best reflect the changing fabric of society. It was introduced by Elinor Ostrom, the first and as yet only female winner of the Nobel Prize for Economics Sciences (in 2009).[57]

In the commons model, a common resource is managed and maintained by groups of people based on an equal and shared interest in the resource.

The *key elements* of commons are:
- The availability of a common resource with economic, social, and environmental value for people's lives, survival, and interrelations in society. In the literature, such a resource is referred to as a common-pool resource, a common good that is a source for the economic basis and quality of life (pool resource).
- A relevant selection of citizens has a common interest in ensuring adequate management of this common resource. These relevant citizens are the users of the resource and therefore also the stakeholders and participants in the management thereof.
- Adequate management in the shape of collective management by the relevant citizens, according to the principle of equality (although there can, of course, be different echelons within the group in terms of roles for historical or economic reasons).

The commons model was first applied and studied in small-scale village and agricultural communities for common resources such as grazing pastures for the villagers' cattle or ponds or specific sections of the sea where all stakeholders could fish. The Netherlands has a long tradition of this kind of self-management by citizens, such as in so-called 'meents', common lands and squares in villages that were managed and maintained by all villagers jointly.[58] Later, the concept of common property was taken to a broader level to include the routes and purity of irrigation canals and common power supply. Urban developments including parks, central buildings, or market squares are also increasingly approached in this same way, as a common-pool resource for residents to manage jointly. Bologna, in Italy, is a well-known example of a city where the local authorities have teamed up with civil society on a larger scale in experimenting with so-called urban commons. The focus is shifting from physical common resources only to more general or social issues, such as people's sense of security on the streets and in their communities. It will be clear that the above definition of the nature and scope of commons as an administrative model can cover a wide range of common interests of groups of citizens (and thanks to modern technology of increasingly large groups of citizens), from community management to recreational areas, from local schools to sports facilities, and ultimately for a lot of things that are currently managed by public officials, both on a local and on a national level.

The major issues that this revolutionary shift in the interests and influence of the institutional triangle will provoke, will, besides the defense of their old powers, be focused on property rights (who owns the common good?) and on the quality of commons management (are citizens capable of doing a good job together?). The first issue is one of political will, especially when it concerns government assets and public services. The second is something citizens are going to learn by trial and error, notwithstanding the inevitable naive or arrogant, non-fact-based criticism saying that the government did a much better job at managing the common good in question.

An important underlying issue is how committed these citizens really are to solidarity in these private, self-management circumstances, initially only within a familiar circle of a local community, but in modern times on a much larger scale, also in a geographical sense, even up to a global level. The virtual communities that are arising now are often based on common interests (the so-called bubbles). In Western nations, solidarity (between the sick and the healthy, between the employed and the unemployed, and between the rich and the poor) is often assumed to be something that exists on a private individual level: voluntary efforts and coordination, voluntary contributions and donations. Collectively-organized solidarity often comes in the form of government-imposed taxes to fund civil entitlements in certain areas, ranging from health care to social security, sometimes (also) through a collective, compulsory insurance system with the weight of the government behind it that forces people to contribute by charging them premiums. Examples of such systems are plentiful across the globe, ranging from state pension plans to public schools. They constitute a more compulsory, top-down imposed, anonymous, and bureaucratically managed sort of solidarity, not the kind of pure solidarity in the private domain such as volunteering and philanthropy. This differs significantly from what will be required here from now on, which is for bureaucratic systems that often inherently lead to management based on the supply side, to anticipate more powerful and influential individual and collective demand! It is ultimately about an amplification of civil society's power to get organized, which is nothing new, but which is now infused with greater citizen power, thanks mainly to new technology. The big political questions with respect to these collectively funded public services will therefore be whether citizens' newly acquired power should be reflected in greater formal and legal power in comparison to politics or management or the professionals working in public services. Such greater power can come in the form of a right to a second opinion, the right to claim a greater stake in public services (either by paying extra, or by actively getting involved), the right to take over certain services when a group of citizens can do a better job (right to challenge).

This conclusion echoes my previous book, which dates back to 2015 (in Dutch): *Burgerkracht met Burgermacht*. The basic idea behind this title (A Stronger Civil Society through Citizen Power) is that a strong civil society is a timeless concept. The Netherlands has a long tradition when it comes to building strong civil societies, it is, in fact, a prime Dutch export. In the 16th and 17th centuries, when the Dutch had colonies all over the world, they exported their civil society ideal to America, to New Amsterdam to be exact, which later became New York (see also Note 3 about the triangle of state, market, and civil society and the link to the tradition of a powerful and active society in the Netherlands). Unfortunately, civil society has lost a lot of its clout over the centuries, due to decades of denial, political arrogance, and market interests that have silenced civil society. Thankfully, the coalition agreement of the current Dutch government (which came into office in 2017) includes a number of promising sections on citizen power: right to challenge, allowing housing, parent, and care cooperatives to provide public services, and acknowledgment of the importance of and the entitlement to personal allowances such as a voucher system for care services, which gives citizens a financial and actual say in their care arrangements. These examples show that there are certainly serious legal instruments that allow governments and the public sector in Western nations to anticipate and tap into citizens' initiatives and desire to get more proactively involved in the public good.

Citizens' growing influence and increasing organizational capacity is making it more important to maintain a constant focus on civil society. We are going to have to adopt a fresh new and open approach to civil society. During all those decades behind us, civil society was viewed and judged from the perspective of the other two legs of the triangle, the state and the market. In this perspective, these latter two were dominant, as they had the power and the financial clout, and greater interests and more means when it came to framing public perception of the role and potential of civil society. Politicians referred to civil society only as either 'angry citizens,' 'calculating citizens,' or 'not-in-my-backyard citizens.' Earlier in this book, when I outlined the successful German wind energy initiative (see page 64), I explained how this kind of behavior is provoked and reinforced precisely by the top-down approach and bureaucratic 'solutions' implemented by the government to which citizens can only react, because they are never actively involved. Again, we can see how the perceptions of the (in)competencies of citizens are basically colored by public officials' own interests! It is fascinating to see that the triangle is spot on, as the state does not automatically assume citizens' perspective, not even in democracies. In the eyes of the market, citizens were merely consumers who only looked at the price of products and services, and who did not want to get involved in companies' practices and policies. Framed in this way, citizens and their citizenship never stood in the way of these parties' own interests. For politicians, this framing of civil society was aligned with the idea that politics had power and control over things that citizens were seemingly clueless about and were not even interested in.

Citizens were framed as being selfish and too self-interested to engage with the 'common good' and the 'public cause.' The market reveled in the belief that only products mattered, and not the sometimes amoral or money-grubbing and status-seeking behavior behind it, which continued to be what the board's power was based on. A strong civil society means, among other things, that citizens become more mutually engaged and show greater solidarity with the vulnerable than the dominant triangle parties of politics and market ever did. Citizens then also trump politics and the market in terms of organizational capacity, thanks to new technology, which instead of merely protesting against the traditionally dominant parties is increasingly used to help and care for each other in society.

The State's Struggle with a Strong and Vital Civil Society

In this book, I am using the term revolution for a good reason, because even though it is sparked by technology, it is ultimately a revolution of the people, their communities, and interrelations in the triangle of state/market/civil society. Especially for a dominant state that was so convinced that they were doing a good job for citizens, this means a tremendous turn in their attitude towards those citizens with their greater volatility, swarm behavior, and organizational capacity.

A fine example of how the state and politics in the Netherlands completely misjudged this change was the concept of 'participation society' that the Dutch government floated to describe the major transformation of the traditional welfare state. The government believed that citizens could and wanted to do more themselves. Although this was a positive and contemporary belief, it was completely undermined by the fact that the government used it only as a way to justify sweeping budget cuts. Citizens had to and should do more, but they had to do it for free and with fewer guarantees in times of need, because the government had a financial problem. It was a kind of reversed solidarity, not one of citizens helping each other, or even of the government helping all citizens through collective securities, but really one of citizens helping out government. The term itself already shows that they did not put a lot of thought into it. It is a dumb pleonasm. After all, when there is participation, there is a society, and vice versa. Not only government had a misconception of the modern citizen, the market, too, saw these more autonomous and emancipated citizens mainly as 'critical voices' or, on the eve of the disruption that the market did not yet see coming at the time, 'browsing-not-buying' citizens (consumers would increasingly go to bricks-and-mortar stores to browse and try on items, but then buy them cheaper online). Both parties, politics and market, thus basically promoted perceptions of citizens and civil society that suited them and their interests, painting them as passive and selfish, or the other way around as active citizens, for which they could, in turn, reproach these same citizens.

This lazy, self-serving perception of citizens, their voters, was clearly crushed in the most recent edition of the world's most important elections, the 2016 U.S. presidential elections. U.S. voters elected, albeit with the help of the electoral college system, and therefore not in an absolute majority (popular vote), the inexperienced, erratic, and error-prone Trump, whose intellectual output was limited to tweeting rumors and a stint as a TV presenter, over the experienced, professionally trained, balanced, seemingly rational policy junkie and stickler for detail Hillary Clinton and her thorough and calculated proposals. It showed that people want something else from their politicians, not only expertise and so-called professionalism. While to politicians and political parties that select them and give them a public platform, 'politician' is increasingly becoming a profession, citizens have totally different ideas. Perhaps citizens, more so than politicians themselves, have a greater belief in the original intentions of democracy, and are looking for more emotional commitment, the same credible feelings for the same cause as voters, and a willingness to stick one's necks out for difficult issues (and therefore have these truly addressed). This kind of attitude that citizens want from their politicians is aptly summed up by that famous Bill Clinton line: 'I feel your pain.'

The market always thought that as long as you do not mention the background of your products, customers will not be interested in it and keep buying your products from you no matter what. This misconception was already entirely blown out of the water by well-organized NGOs such as Greenpeace (who exposed harmful environmental impact) and Occupy (who highlighted cases of pay and treatment inequality). As far back as in 1998, oil giant Shell was forced by pressure from NGOs and the general public to scrap plans to dump an old oil rig in the Atlantic. Nowadays, every single citizen who sees something scandalous or suspects some kind of abuse is empowered to kick up a stink about it, showing how passive consumers can turn out to also be committed citizens with citizenship-based ideas about the environment, inequality, crime, and corruption.

> One example is how rapidly word of the KPMG/Bell Pottinger scandal spread across the globe. Accounting firm KPMG and PR giant Bell Pottinger were involved in the corruption practices of South Africa's Gupta family, who were strongly linked with the then president of South Africa Jacob Zuma, who was also largely believed to be corrupt. It was a case that in less technological times few would have heard of, or even understood, but which in our modern global village spread like wildfire and in great detail thanks to numerous news and other informal websites, allowing anyone who was interested to get a detailed account of what was going on. As a result, the KPMG partners involved have lost their jobs, KPMG has been banned by South Africa's auditor general from auditing public institutions in South Africa, and Bell Pottinger has gone bankrupt. The information machine keeps churning out more and more news, which instantly goes global. This latter aspect leads to an immediate impact in other countries as well, on the head office, and the stakeholders, such as current clients across the globe, of a globally-operating firm. The results of such a wave of negative reporting that hit vendors, employees, and customers are unpredictable, wide-ranging, and cannot be brushed under the carpet or controlled through traditional PR practices of denial, diversion, and different representations. Obeying and responding quickly to the new public opinion is the only real option.

The old interests-based ideas of autonomous, all-knowing corporate governance with passive consumers who only look at value for money needs to be overhauled. In today's economy, the re-emerging bartering mechanism is replacing a lot of buying power and illusions of scarcity. As it turns out, there are far more privately-owned goods that owners are willing to swap or sell than many companies and public service providers thought. Not only does the bartering economy mean that people are not spending money with companies, it also causes prices to drop as the scarcity bubble is burst. In the same way, self-organization in civil society is also replacing part of the public services sector, with citizens demanding that traditional providers in this domain be open to partnerships and collaboration instead of always claiming professional superiority. The ability to produce and share opinions on an unprecedented scale means that public opinion is now truly public and that direct democracy already exists as public opinion has real influence in the political domain (especially on front-running politicians who are tuned in to modern times). Like the market before, representative democracy will be disrupted if it fails to embrace relatively new tools such as online polling, citizen panels, and referendums. So far, I have seen in many countries across the globe how representative democracy is looking away or at least still has the illusion of being in charge of what happens next (while taking their time and adopting a wait-and-see attitude), just like the CEOs of so many companies that have meanwhile gone out of business due to their CEOs' sluggishness.

Over the past few years, steps have indeed been taken in the changing relationship between government and the governed, but they were extremely arduous, involving major ideological confusion, also due to the use of that most misleading of concepts, 'participation society', and the underlying misassumptions. Steps were taken in three phases.

Phase 1: Sympathetic focus on citizenship and civil society, but on the back burner and from a historical rather than a strategic perspective
During this phase of the transition, many speakers and writers, including myself, continued to draw attention to the origins of many of today's public services, ranging from health care to pensions, from elementary education to village life and living environment, out of a strong civil society and active citizenship. They pointed to the power of socially engaged citizens, the major importance of civil leaders as part of social elites as pioneering and active citizens. And yet, the underlying reasoning was often driven by a historical perspective, while past performance is no guarantee of future results. If nobody believes in socially engaged proactive citizens or wants to give them space in the overregulated,

often state-controlled contemporary public services landscape, there will be no socially engaged proactive citizens, simply because there is no arena for them to get active in. The triangle I described at the start of this book, the three pillars of state, market, and civil society on which Westerns nations' constitutional structure rests, did not come out of nothing back in the 1990s when I first outlined it, because in those days the latter pillar was often overlooked in public and political debate, as most poignantly confirmed by the late Margaret Thatcher herself when she said: 'There is no such thing as society'.[59] Coincidentally, there were a few scientific studies published at the time that proposed a similar triangular definition, claiming that citizens and citizens' initiatives were overlooked in the public debate about privatization, which seemed to focus only on a choice between state and market. Civil society had basically been placed on the back burner as the real political fire was raging in privatization, market forces, outsourcing by or competition between public service providers and subsequently new public management, with the consequent 'businessification' of parts of government that could not be farmed out to the private sector. On the street, in local communities, and at sports clubs, civil society continued as normal, albeit underground, at a 'safe' distance politically and outside the control of both the market and the government, namely in volunteering and charity. Active citizens were still there, and we were often reminded of their historical value, but they were not taken seriously in a modern setting, neither by politicians, nor by public services. Citizens were expected to be thankful for the support of selfless others through charity events and donations, accept official decorations from the authorities for their volunteer work, and be passive consumers of public services. Citizens were kept out of the real decision-making process and outside the design process for public services, but politely thanked for their voluntary help.

Phase 2: The transformation of the welfare state through top-down involvement of so-called more citizenship
The main thinking at this stage is that active citizens can and must contribute more to collective and public facilities, because government is getting stuck in many areas due to overly costly, overly bureaucratic, and overly standardized public services.

The government cannot do it on its own. In fact, they often turn things into a bureaucratic mess. And on the other hand, we are seeing how active citizens are able to take better care of themselves and others than a standardized public service offering ever can. Of course, there is nothing wrong with professionally organized public services that are funded, monitored, and controlled by a strong government. This generates standard quality across the full spectrum of public services and solidarity with every single citizen who is entitled to use these services. The old duo of government and demand-driven public services has brought many western nations a long way. But what strikes me is that this success required us to ignore or even eliminate citizens' initiative, influence, and collaboration. The new disruptive technologies now, once again, support citizens' historical, but forgotten demand and opportunities to get involved a lot more, setting new requirements for the professionalism of public services. This old attitude of ignoring and denying citizens' involvement is now a superseded attitude. Just take health care (being health conscious will improve your quality of life and keep you healthy during the vulnerable years), education (the best learning performance comes when students work hard and in a disciplined manner), your pension (putting money aside for later is something you should start doing as early in life as possible, as it offers greater security than state pensions or entitlements), to name just a few. Here, too, politics and public services need to learn from the market's strategic responses. The power of new technology must not be denied. The best response is to engage in an innovative combination with these new technologies and actively incorporate citizens, their wants, and their potential on the supply side, both on an individual and a collective level, wherever it occurs.

Earlier, I described this using the Dutch government's ill-considered and erroneous concept of 'participation society.' The bad news for the government was, of course, clear right away. Citizens would not be roped into the government's cutback plans, would not be used as a tool to allow the government to cut spending on public services. Asking citizens to do more, while also requiring them to pay more and get less in return, was not exactly a great stimulus package to get citizens involved. The good news, however, is that it does show that the government is starting to see the downsides to the demand-driven system of public services, especially due to the inherent properties of government itself, which are not exactly easy to rectify or avoid. From the 1980s onward, market forces and privatization of public services were therefore embraced as the solution, out of a sentiment that was best captured by Ronald Reagan when he said: 'The government is not the solution to our problem, government is the problem.' Of all the privatizations we have seen since then, so many have failed by now that it was clearly not the panacea many thought it would be. Greater involvement and influence for individual and groups of citizens, also based on the triangular design of nations, then seems a suitable alternative.

It comes with major benefits:
- it sets the scene for active citizens who collaborate and adequately take care of themselves, which is better for themselves and for the effectiveness of public services, as pointed out above.
- citizens get more say and influence, encouraging co-production based on personal authority and potential, driven by what citizens need and can handle. Services become far more customized and individualized, rather than designed by bureaucrats or professionals, who would only turn to standardization and protocolization again. Instead, citizens come up with suitable solutions themselves.
- it comes with scope for innovation, start-ups, and social enterprises who adapt current services to the new age, and who innovate and introduce different perspectives.

Although the public/collective costs of public services will not necessarily come down as a result, it will boost citizens' voluntary, and perhaps even unpaid, commitment, as well as their philanthropic involvement and the effectiveness of services. All in all, it seems to me that this is more something that public officials should consider part of their responsibility, and where they are best placed to act effectively, than something citizens should organize. At most, citizens will be the ones paying the bill afterwards, through compulsory insurance premiums and taxes, but they will also be the ones who initially stand to gain the most from well-organized, open, and co-produced public services. Budget cuts are inevitable sometimes, that is just the way it is, but governments should not sugar-coat the need for cutbacks in misplaced messages, they should just intervene.

Phase 3: Disruptive citizenship turns the playing field on its head.
Citizens can claim, organize, criticize publicly, and arrange counterexpertise. Their dependence on the decisions and rules of public service providers is declining significantly. The question is to what degree and how many services will be organized by citizens themselves, or in an equal partnership with public service providers. How dominant will the government continue to be in this role?

The positive result of both previous phases is therefore that minds were primed for the alternative of active citizenship. What is completely new is the extent of the power that citizens now have thanks to new technologies. This will take some getting used to, especially for politicians and providers of public services.

15
Building a New Civil Society

When it comes to assimilating the new role of civil society, there are five things we have to learn to do.

- *Identify the values of citizens.* What makes citizens alert, rebellious, enterprising, or inspires them to get organized? What is their underlying mindset? Why do they want to do something about their environment, their neighborhood, their part of society? Why do they even make the effort?

Numerous studies and observations have unearthed the following values pattern. It starts with a public or social issue that you, as a citizen, are concerned about and you are sufficiently emotionally invested in it to want to get involved. It can be anything, ranging from the need for more renewable energy for your street to the need to do something about homeless elderly out on the streets of your neighborhood, poor education for your children, or unemployed youngsters hanging around in the street. Then, you see and hear that fellow citizens in your area have the same concerns. They are experiencing the same problem as you, a problem that will not just go away, and they realize that something needs to be done about it. The key components of this pattern of citizenship values are therefore:
a.) feeling personally invested in a public or social issue, b.) outrage or concern when certain social problems are left untackled by the authorities, c.) focus on fellow citizens that may see and experience the same problems, and subsequently d.) considering it your civic duty to actually do something about it. As far as this final step is concerned, I have already outlined that the question for these citizens to answer in this respect is whether to launch a collective campaign to get the authorities to act or to take action themselves to do something about it with other citizens.[60]

■ *Design the best-possible collective initiatives.* At this stage, the hard part is that there is often a broad array of possible initiatives you can take, whereby your choice will never only be based on the original values and resulting concerns and desire to take action. Possible action to take can range from appealing to official bodies to do something, writing angry letters, getting the press involved, buying things yourself, applying for a subsidy, setting up a crowdfunding campaign, to volunteering, to name a few. The choice to make is partly a rational one, based on what would be most effective, best suit the objective, and the easiest to actually do. But there are also very personal, sometimes even emotional considerations that go into it, such as 'This is too costly for me to do,' 'I have to do it together with a neighbor I don't know' and 'Have I not paid for this already via this or that government agency?' When it comes to wielding the power of civil society, all kinds of addictions to old structures and habits come into play that only impede citizens' initiatives. This is a very potent mechanism, because it is anchored deeply in citizens' psyche. The main obstruction is seen in the early stages. Not in the practical execution, but rather in the sinking in of the realization that you as citizens can and must do something together, which is at odds with the institutional relations and expectations that have grown over decades. Citizens' long training in passive consumerism by politics and public services can and will provoke this psychological mechanism. They are not easy to kick, the addictions to agencies that 'I have been paying for this all this time,' to public officials that 'I voted for,' to providers of public services 'who are in charge,' and to our own passive attitude as consumers: 'is it up to me to do that?' and 'hold up, I also have a job, you know.' This is, in fact, where the basis for leadership lies. Engaged citizens who want to take the lead, no matter in what context, need to realize and do several things.

They need to be able to think beyond the formalities of their current institutional position and turn the informal and actual wishes of citizens into action. Potential leaders need to adopt and represent the same citizenship values that lead to citizens being committed to an issue and wanting action, and thus acquire authority in civil society.

■ *Who will take on the leadership role?* Some citizens display the necessary leadership, take the lead, choose from the possible actions, and start organizing things. This is often also inspired by a combination of outrage and concerns on the one hand, and sufficient experience and lack of fear to step up to the plate on the other hand. I therefore consider the underlying values pattern, partly based on my doctoral research, as a combination of 'being passionate about a public and social problem' and 'being enterprising, strong-willed, and impatient.' This second aspect is crucial and often clearly visible, and all the more so after many decades of ingrained routines created by the dominance of state and market. Over all those decades, citizens' initiatives were not only considered unnecessary, but also actively discouraged or thwarted, if only because companies thought they would otherwise go out of business or politicians and civil servants thought they would lose their positions and ultimately their jobs. Enterprising citizens therefore need to overcome these routines and realize that it is now time civil society stepped up and took action.

■ *Proceed to voluntary collective action.* Citizens need to realize that merely protesting and complaining on social media alone will not cut it. Practical, visible, effective, joint action is needed. This is yet another realization that breaks an addiction that has grown over the years, an addiction to institutionalized participation and having a formal say, to paper-based action through angry letters, to complaining to your neighbor and hoping that they will do something. The risk of people's propensity to vent on modern social media is that it will briefly make them feel better and perhaps even proud, only to then return to the order of the day, in the – sometimes justified, sometimes vain – hope that those responsible or the relevant public bodies have heard you and will act on what you said. Sometimes they are right, because public opinion can now act on your complaints and this generates political influence, but most often it does not.

■ *Organize together.* Finally, and this is where modern technology proves most helpful, it is about organizing and sharing something together. As I pointed out, step 1 is that of shared concerns and outrage, which is followed immediately by the step of citizens realizing that more action is needed than the usual, well-practiced, and learned routines.

Concerns and ideas for actions to take in response to the concerns are shared far quicker than before thanks to modern media, and in a far more structured, transparent, and open manner.

16

Conclusion: The Digital Civil Revolution Impacts Our Citizenship

I have summed up today's disruptive technologies as a globally functioning combination of Internet, social media, and user-oriented websites and platforms that are accessible to any individual. This highly efficiently functioning and new IT chain has already acquired huge influence in the marketplace, especially through the use of platforms, which are basically companies with operations based on the bartering and virtual assistance enabled by these platforms, hence the term disruption. My point is, however, that this new tool has revolutionary impact and will have even more revolutionary impact for everyone, albeit less visibly so than in the market, but also on the state (politics, civil service, and public services), and more than anything on the clout and power of citizens, both collectively in their citizenship and citizens' organizations. The trinity of state, market, and civil society is starting to lean over to the civil society side, while the shape and organization of civil society is changing radically. Despite my eagerness to embrace this new civil power, supported by disruptive technologies, I must also draw the rather paradoxical conclusion that such civil power can only arise within the right system of government: democracy. Only in a democracy citizens have the right to vote, speak up, associate, self-organize, and launch citizens' initiatives. In fact, in non-democratic contexts, the technology is likely to be abused to better monitor and control citizens. My analyses are therefore intended to save democracy from the imminent disruption, but, as market disruption has already taught us, it can only be saved through strategic insight, an open mind, and adequate leadership, and not through denial, ignoring, looking away, or defensive behavior.

Despite decades of rhetoric in democracies about 'putting citizens first' and 'we are doing it all for the people,' this power shift will not be a smooth one, not even in formal democracies. All the established parties, ranging from politicians and existing large-scale providers of (standard) health care, energy, and education to experts and professionals who thought they had a monopoly on knowledge and paternalist officials who allegedly know best for others (as long as these others listen and behave as vulnerable as they think they are) will resist against this potential threat to their power and position. Such resistance is a pity and will delay an adequate response, but what it shows more than anything else is that these parties need to learn from the many bankruptcies in the market as a result of that very behavior of ignoring, talking down, taking small inept steps, or not even seeing the power shift and civil revolution coming at all.

It is regrettable that we are already seeing in the public debate, which is actually partly intended to assess the consequences of important developments, especially disruptive ones, on time and adequately, as this book has set out to do, in part through widespread discussions with the officials involved and experts in all kinds of areas, that many opinion makers are shying away from open debate on this hugely important matter. Needless to say, a power struggle is always also a struggle for power over meaning, interpretation, and framing. Throwing falsehoods around, bringing on the same threatened experts to argue the opposite, discrediting citizenship, and quickly and explicitly highlighting errors or scandals in civil society, such as misuse of public funds, discrimination of certain groups of the population, and concealed self-interest in public initiatives, these are all things that are happening as we speak. The best example is, again, Donald Trump, who became a prominent public figure first and then won elections by making clever use of new IT infrastructure to publish unfiltered messages and spread rumors and fake facts, and who now, as the President of the United States, complains about fake news and the power of the media, which he had actually also done during his campaign to some extent. In the end, this fabrication of victimhood, with the media being the aggressor, served him well. My appeal is for citizens to learn to see through this political and public rhetoric and to build and rely more on the horizontal sharing of data, facts, opinions, and debate.

In this strategic analysis of the ongoing Digital Civil Revolution, the following key points make up an outline of the response we need in terms of new, civil leadership. In the following, Part IV, my primary aim is to outline the required nature of such civil leadership, following on from the above strategic analysis. The key points are the following:

1. The new technologically created reality touches directly on our human existence, which is why it is not, in my view, merely the next phase of the ongoing process of industrialization, but rather an entirely new, next revolution.

2. Every revolution is always a power struggle as well, there is no room for neutrality or nuance, only with hindsight, but not in a strategic look ahead. Politics is also caught up in this power struggle, both in terms of fighting for its own survival and in terms of changes in how a nation and a people can be ruled. All parties in the new media landscape that deal with news, public opinion, and commentary are also part of this power struggle. And finally, the power struggle affects democracy as a form of government in its design and adaptation. After all, the power struggle shifts power toward citizens in the democratic context, which traditional parties will have to get used to and learn to tap into.

3. Ultimately, this revolution therefore also touches deeply on the question how citizens and society can and should be governed. Parties will have to figure out how to deal with a public opinion that is truly public, a public forum that is always on, the swarm behavior of continuously, better, and increasingly massively interconnected citizens. In actual fact, below the surface, it is all about the disappearance of all pretensions of top-down government, as the shift is toward complexity theory, swarm behavior and interrelations, toward networks instead of hierarchical government. No matter how paradoxical it sounds, but while governments have access to more and more data, have started to embrace big data technology, and are increasingly trying to monitor, discipline, nudge, and control citizens in all kinds of new ways, their control options and authority are diminishing.[61]

IV
Civil Leadership

Even though new technologies can have a disruptive impact in the market, in politics, and in public services (which is initially disconcerting, because these institutions do have (public and social) value), the undeniable positive aspect is that they give citizens more influence, knowledge, and power. The underlying opportunities for a better society and institutional order can only be seized by captivating citizens on one side and rulers and institutions on the other through a different brand of leadership: civil leadership. In terms of values, this leadership that is needed must be aligned with civil society and with what citizens want to see and follow. It is leadership 'by one of us, a fellow citizen.' But it must also be a suitable fit for boardrooms and administrative positions, because this is the only way that authority can be re-established in the public arena. This new kind of leadership is therefore a bridge between ascending citizenship and the required changes to institutions, between citizens and administration, between disruptions by the inescapably rising citizen power and the ensuing innovations in politics and the public sector to accommodate citizen power.

17
From Disruption to Civil Leadership

The new strategic context that is engendered primarily by the massive impact that new technologies are having on mindset, society, and horizontal citizen organization, and with that on citizen power ('it's a new mentality of citizens, not just technology, stupid'), must certainly lead to new leadership. This is basically the most important strategic response: to get the organization and the domain ready for the revolution on time, to face the future with an open mind, and to get citizens and employees on board in pursuing the necessary changes. The biggest challenge posed by the disruptions outlined above is one that has been widely covered in strategy literature. We have known for some time now that strategy is not a rational process where the future is, as best as possible and preferably in quantitative terms, estimated based mainly on quantitative analyses of the past, and options and scenarios are outlined as the basis for rational choices between these scenarios and options. The real test of strategic intelligence is how you handle and respond to the major and unexpected effects of disruptions, effects that cannot be estimated based on analyses of the past. CEOs at numerous companies across the market have shown how not to respond to imminent disruption. Instead, old routines, presuppositions, habits, and perspectives need to be abandoned and we must embark on the journey toward the uncertain and unknown with an open mind and even some anxiety, as the outcome is far less certain than everyday practices from the past. This is one of the reasons why, in my view, some level of permanent uncertainty and an edge of paranoia is actually a good basis for true strategic thinking and cognitive psychology is one of the building blocks for strategic intelligence (see Chapter 3).

Not only do we need more leadership, we need a different kind of leadership, based on different values, rooted in citizenship, because new technologies are empowering citizens and we no longer have to wait for politicians to finally realize what is happening and to want to adjust their 'policy' accordingly. Leadership has also become a widely researched topic in public administration and management literature, while also featuring heavily in courses and debates. In the first part of this book, I added to the debate by outlining the underlying disruption of the traditional management and policy industry (see Chapter 3).

I have identified three major movements that underpin and fulfill the need for a different kind of leadership. This new civil leadership is needed as a strategic response to and for the most fruitful handling of the fundamentally new strategic context created by the current Digital Civil Revolution.

a. The required addition to traditional management theories consists mainly in greater emphasis on *the personal side*, the drive, the charisma, the underlying set of values and attitude of the person who manages or leads. Management literature published so far fails to adequately focus on this aspect. This means that *the position* from which leadership is displayed also becomes more personal and informal. A leader is defined as a leader by spontaneous followers who recognize and see that this person is delivering leadership, taking the lead in an inspiring way, in a direction he or she has chosen and which credibly matches the person, prompting people to – spontaneously – start to follow him or her. U.S. Secretary of State Henry Kissinger defined, entirely in line with the foregoing and very aptly, a leader as 'someone who takes people where they would not have got by themselves'.[62] In fact, formal positions may put a brake on true leadership and the associated following, as many formal positions come with routines, procedures, standard expectations, and hierarchical obedience, both for the public official himself or herself (who, after all, is rooted in twenty years of traditional management thinking) and for his or her immediate environment.

First and foremost, it is about the person behind the leader, about character and deep-rooted virtues and values, in someone's life story and attitude.

Next, it is about the skill to get others to join in, also in tense times and with an uncertain course.

b. Still, management theories and practices from the past decades have also given us an idea of this kind of new leadership. Performance at the highest levels that involves major responsibilities also calls for certain *administrative skills* to retain and fulfill an executive position in the public or private sector. Politics at the top, boardroom dynamics, personal ambitions, characteristics, and motives of others who also operate at the top or want to be part of the top must all be dealt with. Leadership without a formal position is very possible in a concrete human circle, such as a team, neighborhood, or association, but is much harder when it comes to large-scale bureaucratic organizations and institutions, of which we happen to have so many in the public domain and business, so in the real boardrooms. Leaders who lack administrative skills will soon lapse into naive argumentativeness, administrative conflicts, or even chaos.

The third factor is therefore the skill of being able to make the right decisions, while securing and using the position you acquired in a politically skilled way, so basically the combination of power and morals.

c. And finally, and most importantly, leadership needs to *operate visibly, consistently, and effectively based on values.* This is gauged mainly through deeper why-questions surrounding leadership, such as: Why does he or she want us to go in a certain direction? Why should we follow him or her? Does it serve the general position and future of the organization and our existence within the organization, is the action taken with that in mind and needed for it? How does this action, which the leader is calling for, contribute to the interests of society and the long-term interests of the organization? A values-driven approach and explicit references to it will boost the credibility and direction of the leadership. Values are crucial here, precisely because we are dealing with disruption. As old values patterns may no longer be valid, values may need to be reassessed and redesigned. The institutions based on the values will also come under debate or be called into question, including the form of government, public services, formal or legal bases of certain relationships, such as with respect to banks and money, contracts, and civil rights. The biggest change that is now imminent concerns open strategic insight into the social impact of the ongoing technological revolution and the associated leadership that is providing people with direction in these confusing and chaotic times. After that, a string of similar institutional changes will be needed over a very long period of time. After all, it is about shaping a revolution that transfers power to citizens and citizenship (meaning that everyone's behavior needs to display an appeal to citizenship and civic responsibilities), and particularly about a strategic disruption that must have a psychological effect: people searching for new truths, and so also for new values, which leads to feelings of insecurity and a deep, almost philosophical quest. The ability to explore such a quest, is something that many managers lack or have unlearned. As a result, any kind of deep psychological shift, like the one we need now, will surprise them as an unexpected new requirement that their competencies have to meet, and is therefore very complicated.

This brings us to the fourth feature, namely that of a continuously open and smart assessment between the new strategic context and the right steps, measures, and decisions. As an extra skill that must lead to a desire to keep learning from this practice and from one's own choices in the same cleverness and strategic steps.

The good news is that our thinking about humans, humanity, and therefore about leadership as well has been systematic and at a high level for over 2,000 years, and that we do not solely rely on the latest state of the art in modern science for our new insights. This is a good thing as the new revolutionary, technological context and its impact on leadership is probably taking modern science by surprise as well. Could it be that our modern social sciences knowledge is now also being disrupted?

Approx. 2,300 years ago, Aristotle already spoke of the importance of values-based and virtues-based balancing in a strategic and administrative context with smart strategic action, which he referred to as *phronesis* (practical wisdom). Aristotle's thinking and analyses will reverberate in the rundown of key elements of new leadership in the next section.

18
'Good' Leadership Can Save Citizenship

The analysis in Part II showed mainly the impact of the new developments on our human existence and human functioning. Continuing from there, I am turning to the concept of 'citizens', as the human element prevails in this concept, albeit not only in a philosophical or ideological sense, but also in a more professional and organizing sense. It therefore both contains a social element and implies collective organization and communality toward modern governments and market parties. This choice is made because we need a concept that captures people on a very personal level, also individually, in their survival, continued existence, and mutual functioning and interrelations on one hand, but that also represents and invokes the professional side of their input and influence toward both other parties of the triangle, the state and the market. All of this is encapsulated in the concept of *citizens* and their behavior and attitude, and the values pattern of *citizenship*. Also and primarily in the roles beyond the traditional, interests-driven perceptions of citizens as purely passive consumers or passive voters by those other parties (state and business), who were dominant until recently.

What is Citizenship?

In much of the literature, citizen and citizenship are defined and viewed mainly in relation to the state. This is because that is where the concept originated. The European cities of the Middle Ages were the first accumulations of land, companies with regular folk with an overarching legal say and order, and which included a formal and organizational place for people to take part in administration and management. This kind of say and the recognition of residents as citizens were subsequently transplanted as an institutional order from sovereign cities to their larger-scale successors, the nation states (obviously also with forms of government such as monarchy and oligarchy; the outlined urban culture and governance are not seen in all national constitutional legal orders of state). Until today, this is visible in phenomena such as the political struggle surrounding integration and immigration, and therefore in the selection of persons who are recognized as citizens, with all rights and obligations that come with it. The main approach is still the formal and constitutional recognition as citizen of a town or country. This is coupled with recognition by the citizen of his or her compliance with the rules and laws of the governments, such as with respect to taxes, property, and legal competency.

> *In the summer of 2010, I was on vacation in France. At the time, the then president of France, Nicolas Sarkozy, was stirring up wide-spread debate about crime, especially following attacks on public servants such as police officers and paramedics by what he referred to as 'immigrants.' These immigrants were actually French citizens (albeit second-generation), or from groups of people who had been living in France for a long time and more or less tolerated groups such as Romani people. Sarkozy wanted to have these people deported or to have their French citizenship revoked. In doing so, the state would be officially distinguishing between 'stable citizenship' and 'disputable citizenship.' Political commentators generally concluded that Sarkozy had started his re-election campaign early and was basically trying to appeal to right-wing Le Pen voters.*

I am, however, also emphasizing the other side of being a citizen – which I do not solely consider a formal legal relationship with a government. To me, it is more about citizenship as an extra denotation beyond that. Citizenship is an attitude, a values pattern and solidarity, individually and mutually, sometimes focused on a government but without being fully dependent on it or having to follow its dominant vision. This is what political scientist Herman van Gunsteren called 'public office of citizen' or: ' citizenship as an office.'[63] In fact, the concept of 'civil service' captures this line of thinking very eloquently. This office is more than a right ('the right to have rights'), it also encompasses the desire to play an active role, to have ambitions, wanting to do your bit for the common good. It is therefore also an obligation, a sense of duty: to want and be able to contribute to the public cause. This kind of citizenship already existed in the same medieval towns where 'citizens' were legally and administratively 'invented', where that same citizenship was the basis for individual and communal action and collaboration with and sometimes in protest against the government. This is sometimes referred to as the republican approach to citizenship, because it does not take citizens as only subordinates of a king, emperor, or a state and its administration. In this approach, the citizen is an independent institution in its own right, with civil rights, but also with roles, contributions, and entitlement to a critical attitude, also toward that same government that bestows and guarantees civil rights. Thanks to this approach, the government cannot rely solely on active citizenship and solidarity between citizens in self-organization or commons. It must, in fact and at the same time, be acknowledged that that can lead to a difficult relationship with that same government: '[…] political power is never neutral, but always implies elements of discipline and normalisation.'[64] 'Citizenship is more than a (legal) status – it is postulated on autonomy and the capability of exercising good judgment, so that the citizen is capable of "both ruling and being ruled"' (ibid., p.209).[65]

Also toward market parties, people are stepping out of their passive consumer role, behaving as good citizens and demanding that companies do the same. This latter demand has already led to the coining of the term *corporate citizenship.*[66] Companies, too, must focus on the social interests of the society of which they are a member, such as in the area of the environment, working conditions, and fair pay, and they must do so of their own accord, from their own mission and values, without being prompted by public protests from modern citizens.[67]

The attitude of citizenship and the associated values are essential in coming up with the best possible response to the ongoing disruptions. This, too, touches primarily on leadership as an expression and safeguarding of, as well as communication about, these values, hence my assertion that a new kind of leadership, civil leadership, is necessary as a strategic response to the threat of disruption. People must be engaged as fully-fledged citizens.

In the long run and structurally, the revolution of the new technologies is already visibly leading to a fundamental transformation of our humanity, our view of humanity, and our citizenship, on both an individual and a collective level.

There are two other factors that sometimes further complicate matters: the technological innovations and the practical implementation thereof on the one hand, and the public power struggle on the other (which is, of course, not publicly acknowledged and recognized as such, because that is always the best power strategy to begin with).

As far as the technological issues that are requiring our focus both on the innovative side and on the operational side are concerned, these still need a lot of adaptations and applications, as well as to be implemented and become functional everywhere. This is not only about worldwide infrastructure, both of hardware and software, but also, within all kinds of organizations, about learning to go along with it, serving clients with modern services, starting platforms yourself, trying to take over smart innovative startups and integrating technological solutions, and having all external communications under control. We are also, especially in terms of public opinion and the public and political debate, in the middle of a power struggle caused by its impact on all institutional relations and positions of power. It is a revolution in the institutional relations, which traditional 'pundits' and 'experts' have failed to explain and analyze properly, because they owe their positions to the old media landscape and are now forced to reconquer their positions of authority. This leads to widespread professional unrest in these circles, due to doubts about their survival (politicians), relevance (journalists), and authority in the public arena (professors, experts, members of the public acting as such).

Both elements of the ongoing technological revolution, the ongoing new technological steps, possibilities, and applications and the ongoing struggle for power over sensemaking, interpretation, and framing are in themselves already leading to major confusion, not only among citizens but certainly also among public officials and executives. The underlying key question that is not yet addressed adequately amid this confusion is the need for clarity, new roles and an outlook for the future of the new humanity and new citizenship. Also in this respect, there is a great need for interpretation and renewed structuring, which is a need that traditional opinion leaders will struggle to fulfill, because they are (subconsciously or in a state of denial) focused mostly on themselves and their position. Every stakeholder, every citizen, seeks a path in this new world with these new tools, and will need meaning and guidance as well as to be presented with hopeful actions: recognizable, specific, committed, and future-focused leadership. Getting people to buy into the best responses, the underlying assumptions, and the requested values and necessary thinking hinges on leadership. These revolutionary times call not only for more leadership, but also for a *new brand* of leadership: civil leadership. This is due to the nature of the revolution as analyzed above: more citizenship, more citizen power, greater emphasis on civic values, better alignment with a powerful civil society, especially in leadership.

This kind of leadership is so necessary because this revolution, like all previous revolutions, is accompanied by danger and risks while it may also trigger violence.

The Risks Involved in New Technology

As I have explained previously, my eyes are not closed to the hidden and sometimes open manipulations of and on the new channel, manipulations by commercial parties such as the owners of the channel or platform, and by the providers providing the technology, as well as through the use of big data, microtargeting, and algorithms. And neither do I close my eyes to the fundamentally different functioning of the platform economy, with its reliance on a large network, both on the supply side and on the demand side, but also on flexibility and real-time choices, which is having major impact on the labor market, where people are basically forced to adopt similar flexibility. We did not need the Facebook scandal in early 2018[68], when it was revealed that Facebook had been cooperating, either openly or tacitly, in targeting and the spreading of rumors by a firm called Cambridge Analytica during the U.S. presidential election, to realize that Facebook uses users' personal data for its own purposes and that selling these data on to third parties is actually Facebook's core business. Governments were late to react, as always, as they should have been regulating this market and seen to the protection of personal data well before the scandal hit, but it is still a good thing that they are now truly getting involved and starting to regulate this channel. This does not mean, however, that I am part of the camp that abuses such critical notes to restrict citizens' say, opinion making, and data sharing on websites, social media, WhatsApp, etc. In my view, citizens' freedom on the new channel need not be curtailed by clearly needed better regulation of market forces and privacy protection with respect to products and technology of companies that have meanwhile acquired a global monopoly in their respective markets. This is ultimately also a monopoly on concealed use of personal data for commercial purposes (such as by selling advertising). On the hand, we can conclude that many governments are slow to get off the mark when it comes to personal data protection, so much so in fact that even the sluggish and highly bureaucratic European Union actually looks agile and is even leading the way on a global scale with its new personal data protection regulation. And on the other hand, we need to be careful not to condone a new conservative coalition of market lobbyists and politicians that wants to overregulate personal data protection and restrict open and direct sharing of data and opinions between citizens. Dictatorships have been curtailing citizens freedom in this respect for some time now, and there is no guarantee that a coalition of democratic politics and market lobbyists representing the business leaders of today will not want to go down that road as well. The new direct channel, no matter how manipulated it is, offers scope, exposure, and the possibility to share news and information produced by citizens themselves. With hindsight, the old manipulations of data, information, and news on the old channels are consequently becoming crystal clear to these citizens. For the general public, which increasingly feels a personal connection to news and media, because it is coming from within the population and is actively shared between citizens, the new competition between the three media channels leads to more transparency and openness, also with respect to the old manipulations on the traditional channels of written press, radio, and TV.

Paradoxically, this misuse by commercial firms and politicians is also testimony to the importance of the new channel as a source of power within democracy and therefore for public opinion as well. Putin would never have taken to social media if it were not such an effective way to meddle in Western democracies. Perhaps we needed this criminal abuse of social media to open our eyes to the power of this new channel that is openly available for use by and for citizens. Manipulation of news is, of course, as old as humanity itself, originating in gossip and backbiting in small groups. These kinds of scandals and manipulations do not erode the value and fundamental power sources of new, social media, but they do make us more alert to such possible manipulations and abuse of power (and therefore thankfully also to administrative practices surrounding old media), and consequently to the need for regulation of this channel. So be it, just like you cannot make an omelet without breaking eggs, you cannot have a revolution or a power struggle without a fight and some aggravation.

When institutions and the balance of power shift, many things can go wrong. From uprisings for negative or self-centered reasons to the wrong actions. Something else that can no longer be concealed, just because technology now facilitates it exponentially, is the exclusion of people from groups, as the fact that groups are so much easier to organize thanks to new technology also means that any kind of exclusion instantly stands out. Why would the new technologically driven capability of creating greater and stronger bonds automatically also lead to an attitude of seeking out such bonds? Earlier, I detailed the huge influence that new technologies are having on mindset, social relations, and behavior, but this influence can also create negative results. These same technologies may just as well stimulate and bolster the entirely wrong kind of behavior of people, both toward themselves and toward each other. Commercial parties are not the only ones who can lock people in information, news, and network bubbles, as mentioned above, as people can now also do this themselves, possibly even with the help of new technology. Locking yourself in a self-imposed mental prison has become one of the options. New technology promotes and facilitates this old behavior, although the good news is that it really stands out now if you do so. What you see and judge inside your bubble ultimately depends on your view of mankind. Are you mistrusting of people, possibly partly fueled by politics or market, or can you see their positive potential and needs? Citizens' greater capacity for self-organization is not only a factor when it comes to the noble motives of good citizenship, but also in traditional not-in-my-backyard behavior in protest against inevitable higher taxes or against interventions in the neighborhood that will indeed improve quality of life in the area. There will also be more room and influence for informal bad leadership that manages to get neighborhoods or even sections of the population to follow a leader in mistargeted actions and protests. I already mentioned the risk of demagogues appearing and getting huge numbers of people to follow them. But this ultimately only reinforces my point that the revolutionary impact of disruptive technologies on human existence and communities primarily creates a need for new civil leadership.

The Need for 'Good' Leadership

Building on the above observation, the following matter becomes even more crucial: there is also an urgent need for Good leadership, based on the right values, with the right direction, the right appeals, and the behavior to match. 'Good' with a capital 'G' because of the values-based, ethical, and moral dimension. It is not 'good leadership' in a technical sense, based on the question whether the leader has achieved results and hit targets, and done so in the most efficient and effective way possible. Has the leader, under the circumstances and given the objectives, tasks and position, acted in way that can be classed as correct and effective in a practical and technical sense? Have the objectives been realized in an effective and efficient way? Are the appropriate steps being taken? What I mean by Good leadership is morally good leadership, meaning leadership with the right intentions, focused on humanity and citizenship, the right behavior and the right values inspiring this behavior. Precisely because of the need and scope for different and more informal leadership among people themselves, it is all the more important that such leadership be Good leadership as well. The influence and effectiveness of the leadership are becoming more important, which is the technical side of leadership, but so are the nature and underlying values. This is basically the opposite end of the political debate that is dominant in Western countries today, the debate about 'the elite' and its selfishness and how the members of this elite turn their backs on the people they are supposed to lead. By Good leadership, I mean that the discussion should not be about 'elites' and who is unjustly classed as such (the 'castes,' 'closed inner circles,' 'cronyism,' including the flawed behavior of shielding each other and isolated closed networks for the exchange of favors), but should instead be about the nature, attitude, values, and expectations of the kind of leadership that is needed. It is effectively a call for a new social, human elite rooted in citizenship values. That said, it is perhaps not wise at this time to speak of a 'new elite,' given the current fierce public debate about the phenomenon of 'elites'. My view on this civil leadership addresses one of the big criticisms in this current debate on 'elites' that incumbent elites in essence seem to select new entrants to the elite themselves. It is a much broader group of all kinds of people that can apply for 'civil leadership' and the process of selecting them is much more informal, spontaneous and citizen driven than most of the selection processes of the criticized elites.

19
Eliminating Misconceptions:
What Is Leadership?

Having analyzed the revolutionary impact of disruptive technologies and called for Good leadership as the much-needed response to the ongoing revolution, I will now move on to a question that touches on the actual contents of leadership: what does this brand of leadership look like in terms of features, philosophy, principles, and examples, so as to be able to better recognize, judge, cherish, and stimulate it in our personal environment and even in ourselves?

1. Leadership is **personal**, not necessarily linked to formal positions. In fact, there are hordes of people in high-level official positions who show no leadership whatsoever. '*….think of how many presidents or prime ministers you can recall who succeeded in taking the country in a new direction, and a direction they intended to go in. Most of these famous people fail.*'[69] That said, they are by no means mutually exclusive, it is very possible to have the right person with the right kind of leadership in a high-level position. It would actually be ideal, as it would be aligned with what leadership is intended to be, as well as with the expectations of the people who are led by the leader. In fact, to get people to follow, also on a more spontaneous basis, it is certainly helpful to lead from a position of power and influence, as people will then sooner be inclined to listen to your message and take it seriously. Leadership is also shown when someone goes over and above what is formally required given their position and duties. It is precisely this kind of going beyond the call of duty that turns a top-level position in public administration and executive positions into one of leadership. To distinguish between power based on a formal position and authority based on personal actions, charisma, and inspiration, we can look at the following feature of leadership.

2. Leadership is characterized by a **spontaneous following**, people who follow a leader, recognize him or her as their leader, and adopt,

execute, and support his or her course and ideas. This kind of following is considered spontaneous because it is not borne out of subservience. It is not borne out of a subordinate position. However, this distinction is difficult to make in practice, as people also tend to listen to someone because they have power over them. People are not always willing to openly admit that they do not understand a word the formal boss says, say that they consider it nonsense, or even claim to have a better idea themselves while he or she still has power over them.[70] This criterion is the clearest when used in informal groups without a formal hierarchy or differences in positions. Within such groups, anyone can, in principle, be the leader and only few actually acquire that role spontaneously thanks to their followers. These others decide whether or not you are a leader. Self-proclaimed leaders, as there are many, because leadership is all the rage these days, simply have not understood how it works, and probably do not even know whether they even have spontaneous followers or not, and are therefore probably not a leader.

These first two features tie in with my claim that disruptive technologies are leading to very different organizations: more open and more like networks, less hierarchical, less formally structured, barely definable in terms of standard management. The personal is increasingly incorporated into the organizational, which can even lead to traditional organizations becoming separate units within much more diffuse internal and external networks.

3. **Urgency context: there must be a need for leadership**. Leadership is hot, everyone wants to be a leader or show leadership. It is partly a craze fueled by jubilant and hagiographical literature glorifying the successes of so-called leaders. Like I said previously, anyone who has success or claims to have had success is soon perceived as a leader by others and certainly by themselves. The main ingredients of this kind of leadership are an explicit formal top-level role (which is where the managerial mystique kicks in), visible success or at least a provisional veneer of success, and more than anything the claim that the success is due to the leader's personal effort, plans, and motivation. It is therefore good to realize that this kind of leadership, as well as the kind of leadership targeted by demand for 'more leadership', is not always good and not always necessary, and will certainly not always contribute to

society or the organization. Leadership is possible and desirable only when there is a strategic need for it. If there are no major changes or turbulences in the immediate environment, if there is no urgent need to break down routines, habits, and structures, and if most of the work can be done on a business-as-usual basis, there is no need for leadership. In fact, it is then likely to be a hindrance when someone is overly eager to show leadership. In those cases, the existing hierarchy and existing approaches are more than enough, as everyone simply does 'their thing' and executes the current routines as best as possible. The standard management functions of planning, organizing, coordinating, commanding, and controlling, and the organization in its current operational state, will suffice in those cases. Someone with a different view who wants their team to follow him or her in an entirely new direction will then, no matter how charismatic and rhetorically gifted, not get a chance to rally people, but there is actually no need for it, which the followers will then instantly realize. The first step of leadership is to get people to join you in your concerns and strategic uneasiness, to get them to buy into your 'definition of the situation.' If there is no factual basis for your definition, rhetorical skills alone will not get you very far. This is a tricky point in practice. When a leader fails to get his or her team to join him or her in major changes, the question is: why?. Was it because there was no real reason for the changes, or was it because he or she fell short in getting the strategic problem, which was indeed a real problem, across? Was it a failure of leadership or because there was no strategic reason for the changes? Was the leader right or were the followers (who pulled out) right?

This feature also makes that leadership is mainly relevant in times of need, problems, and strategic issues. This often also leads to social turbulence surrounding the leader. Such turbulence can manifest itself in resistance, arguments, pulling out, and sickness. This, in turn, potentially leads to perceptions such as 'leadership is trouble' or even more stinging: 'this leadership is trouble.'

There are two things to note here:
- There is no objective truth on leadership, it remains a social definition that depends on many different factors and relations in situ and perceptions of stakeholders; even when using scientific empiri-

cal methods, the 'reality' based on a so-called unique, true and objectively measurable definition, no matter how measurable it is, will never surface. This realization is now causing social sciences to increasingly turn to methods from anthropology, such as participatory observation and action research.[71]

- When there is indeed this kind of social commotion around persons and their actions, it is most likely 'leadership' that you are seeing. When there is no ado about persons, you will probably be dealing with obedient and anonymously operating management, which intends primarily 'to keep things going,' 'organize things properly,' or 'do a good job.' Whether this ultimately is successful leadership remains to be seen. Again, 'objective' observation is problematic here, as only success will prompt people to call it leadership. In day-to-day practice, the term 'leadership' still has such a positive connotation that people often wait until afterwards to use it with hindsight, when it is backed up by success. In many autobiographies of leaders, leadership is claimed with hindsight, because one can base it on (perceived and personally attributable) successes.

4. **The good leader: moral and/or technical, or both?** The need for the *morality of leadership* has been a topic for debate in leadership literature. My definition of Good leadership (to set it apart from regular or even bad leadership) is sometimes twisted as follows: only Good people with Good intentions and Good values can be called leaders. This basically leads to Leadership with a capital L: we reserve the label of leader for morally Good People with leadership qualities and a position of leadership.[72] Personally, I prefer to distinguish between Bad and Good Leadership[73] (with a large, complex, and nuanced bandwidth in between of 'somewhat Good' or 'somewhat Bad'). Both kinds of leadership are seen in practice, and both can have the first three features (personal, spontaneous followers, strategic need). As a leader, Hitler also checked these three boxes, but no one, barring perhaps a few remaining neo-Nazis (followers!), will still refer to him as a leader.

Another important point is that this topic of Good versus Bad emphasizes the leader's personal values and intentions. There are, however, two critical side notes to make here.

a. We only know these values and intentions insofar as we can infer them from the behavior and manifestations of the leader himself or herself. We ultimately end up having to interpret the behavior and manifestations to pinpoint the actual values and intentions. We can never be sure, though, and we might just as well be dealing with a leader who is just very good at faking, concealing, or airbrushing his or her character and intentions.[74]

b. The reason why someone follows a leader is probably often inspired by the prospect of a result that approximates the intentions and values presented by the leader. A leader who only has a good story and/or good intentions, but who fails to reach a result that is in line with this story or these intentions will soon lose his or her authority and leadership. Good intentions alone are not enough, however much they initially helped the leader acquire a considerable following based on honesty, authenticity, and consistency between behavior and message. This also leads to the conclusion that, in executive reality, there is not a great difference between good management and good leadership. The ideal with respect to the result would be to have these qualities united in one single person, and failing that, the next best thing would be for the leader to have a knack for surrounding himself or herself with good managers and giving them the space to do their important work. '[…[you need managers to run the world before, during and after the revolution'.[75]

There is also some friction between the leadership features listed above, especially around the assigned values pattern and the spontaneity of the followers, such as between the leader's values and the values of the followers, also in their followership: why are they following the leader? The leader's values need to be aligned with those of citizenship and civil society, and therefore with the behavior and motivation behind the leadership. The leader points the way toward a certain social result and in tackling major social problems, also based on his or her personal values, such as solidarity, care for the vulnerable and the weak, or a drive to improve public services such as health care, education, etc. The leader will often do so beyond the call of duty of the organization as a whole. He or she is effectively taking his or her social pursuit to the extreme. The question that arises is then what makes followers spontaneously follow the leader's example. This basically presupposes that they – spontaneously, unprompted, albeit somewhat triggered and encouraged by the leader – are themselves advocates of and adherents to citizenship values. A traditional followership pattern based on the question of 'what's in it for me?' will therefore not work in this case and also lead to followers not recognizing this kind of leadership. It could even lead to an internal political struggle between the representatives of the social values pattern and the people with this more traditional pattern of values.

5. **No matter how personal it is, leadership is linked to an organizational context and position**. No matter how personal leadership is in terms of, for example, behavior, actions, motives, and approach, it is naturally also linked to the organizational context and therefore to the aforementioned institutional changes. You could say that many of the aspects mentioned above, such as good intentions and the pressure to legitimize, can be linked back to this point on the interface between leadership and organizational context. You are a leader based on a certain position, such as a job, status, name, means, and team. This not only goes for leaders whose leadership is linked to a formal position in for-profit or not-for-profit organizations, but also for someone who operates from a more informal kind of active citizenship. This is also a kind of leadership from an organizational position, whereby the organization may be no more than a network with a certain identify or demographic composition, while the way you approach the network determines the impact of your leadership. I am explicitly mentioning this because it is yet another point where there is a lot of romanticizing of the phenomenon and concepts of leadership going on, as if structures, power tactics, and struggles for a certain position and status cease to matter as long as you operate with the right level of passion and enthusiasm. In most literature on leadership, power and money do not or barely feature, as noble causes and good intentions are believed to be all the fuel a leader needs. This is, of course, not accurate. Laws, people and other (power) positions tend to get in the way. Civil leaders, too, need a healthy dose of political and tactical nous, and therefore need to have studied the political analyses and advice like those of Machiavelli. In these matters, we can perhaps learn the most from executives who formally operate in top-level positions, even though they themselves will seldom openly admit that they have gotten where

they are thanks to their political skills. Like seasoned politicians do not benefit from transparency on their strategic intelligence (while entrepreneurs do), as was analyzed before, executives do not benefit from transparency on any political skills they employed to get to the top-level position they acquired. Perhaps that the great focus on leadership in these circles is partly based on this: it is better to boast about your solidarity, personal commitment, and good intentions than about your success in reaching an important formal top-level position. Still, what every civil leader needs to do in this respect is to learn from the past two decades of professionalization in the management domain. There are four elements in these management practices and training that you, as a civil leader, need to consider and be able to use in mutual correlation, no matter how contradictory they sometimes are:

a. *Struggles for position*: being able to get your way, either by pursuing a position, or by effective deployment of the associated means of power, such as authorizations and finances.

b. *Position elements*: Responsibilities, expectations, and objectives from your formal position, appointments, and mandates, which you can invoke internally and externally and which are very important in getting people to follow you.

c. *Values*: What is it that you personally want to achieve and add, why, and what are your considerations in doing so? This has been covered above, while the next section will go into (possible) specific details of these values. It is important here that you, despite the need of the struggle for position, not lose sight of this aspect. If you were to, you would become an apparatchik or impersonal manager, like so many others.

d. The overarching matter, and this goes beyond Machiavelli, is: *what values come to the fore in how you present yourself and in your behavior*? After all, Machiavelli's focus was on, and his observations and lessons were about, the behavior and actions that a political leader has to adopt to conquer, retain, or execute a political position. This is the ultimate political effectiveness, which happens to be based on the equally 'objective' (in the sense of not being colored by moral considerations; Machiavelli is consequently often considered the father of political science) as astute observation of the political behavior he saw around him. At the end of the day, the good values of these political leaders seem of little relevance to him, as only the result in terms of power and political positions in his observations and analyses matter. That said, he lets his criticism of this selfish behavior and his criticism of monarchs, popes and dictatorships certainly filter through. This portrayal of his philosophy is somewhat in line with the one-sided interpretation by many that came after him. In his writings, Machiavelli often also emphasized, contrary to this portrayal, the importance of 'virtu', which translates as a healthy, vital personality with an eye for the interests of society.[76] Given that values are so crucial for the social aspect of leadership, while politics and a formal position are also indispensable for effectiveness and accruing a following, this is a crucial point. It is precisely this problematic and rare combination, of values and good purpose on one side and the political struggles and skills on the other, that is often not suspected behind persons with a formal power position, while it is actually of great importance. Most writing on leadership comes from academics and management consultants, who often have little or altogether lack internal political experience and seldom have actual experience in executive positions and high-level public administration. They therefore fail to highlight this fundamental dilemma between purely political struggles for position on the one hand and having an intrinsic values pattern of help, solidarity, and civil commitment and expressing it in leadership on the other hand.

20
The Building Blocks of New Leadership

This integral mix of administrative effectiveness and a values-based drive, which used to be captured in separate elements such as good character or good intentions, while it is now taken as passion and objective of administrative practices, is the crucial new correlated core for leadership. The new creative mix of power strategies and morality is, consequently, not only an external sign of efficiency and effectiveness, but also an internal matter for the leader personally, one of integrity, a values-driven attitude, and personal effort. There is, of course, also a link between these external and internal aspects: leadership is most effective when the people around you believe in your integrity and your personal commitment to the course you have charted and the destination you want to reach with them. The ongoing disruptions are leading to new combinations that also have to be reflected in the new nature of leadership, which is where I see many executives in the public and private sector go wrong these days.

This is because these are new combinations of what used to be separate worlds, at least in theory and concepts of governance and management, partly due to a misconception of professionalization of management. It is then about *values-based rules*, such as for the development and application of governance codes,[77] *values-based politics*, which is power combined with values and good causes, *values-based rhetoric*, which is the ability to convince the crowd of your integrity, good causes, and good character, *sanctity with practical wisdom*, which are good intentions and good character applied to the administrative and strategic context and challenges, while fulfilling these good causes as effectively as possible.

The core of these outlines of leadership is therefore **character** in the broadest sense, backed up by values, skills, and personality on the one hand and **wisdom** in considerations, direction, and positional and organizational requirements on the other (which is also covered in the below section on the philosopher who outlined it as 'phronesis' 2,300 years ago, Aristotle). After all, who does not love these human and idealistic traits in a boss, spouse, or neighbor?

In the following, I will give a rundown of the building blocks of leadership that I keep referring to here and which seamlessly blend into the specific version of leadership that I have branded 'civil leadership,' along with a specification of the special elements of each one.

Building Block 1. Character & virtues (**human**): What is the character and what are the virtues underlying the leader's consistency, honesty, credibility, and behavior, which determines what kind of person he or she is and to what identity and relations with other people does this lead?

Building Block 2. (Ability to) achieve results (**manager**): Leadership is no good to us if it cannot achieve results in the direction that the leadership claims to steer. This is not entirely up to the leader on his or her own, as results can be achieved by gathering a team of managers around him or her, which is also a management skill: delegating tasks and responsibilities to the right people in an effective division of labor is still the core of what management is all about (as claimed in an early definition: 'getting things done through other people').

Building Block 3. Making adequate assessments in this administrative and strategic context (**practical wisdom**): 'Good' is both good in a technical sense (effective and efficient with a view to the intended result) and Good in a moral sense (making the right choices based on the right moral considerations and virtues). It is ultimately about making the right choices and doing the right thing within a certain context, which cannot be captured in general rules, protocols, codes, or checklists, as the leading person and the strategic and personal context are the defining factors.

Building Block 4. Getting people to follow in the chosen direction and buy into the underlying choices and intentions (**leadership**): This is the core of all leadership, as quoted before: 'getting people where they wouldn't have gotten themselves.' But the above building blocks of character, management, and practical wisdom are worthless if the leadership is not aligned with the context, people, and desired direction.

Building Block 5. Attaining, using, and retaining a formal and/or informal position in the relevant circle of people and means (**politician**): Again, leadership, practical wisdom, and being a Good person will be inconsequential if the leader is unable to build and conquer a position of authority and even power. In the eternal struggle between power and morals, between authority over others and moral justness, a leader who ticks all the above boxes but does not master or is unable to persevere in the human political game is all but useless to us.

On top of this general outline of leadership based on the above building blocks, there are several specific elements that are needed for civil leadership.

21
The Key Elements of Civil Leadership

My core argument is that the only response to visible and ongoing disruptions of political, public, and social mechanisms and institutions is **leadership** (see Chapter 17). It does require, however, this leadership to be driven by values and able to engage in the power struggle that is part and parcel of any revolution. And given the great misconceptions of leadership, I have also tried to define this in as specific terms as possible. In doing so, I focused on the difference between 'Good' and 'bad' leadership, as the leadership we need is **'Good' leadership** (see Chapter 18). My definition of 'Good' leadership subsequently led to my rundown of five elementary buildings blocks of this kind of leadership, also as a way to counter dominant leadership myths (see Chapter 19). Owing to the need to tap into the strategic context of an increasingly powerful civil society and the threatening disruptions of public institutions, we need a specific kind of leadership: **civil leadership**. The thing now is to zoom in on the defining elements of civil leadership, within the outlines of leadership and 'good' leadership as presented above.

The following are key elements of the new brand of leadership we need, civil leadership.

- **Values**: There are certain values that are key to and in sync with civil leadership and that are based on intrinsic, well-tried citizenship and the associated citizenship attitude.

Private attitude for public value: In all their actions, new leaders are close to the private world of citizens and *civil society* and work for society, for *the common good*. In modern times, elected politicians simply can no longer claim to have a monopoly on the public interest and being the only ones who solely and exclusively look out for it – on the contrary. This has great consequences, such as the fundamentally changing vision on citizenship and civil society that I presented above.

This also calls for a different vision on the economy, market, and business. The outlines of such a new vision are also emerging in the changes in economics (see Note 18, for example). Companies no longer only look after their own best interest (thus indirectly contributing to overall prosperity and therefore the public interest),[78] while conveniently leaving the public interest in the hands of politicians, as they are increasingly forced to shift their focus to the pursuit of social goals as part of their integral strategic objectives and considerations.[79] This does, of course, bring to a head the question of whether (democratic) politics, the third leg of the triangle, actually adds value! And perhaps the step to new civil leadership is greater for politicians than for anyone else. After all, it requires them to break their habit of 'always knowing what's best' from their elevated formal position when it comes to what is needed for citizens and civil society or what orders they hand down from their position of power. This is where the switch from formal high-level public administration to civil, credible, reliable, and authoritative leadership may be the hardest to make, as many still largely assume that their formal democratically acquired position gives them the right to know what is best for 'their' citizens. But now, these citizens have the power to verify whether politicians really know best, as well as to counter their claims and decisions with other information and have the voice to openly oppose them.

Such a fundamental rethink of the concepts, visions, and frames that underpin the Western institutional order is an essential element of any revolution.

Both these features converge in *public passion and commitment*, as a characterization of the direction and nature of civil leadership. The legitimization of this leadership is closely linked to a credible and visible reference to the leader's personal commitment to and passion for the common good or the issue that the leader wants to tackle. Motivation and leadership, as well as the intended social changes for the common good are mutually reinforcing here, creating a powerful feedback loop. Given that leadership is personal and followership voluntary, both the motivation and the public passion based on it are crucial for the direction and effectiveness of civil leadership.

- **Citizenship in the boardroom**: Even though these kinds of leaders have a formal position as the boss or manager, they will show their citizenship vision and values in the boardrooms.

Both these latter points are crucial in the orientation of civil leadership. There is, probably due to the association with the term 'civil,' a strong tendency to position this type of leadership exclusively in the realm of the informal civil society: neighborhoods, districts, sports clubs, volunteering in health care and education, local initiatives for support for the vulnerable, charity work. My definition of this kind of leadership departs primarily from a citizenship-based set of values, meaning that I see the goals and passions of this kind of leadership as focused on the broader common good, as that is the core of their orientation on citizenship. This type of civil leadership is therefore not locked in purely informal sectors or the charity sector, such as volunteering or philanthropy, but can also be found in the boardrooms of major corporations. And within that domain not only in an informal team-based context, but even in formal executive positions, also at major organizations, both non-profit and for-profit ones. There is therefore also citizenship in the boardroom, to which the ever more powerful civil society is increasingly appealing.

- **Strategic intelligence in a new era with new problems**: Leadership will only acquire (informal) status and authority toward followers if the leader delivers on his or her promises and makes things happen. So, there is a technical side to good leadership: to formulate feasible goals, take steps to achieve them, set up the right actions at the right moment involving the right parties, using charisma and communication skills as and when needed. Civil leadership that only has the first three features will be of little use to us, as it would likely get bogged down in good intentions, attitudes, and motives that are not converted into successful action. We therefore need civil leaders who understand the new strategic context and display successful leadership in this context by taking the right steps at the right time.

Values

Values are the underlying preferences and motives that determine the concerns, dislikes, or worries that lead you to believe that certain interventions and actions are needed or beneficial. They are the fundamental, deeper, often subconscious and not explicitly shared ideas that matter to you. They are often rooted in your upbringing and childhood experiences, handed down by parents, siblings, friends, or learned in the street. At a later age, they turn into preferences and leanings, also in a political and public sense, as well as into commitment to certain causes. Values are furthermore an important factor for the credibility and reliability of leadership. Assuming that you are asking people to follow you in steps toward the unfamiliar, it is precisely this kind of substantiation based on personal inspiration that is of crucial importance.

Two factors are crucial for leadership:
a. What values do civil leaders have?
b. How do these values drive their behavior and actions, which are impactful thanks to their leadership?

In my PhD research into civil leaders, I stumbled on a consistent and recurring pattern of values. On the one hand, these leaders were focused strongly on the public cause, on society, on the community they represented or were even a part of, sometimes also based on their own childhood. What was most important to them was to do something, be instrumental, tackle issues, even by going against current guidelines or routines, for this public cause, for this societal problem, or for this group they belonged to or represented. On the other hand, the leaders I studied were also enterprising and self-willed. They saw new opportunities and new approaches in defiance of habits, regulations, or procedures, and ultimately seized them and put them into practice themselves, despite the resistance, aversion, or even regulations. Their passion for the public cause saw them break down barriers to do their personal bit for it. So, they were by no means saints or 100% virtuous. They showed their character, self-will, and entrepreneurial spirit on the one hand, and their values on the other, whereby these values explain why they engage with certain issues and are willing to overcome resistance or opposition for them: true leadership.

For a good outline of the various patterns of values, please refer to my dissertation and the subsequent work by Arjo Klamer:[80]

Market-Based Values	State-Based Values	Civil Society-Based Values
freedom of choice	(social) justice	responsibility
consumer sovereignty	solidarity	loyalty
independence	collective interest/ serving public cause	connectedness/ bonding and bridging
result oriented/ performance-based	legislation	(social) caring
entrepreneurial spirit	consent/consultation	generosity
objective validation	equality	communality
individuality	democratic procedures	citizenship
individual responsibility	objectivity	respect
	sustainability/stability	privacy
		self-actualization

Considerations that are made in applying values in leadership are also an important factor. No matter how noble each value is, ranging from 'honesty' to 'connectedness', from 'reliability' to 'social justice', or 'opportunities for the most vulnerable,' the pros and cons must always be weighed. Such weighing is ultimately based on the two core elements of leadership, namely character and wisdom (which Aristotle defined as 'practical wisdom,' phronesis, see further explanation on page 162 and note 82). It is an assessment of the context, which is the practical side of practical wisdom. Values have to be offset against strategic challenges, the available funds, legal requirements, team spirit and composition, etc. No matter how great they seem, those lists of values and virtues that the civil leader claims to represent and wants to live up to in his or her behavior and that of the organization, there are no standard rules for weighing up these values and virtues against these kinds of factors in an administrative context. And then there are the position elements that come into it, as I referred to previously in the passage about Machiavelli, and the dilemmas this creates between politics and power and morality. The right values are meaningless when they do not provide a response in times of need or have to be implemented by an arguing or disintegrating team. And neither do these noble values of a civil leader have any meaning when the leader is unable to get his or her way, lacks a position with potential and possibilities or fails to utilize his or her position, or has a history of errors that taints his or her authority.

The following will need to be weighed up against each other:
- *your values and the effectiveness of your leadership*, as specified above in dealing with 'strategic intelligence': The question when you have a cause you want to fight for is whether you can effectively do something about it from your current position and leadership. Are you able to rally the following you need? Do you have the power and means, or can you get them, to do what is needed?
- *your values and the strategic need under your leadership*: What is needed to convince your environment that your intentions must and can be executed and that business as usual will no longer do?
- *your set of values*: Sometimes, values contradict each other or are hard to combine, such as 'honesty' and 'diplomacy' or 'caring for each other' and 'strong intervention.' The question then is which outweighs which in the specific context in which your leadership is set.

Many discussions about 'values-driven leadership' are about how a lot of people find it hard to accept that these kinds of assessments between values are actually needed, and even prefer to deny that they are. These people are always extremely quick to *sanctify* (morally) good leadership. It is a kind of intuitive reflex of well-intentioned people, who in this way want to show that they understand the 'sacred' leaders and their 'sanctification' and are perhaps very close to that themselves as well. 'Sanctification'[81] is here a designation of their 'own sanctity' by association. Values are good and human, and literally valuable, and therefore something to flaunt and to be associated with. And so assessment of which value is of most strategic or social value in this situation or which value should dominate in the decisions to make is something that is too executive or professional to be associated with.

Next, it is important for the combination of the words 'civil' and 'leadership' to lead to a unique combination of personality and character. Civil leaders are, as pointed out earlier, enterprising, not risk averse, willing to break through rules and routines, and they show solidarity and commitment to the public cause. They are not 'saints' in their behavior, but they may be in their overriding values that drive the result and direction of their behavior.

They are focused on public value and the common good, and innovative and pioneering in this respect. As a result, they are often in the public spotlight, because they have to defend and explain their choices, innovations, unexpected attitude.

And finally, my research revealed the following distinguishing style features in the thirty civil leaders I researched (use them to identify the civil leader in you or in your environment!):

a. They are able to build bridges between elites and workers, as they possess leadership authority in both circles.
b. They are, needless to say, driven by values, albeit in either of two possible ways. There are civil leaders who explicitly invoke their values, in all their conduct, speeches, messages, and choices, and there are civil leaders who keep their values implicit and also defend their choices with 'regular' arguments such as strategy, finances, and external pressure.
c. Also in terms of public focus, I observed two types of civil leaders. Civil leaders who want to do good behind the scenes and civil leaders who manifest themselves in the public debate to do good, if only to publicly defend their exceptional choices, but sometimes also because they realize that others need to be brought round or stimulated, so as to ultimately reach more people.

d. And finally, I have identified two underlying strategies pursued by these civil leaders through their public persona. It is either to mount a defense based on innovation, claiming that the new is better and the way to go. Or it is a defense based on legitimization, claiming that the new fits the mission, decision authority, mandate, and (sometimes partial) public funding of the group or organization they represent.

Values Assessment: Aristotle and Practical Wisdom

Since ancient Greece, we have been able to rely on the help of one of the most important philosophers in this area, Aristotle[82] and his ethics, in making our values assessments. Aristotle emphasizes that virtuousness or endorsing and conveying all virtues (which is exactly what happens in most governance codes) alone is not enough, and not even correct. As far as leadership is concerned, it is ultimately about your practical and day-to-day weighing of those virtues, as you need to strike a balance between these virtues, in the ultimately ethical pursuit of a fairly practically assessable *eudaimonia*, 'the good life for many.' The downside to the currently dominant all-or-nothing approach to values and virtues, as I described before on 'values-based leadership' approaches, is that it does not square with leadership or an executive role in a more classical sense. In this sense, it is a 'layman' approach by people who either lack executive experience or whose approach to leadership is overly philosophical or overly ideological, whose actions are basically too naive and vacuous. As if leadership, no matter how personally and informally it has been defined, can be detached from administrative contexts, power relations, organization requirements, financial possibilities, and dominant cultures. Every elected official, executive, and leader needs to, based on the circumstances and given his or her passion and goals, assess which values are best aligned with each specific situation. Administration and being an executive is about weighing up values in a strategic context and against the goals and effectiveness. The downside to this currently dominant 'layman' approach in this philosophical and executive void is that those who have adopted it also think you can capture virtuous conduct in rules, regulations, and formal and procedural requirements. This is correct up to a point, as the counterpart, 'bad leadership' (in the form of fraud, corruption, nepotism, favoritism), can indeed be captured in rules, regulations, and formal and procedural requirements, namely when it can be judged and penalized in a court of law, ultimately based on the rules of justice. This way of punishing bad behavior also explains why people have started to look for rules of good behavior and good governance. But a misconception arises when people think that values-based and Good leadership can also be assessed and even stimulated in this same way through previously defined rules, regulations, and procedures, and thus applied to the selection of people for positions with power. In fact, this misconception dates back to Confucius in ancient China,[83] and it continues to grow in the present time, as criminal prosecution or public identification and condemnation of 'bad leadership' are directly translated to the artificial certainty of rules for Good leadership, which are subsequently even used in selection and supervisory procedures. It is, however, impossible to stimulate and support Good leadership in this way. After all, Good leadership comes mainly from the character and wisdom of the leader in his or her weighing of values and virtues against his or her objectives and preferences. It is simply impossible to capture the character and administrative wisdom in so-called universal rules and selection procedures based on them.

Whether or not practical virtuousness and wisdom can be learned has been a topic in leadership development literature and practices for some time now. There is extensive fundamental doubt about this. When it comes to learning these personal assets and capabilities, it turns out that practice, exercises, and actual observations are the best resources. Inspired and philosophical lectures about 'ethics' do not produce this real learning. The same goes for supervision, which is often dominated by rules and regulations and ensuring compliance. Whether or not supervision is actually conducive to Good leadership is highly doubtful for other reasons as well. Paradoxically, it mainly produces non-leadership: meekly following the rules and keeping the industry regulator happy apparently makes someone a good leader, which is, of course, a misconception.

Private for Public: The Battle for Civil Leadership between the Private Sector and Politics

Civil leaders can be found across the private sector, in informal and formal settings, operating on a small and a large scale, close to or somewhat removed from day-to-day business, in direct activities and managerial roles, and at all kinds of enterprises, ranging from non-profit to for-profit ones. That is where the basis for citizenship, and thus the associated pattern of values, lies. The same pattern of values is also seen in public officials: politicians, elected officials, and civil servants. Their strategic and administrative context, and therefore their consider-ations in the values pattern differ from those in a private-sector setting, in terms of position, in terms of power sources, in terms of say, and in terms of scope for independent initiative and action. The public-sector role is also different in terms of accountability, mission, perception of the environment, and access to certain forms of public debate (which as we saw before is intrinsically acquiring a more private, citizen-driven nature due to the new media landscape).[84] Consequently, there is tension between these two types of socially grounded and committed leaders, even though their values and the direction in which they intend to take the public cause and society are similar (I will not be going into tensions ensuing from political differences in vision and values, which are, of course, common and even augmented in politics). This is, as you would expect, due to positions and perceptions, also dominated by the part of the triangle that they occupy: state versus market and versus civil society. After all, politicians generally only expect, and consequently only perceive, civil leaders in informal civil society, which is where they are allowed to do 'good' without any kind of real politi-cal influence. As outlined above, this 'frame' of a politically convenient vision of citizenship and civil society will come up for discussion. This pattern of expectations on the side of the government means that insti-tutional friction is expected because of the stronger civil society caused by role shifting like:

- directors of large organizations in the public and the private sector, who start displaying unique, revolutionary, extra committed social behavior, also with their organization, thus raising the social respon-sibility bar for their peers and for politics as their principals;

- civil leaders who are starting to prominently get involved in the public debate, and sometimes criticize or even manage to undo public support for certain government policies, thus becoming a public competitor to professional politicians;
- directors of large organizations who, visibly committed to their goals, products, services, and target groups, start to manifest themselves as voluntarily committed to the good, public cause. This is entirely at odds with normal expectations we have with respect to well-paid, professional managers.

The new thinking based on stronger citizens and a more active civil society as a result of new disruptive technologies comes with two fundamental changes.

First of all, the public arena in which leaders are held accountable and have to show what they are doing is changing fundamentally and drastically. It is becoming more personal, more confrontational, and more open, with more debate and even more conflict.

Secondly, the operating base of civil leadership is changing. Politics can no longer claim a monopoly from their 'natural' position and preoccupation with the public cause or public communications and public opinion making about it. The new public arena is not only further opening up the political playing field itself (by inserting all kinds of newcomers, small single-issue parties, and new politicians who, with public support, operate based on personality and a specific message and who have abandoned pre-cooked party-political routines), it is also paving the way for entirely different forces and powers that determine public opinion and make it visible. This also creates a lot more scope and a 'natural' position in the public arena for civil leaders who intend to influence public opinion or explain why change is needed.

We therefore need to start thinking in terms of 'private for public', or, to be even more specific, 'personal for public' (whereby 'personal' is all about both being close to 'other' citizens and the core element of 'character & virtues' in leadership). The core idea is then that private-sector parties and associated directors and managers also have a responsibility rooted in citizenship values (from which policy and behavior will have to be defended toward other citizens) and have their own influential position in the public arena. The former of these two aspects is already becoming increasingly prevalent in the fact that all kinds of corporate scandals or actions that go against the interests of citizens (so not only harmful in an economic sense, such as swindling or financial fraud) are being discussed openly and that those involved are no longer allowed to get away with it by merely invoking vague excuses, based on the routine of traditional economic thinking and dominant business values that were part of it, like economic need, shareholder interests, or business continuity.

> *One example came in 2018 when the Supervisory Board of major Dutch bank ING decided to award the bank's CEO a huge pay rise. The decision triggered widespread and loud protest, ultimately leading to the bank reversing the decision in under a week. In the context of the analyses in this book, the most striking aspect of this sequence of events was that the Supervisory Board's public arguments for the pay rise, which they even had to present openly in Dutch parliament, lacked any kind of reference to the CEO's alleged good and engaged civil leadership and the bank's Corporate Social Responsibility results. The board presented only traditional conservative economic arguments (the bank had been returned to profit and repaid its bailout debt from the financial crisis to the state) and references to a non-existing international labor market for managers, which they claimed looks only at technical criteria with respect to management, management capabilities and managers' pay. (The trend in this non-existing labor market was supposedly one of increasing pay for incumbent managers, anywhere in the world.)[85] As outlined earlier, managers behave as a caste that takes very good care of itself and that newcomers, fresh minds, and independent thinkers find hard to break into. (In this sense, managers are an entirely different breed from entrepreneurs.)[86]*

Politicians are also facing this new need for 'person for public' as a building block of civil leadership, which will change their attitude and approach in the public debate and public opinion on all those issues that citizens (which in democracies includes voters) feel strongly about.

Democracy is maturing and acquiring elements of Greek direct democracy. Again, the best response to the looming disruption is to recalibrate what we already have through a fundamental new blend of the old and the new, representative democracy and direct democracy.

Citizenship in the Boardroom

As said, this shift is leading to a new pattern of values entering boardrooms. Initially, these values will be pushed in by external pressure, such as scandals that have come to light or gaffes in public communications. It is, of course, a shame that true change on the level of values, which most executives will smoothly endorse when explicitly asked (which explains why many of them want to be openly associated with good causes these days),[87] almost always requires a scandal, conflict, and rumors first. The times that you had hard, financially driven economic decisions on the one hand and public relations, good causes, and corporate social responsibility for purely image-related reasons on the other are well and truly behind us.

In the modern public arena, citizens see right through these kinds of false assertions. They no longer accept socially harmful behavior and will hold executives personally responsible. Luckily for these executives, several features of the modern public arena do initially protect them from the tsunami that may wash over them at any moment, even though most will feel as if it is already washing over them. These inhibiting factors are the following: citizens need to hear about abuses from someone (I outlined several examples of how modern technology increases the chances for this), they must, upon further inquiry, find claims of abuse to be sufficiently substantiated, and these abuses need to resonate and be featured prominently in the daily news stream that permanently engulfs many citizens. These are the new key factors on the direct channel, which are very different from the old manipulations, secrecy, and disregard. I therefore feel little pity for those boardroom executives who suddenly feel caught up in a public storm and start to protest that 'people don't know what they are talking about,' 'economics is complex, leave it to the professionals,' 'you used to be able to convince newspapers and journalists that you were right' or 'the inspectorate and the government were perfectly happy with what we were doing.'

These will be the biggest challenges for executives, especially in public services. It is all about treating citizens' initiatives and citizen organizations in the same way as you treat the formal organization and professionals you manage. In civil leadership, you need to show and foster partnership and co-production. One of the results will be that quality-related issues will have to be formulated more openly from the customer's perspective, and that citizens' desire and capacity to organize and produce will have to be taken into consideration more, without getting bogged down in amateurism. And finally, it is okay for the executive or public administrator to be critical of people's contribution and quality, also when it comes to citizens' input, albeit always in an honest and open assessment, and never with a view to protecting the original traditional public service provider.

Strategic Intelligence and Administrative Skills

Despite the increased focus on the social aspects of leadership, leaders being closer to citizens, the commitment to good causes and values, it continues to be important to learn from and even copy parts of the administrative practices of the past few decades. No matter how technical they are, experienced executives can teach us a thing or two about the importance of getting people to follow (leadership) and that this requires decision-making skills, as well as financial clout, while key others, such as elected officials and shareholders, also have a say in decisions, etc. Civil leadership is impossible without the two essential ingredients of strategic intelligence and administrative skills. Both have already been dealt with at length in this book. Strategic intelligence puts the emphasis on the personal side instead of on the paper reality of strategic planning with lots of figures, quantitative models, rational analyses, and step-by-step plans. Civil leaders need to be able to oversee the arena that surrounds their organization, the interests involved, and the relevant trends, and have a vision for it, so as to design the right steps and actions within the estimated possibilities and limitations.

Civil Leadership as the Future of Leadership

The technologies that are disrupting the market also have massive impact on the public domain, changing it into a different kind of public arena, with much greater opinion-making and organizational capacity in the hands of citizens, as well as disruption of the political marketplace, undermining of standard organizations and management positions, and an entirely different attitude of citizens, as in between citizens mutually, toward the government, and toward the market.

This new attitude of citizens can be compellingly and publicly held up to politicians, business leaders, and public service providers, such as hospitals, power companies, and educational institutions. Concealing, burying, and suppressing news is not possible in the new public arena, like it was – sometimes – in the old media landscape of newspapers, TV, and radio. The existing administrative elite is also changing in its composition. It is no longer in the interest of the members of the elite to cover for each other and conceal unwelcome facts, as they are routed by the transparency of the new media where citizens share information, reveal scandals, and divulge proof of executive errors. Also on a social level, the elites are changing in terms of recruitment and selection. They are opening up to outside influences from the new media channel, which creates space for newcomers who can rely on public support in the public forum. Officials with administrative responsibility are increasingly taking to the public forum to counter or intercept facts or mishaps that come to light or are threatening to come to light on the new channel, where opinions and data are published uncensored. Whenever that happens or might happen, the executive in question had better be on hand to provide an explanation or their side of the story. Citizens are basically forcing executives to show more citizenship in their behavior and in the mission and choices of these executives, whether they be active in the public sector or in the private sector.

Existing relations, which have taken root in institutions and the institutional fabric of countries, contain a preference for certain values. The administration of justice, for example, emerged out of our sense of justice, while philanthropy is inspired by a desire to stand up for and take care of the vulnerable in society. The changes outlined above, caused and boosted by the technological revolution, are fundamental enough to affect institutions and force them to reground themselves on new values. This will also greatly affect institutions such as democracy, public services, and business, as well as the markets, just to name a few.

The sum of all the above factors, i.e. new technology, new impact on institutions and the underlying values, and citizens' newly acquired power, leads to a call for new leadership. One that is primarily a call for a certain brand of leadership: civil leadership. Precisely because it needs to be leadership that inspires people to follow toward an uncertain future and will have to shape, demonstrate, and introduce the new dominance of civil values.

22
Inspiration from Civil Leaders' Practices

What is even more important than all the above reflections and analyses are, and this goes without saying, civil leaders' *actual practices* as a guiding and inspirational framework. What behavior are they displaying and what example are they setting? What are they doing differently? What unexpected approach have they adopted? Where are they deviating from long-standing routines and expectations? Their actual practices will highlight the opportunities and possibilities for civil leadership for anyone who, based on the above analysis, realizes that the strategic context is changing fundamentally, with major impact on institutional relations, and that a different kind of leadership is therefore needed. The question is how to go from analysis to practice, from new convictions to different actions, from intellectual understanding to civil leadership in practice.

Those who have their eyes open to them, will already have seen numerous inspiring examples.

And I do not only mean faraway 'canonized' examples, such as Nelson Mandela or Mother Theresa. They are, as it were, 'safe' examples. Most of those have already passed away, offering role model behavior from a distant past under very different circumstances, and they were deemed successful in hindsight based on their personal intentions and impact, leading to their success being attributed to their personality and actions posthumously.

Neither am I referring only to celebrities such as Bill Gates, Bono or Mark Zuckerberg, who were among the first to tune in to the zeitgeist and start to increasingly raise their profile in the realms of charity, social commitment, and philanthropy. This is actually their most important innovation in their leadership, the transparency of and openly avowed pride in their philanthropic actions and commitment. They are effectively harnessing their celebrity status and marketing clout to help charity, while the old rich elites always practiced philanthropy in silence behind the scenes, with few actually drawing attention to it and publicly taking pride in it. This is certainly all great and very inspiring, even more so because they are breaking down old definitions and expectations that say that fame only breeds vanity and selfishness, and that having a lot of money only leads to anti-social behavior and extravagant hedonism. But these celebrity do-gooders are also 'safe' examples, due to their distance. Most of us will never be so rich or famous that we can forget and ignore the hard choices we have to make between surviving and giving to charity, as these rich celebrities can, no matter how exemplary their giving behavior is. They are nice examples to admire from afar, which celebrities are generally used to, but whether they hit home in a way that will make people change their choices or behavior remains to be seen.

Good examples should be found much closer to home, and in what we ourselves could do or should consider doing. Such closeness greatly boosts examples' potential as a source of inspiration, while they then also become much more of a challenge for any of us. Civil leadership is within anyone's reach, as long as we want to and do actually take it on.

The following characterizations and suggestions from real-life civil leadership practices come from the research on which my dissertation was based. An important choice I made, though, was to limit myself to civil leaders from a private governance context, at for-profit enterprises, non-profit organizations, and in informal active citizenship. From the domain that I previously referred to as 'private for public,' albeit also formal: from private governance contexts. Although I am approaching it more as a private-sector attitude here, close to citizens, it can very well apply to political leaders in a governmental context as well, although this often proves difficult in practice.[88] I outlined these differences in executive practices between private-sector and public-sector governance contexts earlier (in the section about strategic intelligence: 2.6).

It is therefore good to bear in mind that civil leaders are not always saints or rich *celebrities*, and that they can be found in any practical setting, including executive ones. This makes it a lot easier for us all to be inspired by real-life examples close to home. It also makes the associated call for civil leadership a lot more insistent.

The following key and inspiring elements of how they act and present themselves touch directly on insight into their position and behavior in the most objective and practical way possible.

Engage with the Social Issue and the Target Group

Civil leaders' passion for social issues and a certain group in society translates to, as pointed out earlier, unwavering behavior in a certain direction, behavior which cannot be classed as 'normal administrative' behavior. Managers and politicians the world over have, however, always been taught to be aware of what others think about them or of public opinion. They have grown accustomed to conform to routines and habits, as they would otherwise stand out too much as a person. This is partly why many of them fulfill their positions in a somewhat predictable and technical manner, almost anonymized. As a result, no one remembers their manager or town aldermen from ten years ago. Colorless and therefore personless. This in itself is entirely at odds with our definition of leadership. With civil leaders, you definitely know what kind of person you are dealing with and what this person stands and fights for in society (and why, as their drive is often rooted in their personal life story).

Your Social Makeup is in Your Public Passion: You Will Break down Walls to Achieve These Goals

Political effectiveness, which is you getting your way in fighting for the common good, is part of our definition of leadership. Leadership just happens to be all about this (perceived, proven, expected) effectiveness in realizing your personal vision and achieving your personal goals, regardless of your formal position and formal means of power. The personal side of this leadership is therefore not only rooted in your social vision and passion, but also in your personal skills and actions in realizing them. Partly based on their trust in you 'getting things done,' people will spontaneously start to follow you as a leader. This is certainly not a new phenomenon. It was already described by Machiavelli in his political analyses, when he asked whether the end justifies any means. He wondered whether for the sake of effectiveness, the leader's behavior would be allowed to deviate from the values underpinning the goals he or she wants to achieve. Is it acceptable to be effective in terms of your use of power, to play the game and win for the good, public causes that subsequently benefit a lot of people? As the School of Life wrote: '[….] may require what we evasively call 'difficult decisions', by which we really mean ethical trade-offs. We may have to sacrifice our ideal visions of kindness for the sake of practical effectiveness. […] That – insists Machiavelli – is the price of dealing with the world as it is, not as we feel it should be.'[89] Again, we are passing over many analyses by those who believe in 'sacred' leadership, who are generally quick to cry shame over certain means chosen without valuing the social objectives achieved and the underlying unique values of the person fighting for those objectives. In the end, this is part of the 'weighing and balancing of values' in executive practices I described earlier, using Aristotle's concept of practical wisdom.

Actively Liase with Social Powers: Authorities, Media, Decisionmakers; Use Your Position and Network

Civil leaders are not isolated actors in society without a network or an official position. They have a place in the world. They know people and institutions who also know them. So, even if they are motivated and committed on a very personal level, they do realize that they have to accept their network and their role within that network and get stakeholders on board in their struggle for their particular societal goal.

Let Your Passion Drive You, Your Passion Will Drive Others

Passion for the public cause, charity, or target group to which he or she is committed is not only what drives the civil leader out of an inner need, it is also what legitimizes his or her actions and what additionally will get others, who see it, including anonymous and bureaucratic institutions, to follow him or her. The civil leader's passion, which goes beyond mere words and is decidedly reflected in striking actions, sends out a strong appealing message to others. Especially those who, before the civil leader entered the frame, told themselves and others that they were already working on the same issues as part of their formal position and tasks at the responsible organizations in the same sector or for the same target group, are confronted with their own self-imposed limitations and self-perception. It basically disrupts their personal social definition, also at home and toward their family. The civil leader has shown that a lot more can be done than they initially thought, or than they, caught in their routines and habits, were able to see. The civil leader's attitude and passion, and particularly his or her associated striking actions and out-of-the-ordinary behavior, send out a powerful message to others, because they make it harder for them to hide behind (their own) excuses.

The Best Is Not Good Enough for the Public Cause

Pitifulness and good intentions are no excuse for amateurism or concessions. Also in a professional sense, civil leaders raise the bar. As their focus is on social issues, hiding behind amateurism in executing tasks or tackling problems is basically a weakness under the guise of good intentions. Why is it necessary for an organization that has ample resources and a certain status, and that wants to use these resources to enrich shareholders or keep politicians in power, to have a professional marketing or PR department or logistics operations, while we seem to be perfectly fine with civil causes being handled by someone without proper training in their spare time. This is not as straightforward as it sounds, though, as there are cultural considerations and financial possibilities that come into play. Sometimes, there are only these volunteers to lean on. It goes without saying that many civil leaders recognize this fact, but their passion and commitment to the greater good is effectively a form of resistance when the dominant culture leans towards naivety, amateurism, and a good-enough attitude without a valid reason. Civil leaders want there to be a drive in the culture to, despite the limited financial means, always work to a high standard, to always go for the best possible outcome, and therefore also actively look for and listen to that high standard. Too often, charity culture is one of below-par performance, where opportunities for improvement are not seized and expert or professional help is rejected. Good causes hence become a justification of weakness, amateurism, and poor performance in the organization and execution.

Shamelessly Use Societal Support

Many people, companies, institutions, and opinion leaders publicly support the social causes that civil leaders represent and work on every day. That is great, there is no doubt about that, but it does not do a great deal of good at the end of the day. It does not amount to much more than a mental lift every morning. One part of civil leadership is to believe in your goals and the need for your unique approach to such an extent that you want supporters to turn this verbal support into tangible and effectively deployable resources, such as money, professional support, and an active network. Civil leaders do not consider this 'begging for help,' but instead as their entitlement to support and an opportunity for supporters to put their money where their mouth is. The moral leadership of these civil leaders actually comes with forceful, hard-to-parry, moral pressure, a kind of litmus test of the verbal morality of their environment. They are basically popping the balloon of obedient rhetoric and verbal claims of civilization.

Ensure Legitimacy at All Times

This is more of an issue that comes at you from your environment. People are used to a certain kind of behavior, certain facilities, and a certain attitude, and if you deviate from that, especially being an executive, but also from a more informal brand of active citizenship, you will constantly face questions as to the legitimacy of your actions and ultimately your leadership. Are you actually allowed to take on this role? Is it aligned with your job and organization? Should others not have done it, who would perhaps be better suited to tackle the issue at hand? Are the public or private resources you have received and spent indeed intended for this purpose? These questions have to be answered, regardless of how important and indisputable the civil leader considers his or her good intentions to be, regardless of the absence of ulterior motives, and regardless of the fact that he or she is only taking on extra work and not getting any personal gain out of it. Again, having good intentions and serving good causes alone is not enough. The civil leader cannot hide behind them when this kind of external pressure exists and the civil leader is forced to render account. Just like people who perform tasks or provide services, also in the public sector, are not allowed to get away with glossing over amateurism by citing their good intentions.

Only Personal Sacrifices and Choices Are Credible

This is where the values, passion, and legitimization questions for civil leaders converge. It is basically a kind of internal legitimization. Internal in two ways: you legitimize your actions to yourself, so on a psychological level, and to your people and organization, which is the peer or social group from which your civil leadership emerges. Why is it up to me to do this? If this is the right thing to do, why are others resisting or not doing it? What authorizes me to ask this of my people, while it will take up their time, make them work more, is unusual, and sometimes even hovers on the verge of going against rules and regulations? This is where the steadfastness of one's leadership is linked to social objectives.

In your behavior and personal considerations, you have to legitimize to yourself and to your people why you are right to be so steadfast and firm. That the good causes you are working for and your effectiveness in achieving these goals legitimize your actions goes without saying, but how do you account for it to yourself? There is basically only one way. And it involves the personal element of any kind of leadership. You not only have to show leadership in your attitude and how you relate to your environment, and in your charisma and your ability to get people to follow you, but also in your personal choices and sacrifices. If you demand a lot from people for a good cause, you also have to demand a lot from yourself, and make sure everyone knows about it, so as to boost your credibility. So, even though your good intentions and social results legitimize your different approach and path to the outside world, they do not fully satisfy the inner need in your network and team for legitimization, which is satisfied only when you forgo on the benefits of your position or not choose the easy route, not in your private life either. This is also why many people have this lingering doubt about the good intentions of rich celebrities who suddenly present themselves as philanthropists. Is it not just the next step in their successful personal PR through the addition of a sexy modern element, which is largely justified by their old business benefits, and not based on a new personal dedication and sacrifice? Bill Gates and his wife Melinda have, of course, raised the bar where this is concerned, putting a large chunk of their wealth in the Bill & Melinda Gates Foundation, and making the running of this foundation their primary job.

Have, Share and Hang on to a Good Story; Never Underestimate the Power of Rhetoric

There is a lot to be gained in public communications if you are willing to stick your neck out and show leadership on all kinds of societal issues. All civil leaders I have studied faced public debate and had to deal with public interests, which triggered public toing and froing. In that atmosphere and under those circumstances, it is not enough for your public story and discourse to be technically sound, to have solid knowledge of the relevant files, or to continuously refer to rules and how you are, 'and this goes without saying,' sticking to them. The personal and values element have become prominent fixtures in all public discourses. A public, pronounced, and proactive approach is then often the best defense in public debate, which must start with being alert to and prepared for this possibility of you becoming a talking point. The modern public debate swiftly moves on, also due to the modern media landscape I defined in Chapter 8, to the character, personal considerations and interests of the civil leader, often even based on rumors. This was, however, already the case in the old media, and then certainly not only in tabloid journalism. Attacking the other on a personal level when you disagree with them is a trick that has been used in public rhetoric for ages, while the line between gossip and news is sometimes wafer thin in these old media. My advice in this respect is also partly based on

new media technology: we simply must accept that there is a permanent public forum, while research has shown that juicy and sensational
news lingers for longer and is readily shared in the swarm, meaning
that it is inadvisable to completely refrain from countering such news. A
good story with a personal touch, told at the right time, will then be the
most effective. Still, you cannot expect to be able to repair such negative publicity just like that by publishing a good story or convincing an
authoritative channel in the media landscape of your side of the story.
This kind of public authority has all but disappeared.

Go for the Solution, Not for Routine or What Is Customary

Needless to say, this is what is unique, creative, and groundbreaking
about many civil leaders. Their social passion and commitment to the
problem and the target group go so far that they do not want or are
unable to lean on the usual approach in their environment. Their criticism of others is not so much that they are too weak or too obedient,
but mainly that they have chosen the wrong approach. Routines not
only lead to routine attitudes, but mainly to ignorance to what is truly
needed. This is literally the socially enterprising[90] aspect of their style
and character.

Mock Authorities and Rules

It goes without saying that the public position that civil leaders build,
with ample support for their societal approach, also leads to public
influence. Through their actions, they are showing that others are not
doing enough and are shackled by rules and conservative cultures, and
sometimes even hiding behind these cultures. Civil leadership therefore
also comes with steadfastness and personal commitment (hence their
values from entrepreneurship, see page 38, the part about 'values'), the
guts to break or ignore rules whenever it benefits the good cause. This
is, however, based on good strategic insight into that same assessment
based on values: is it legally risky to pass over or ignore these rules?
What will law enforcement and regulators think about my assessment?
Will I be able to rely on sufficient open support from parties and the

relevant target groups who understand my assessment? Do people agree with me that these rules are outdated? In fact, how long have we been waiting for modernization of these rules?

One thing is clear: more than anyone else, civil leaders have taken a stake in the common good and furthering engaged citizenship, away from rules, routines, or habits. The arguments of those who are able to clearly explain why those rules, routines, and habits are necessary and still stand in the way of the genuine good cause will therefore fall on deaf ears when presented to the civil leader, who simply does not want to hide behind them. It was with this in mind that I emphasized above that legitimization of this choice is of crucial importance, as is the public, rhetorical ability to get it across publicly. Hiding behind existing rules and habits is therefore also the easy option.

V
Epilogue

Hope in Times of Disruption and Revolution

The subject discussed in this essay is very much at the forefront of people's minds, both among citizens and public officials. Many are seeing, feeling, or have meanwhile joined in, anticipating the revolutionary impact, using innovations to try to preserve the value added by democracy, free press, and public services. At the same time, many are failing to see or ignoring the revolution that has been ongoing for some time now, partly out of a defensive urge to hold on to jobs that, ironically, will be the first to be disrupted if they keep on dragging their feet. The general conclusion I am drawing here, partly based on the strategic lessons learned in the market, is therefore that both politics and public services need to embrace the new direct channel, the new citizen power, the new input by citizens, and do so as comprehensively and maturely as possible. Market disruption has taught us that the new channel is not one you can trivialize or ignore, you are going to have to embrace it. In the market, this meant having to embrace innovative new business, retail, and service concepts and customer contact through platform technologies. In the public sector, where exposure, support, and power are the primary currencies, institutional positions and reputations are affected, as are the services and how these are delivered, as well as, like in the market, dealings with customers and citizens, which are effectively the same as that is how the person involved perceives and experiences it. Citizen power is here to stay.

This ultimately leads to the embracing of a totally new type of leadership, one that is aligned with this fundamentally new age and inspired by citizenship values, which I have branded civil leadership.

Luckily, there are plenty of hope-inspiring examples of this new brand of leadership, some of which I have presented. But there are many more, in all Western nations across the globe.

Examples of politicians who have taken to new channels (social media) or a mixture of an old and a new channel (such as a physical meetup convened through social media) to render account to or brainstorm directly with their supporters or party members. These politicians are no longer hiding behind meaningless speeches in official parliamentary settings and routinely assuming that traditional media will get the message out to the people and that people still read or watch these traditional media. And, luckily, there are examples of politicians who are really taking signals picked up on the third, direct channel seriously and translating them to the procedures and authority of parliamentary debate.

Examples of administrators of public services, such as hospitals, who are inviting the professionals of their organization to take part in shared decision-making processes and embracing partnerships with citizens' initiatives beyond their traditional mindset of superiority ('only we have the right training for it') or bureaucratic behavior ('that is not how it is done, because it's not in the protocol,' and 'what about my professional liability?').

And examples of citizens, lots of citizens, who have taken an innovative approach in working on public causes in their local community, but also in education, with respect to municipal policies, the energy sector, and reciprocal help and care. They are making widespread use of new technology for such initiatives, such as WhatsApp groups to organize a neighborhood watch, citizen cooperatives, and reciprocal child care arrangements, as well as joint actions for energy production, to name but a few.[91]

Many of the civil leaders from my research, especially the ones operating from a context of informal active citizenship, were initially put in a negative light by politicians, which sometimes also turned public opinion against them, as public opinion used to be influenced more by journalists and politicians together. One example is that of a Dutch reverend called Hans Visser, who turned his church in Rotterdam into a shelter for the homeless and drug addicts, out of a genuine concern about them being neglected and living on the streets. Or Yolanda Eijgenstein, who when seeing the poor elementary education her children were receiving, took an initiative to overhaul elementary education and base it more on children's intrinsic eagerness to learn and character development. They were initially maligned and not taken seriously by politicians and traditional media, which just goes to show that we are dealing with a power struggle here and still have a long way to go, but also that such attempts and initiatives do keep emerging from active citizenship.

If you, after reading this essay, feel called upon and challenged to take such an initiative, I will have achieved what I set out to achieve and inspired you to contribute to a better mankind and society of active citizens. You, however, will then have a long and complicated road ahead of you, which I hope I have outlined adequately to help you on your way.

About the Author

Throughout his professional life, Dr. Steven P.M. De Waal has been looking for a creative and innovative combination of executive practices and academic reflection.

He was involved in administrative practices himself as a strategy consultant to directors of numerous organizations in the public sector, ranging from hospitals to universities and from industry associations to government departments, generally during strategically difficult phases where timely and fundamental interventions were needed. Following this professional work, he became the co-owner, director, and finally CEO of a leading Amsterdam-based European management consultancy and interim management firm called Boer&Croon Strategy and Management Group. While working in this professional and entrepreneurial setting, he also chaired, and continues to chair, several Supervisory Boards, including in health care, public housing, the cultural sector, and professional soccer. Based on his professional background, he was often asked to chair these Supervisory Boards during a particularly difficult stage, such as when the organization was undergoing a turnaround or restructuring. He was also a member of the Dutch Labor Party's (PvdA) national executive committee for five years, during the most tempestuous parliamentary period in Dutch history when one of Europe's first 'populist' politicians, Pim Fortuyn, was murdered.

When De Waal left 'his' firm in 2004, after a highly successful entrepreneurial episode, he continued the Public Space think tank he had pioneered and created for this a separate foundation (www. publicspace.nl). Needless to say, this think tank addresses the main themes that De Waal has been focusing on throughout his career through its mission: 'to create Strategies for Public And Civil Entrepreneurs (SPACE) and promote social entrepreneurship and active citizenship in the public sector'. Thanks to this continuation of the think tank, De Waal was able to continue his efforts to develop and spread the combination of administrative practices and academic reflection through articles, interviews, blogs, lectures, and chairing debates. He is furthermore a member of various international associations in this same context, including the European Healthcare Management Association, Academy of Management, and the International Leadership Association.

He initially used academic reflection in a large number of lectures and talks at numerous management conferences in this and related fields over the past 25 years. To structure, substantiate, and spread his reflections on executive practices and public-sector policy debates, he has meanwhile written five books (all in Dutch), focusing heavily on civil leadership, strategy for the common good, and citizenship. In 2014, his academic efforts culminated in a doctorate from Utrecht University's School for Public Governance and Management with a dissertation (in English) about the subject he had been working on for decades, the value(s) of civil leaders.

It was a natural continuation of his earlier study (Andragology, the study of human development and the institutes, interventions and intentions that support it) (graduated with honors, 1979) that looked for a social science to go with that same subject and therefore also tried to help create a humane and dignified existence for all. This produced a philosophy of science based on a combination of empirical, philosophical, and normative research, whereby scholarly work also constitutes civic conduct that has to advance human development. This is also captured accurately by Aristotle's concept of phronesis, Practical Wisdom. This present book is based on the results of the dissertation and an audience of directors in the public sector at numerous lectures across Europe, in which De Waal continued to explore the combination he has pursued throughout his career.

Based on these insights and experiences, De Waal became a much sought-after speaker at management and leadership conferences and as part of academic programs across the Netherlands and internationally, especially in Europe, including through the Avicenna Academy for Leadership, AOG School of Management's Digital Leadership program,

Blommestein Group, Management Events, Academies for Supervisory Boards in health care, education, and housing corporations, National Register of Supervisory Board Members, and RABO Academy.

Notes

1 Stimulation of active citizenship and social entrepreneurship in the public sector is the primary mission of a private-sector think tank I founded in 2001 called Public SPACE (www.publicspace.eu). For more details, refer to the About the Author section.

2 The original phrase used in Bill Clinton's campaign in the 1992 presidential race against George H.W. Bush: 'It's the economy, stupid!'

3 There are different possible classifications of the revolutions that humankind has gone through, that have taken humankind to the next level, ultimately making humans the most influential and successful species in the history of Earth. This has led some to call the current age the Anthropocene. My timeline of these human revolutions is as follows: the **first** was the **agricultural revolution**: the emergence of concentrated and large-scale agriculture founded on the cultivation of wild grains. We are thus starting at the origin of humankind as we still know it today. I am effectively skipping all kinds of previous (r)evolutions in the development and global spread of humankind compared to other species, the steps that led to what is known as homo sapiens, which were, to a certain extent, also revolutionary in their own right. One of the most important markers in this development is when humans started to live in a kind of symbolic order, which is a uniquely human trait, forged by a revolution that is also sometimes called The Human Revolution, although this is a concept that is widely contested by archaeologists and paleontologists. This typically human symbolical order makes that human behavior and existence, more so than that of any other species, are conditioned largely by concepts, symbols such as art and religious beliefs, collective agreements on the meaning of certain things, and rituals.
In the most recent historical analyses, the advent of a sedentary existence in villages is thought to predate the emergence of agriculture, around 7,500 BC. And agriculture is now therefore thought to have started after that, from around 6,500 BC. Regardless of which came first, it marks the importance of the phase of urbanization, which started around 3,100 BC. By the start of our current era, the 21st century, over half of the world's population lives in cities and urban areas. The **second** revolution is that of industrialization, often referred to as the **industrial revolution**, triggered by the invention and use of things such as cast iron, hydropower, and the steam engine (the first phase of the industrial revolution), electricity, and the combustion engine (the second phase).

A third phase is now often added to this, the phase when electronic and IT technology was first used to automate existing processes in factories and offices, which then is generally referred to as the **digital revolution**. Most of these analyses take the launch of the Intel 4004, the world's first microprocessor, in 1971 as the start of this third phase. Part of this alleged third phase of industrialization is indeed of an industrial nature and driven by technology that further facilitated and automated industrial and agricultural operations in a revolutionary way. But the revolution that we now find ourselves in the middle of is far too invasive with respect to our human existence and human dignity and uniqueness to classify it as a phase of only industrialization as such. The current radical shift that is seeing IT technology take over some of our most human of capabilities, such as information processing and communication, is quite clearly a separate, new intrusive phase in the development of humankind. We are simply not doing the impact of this development justice when we label the effect and purpose of these new technologies as still being a form of industrialization. Therefore, I prefer to classify the new technological phase we are entering now as **a third revolution** in its own right. In my view, this third revolution has a much broader impact on humanity (the technologies are not only adopted in production environments and for production purposes, but across humanity and communities), and therefore have a much more crucial impact on all aspects of how people live, survive and build communities, going far beyond merely facilitating production and providing sustenance. The current conceptual definition as only a follow-up phase of industrialization is largely dominated by the perspective of the companies that are innovating, applying, and managing these digital technologies (which is basically the supply side of these new technologies), and fails to assume the totality of the fundamental human perspective. New technologies that define the technological side of this revolution are used across the full range of human functions and readily embraced in all aspects of people's lives, precisely so as to boost human existence. Even though it is based on the in my view somewhat outdated notion of a follow-up phase in industrial revolution, it is still interesting to point to a comment by Klaus Schwab, the executive chairman of the World Economic Forum, a source above suspicion from the economic and industrial domain: 'We stand on the brink of a technological revolution that will fundamentally alter the way we live, work and relate to one another.' (WEF, January 14, 2016). Agreement on what would be the best possible name for this third revolution is currently still lacking. There are several possible suitable names, such as the new revolution, the technological revolution, the global information and communication revolution, and the new communities. To refer to this third revolution in this essay, I have opted for the term **The Digital Civil Revolution,** precisely because it better captures the huge and fundamental impact it has on our entire human existence, both in individual and collective terms. Another reason behind my adopting this term is that I want to emphasize that the extensive new digitalization technology must not lead to us thinking that humans can, as claimed by transhumanism, be replaced by machines and technology, no matter how intelligent they are.

For the first stages, refer to the scientific substantiation in James C. Scott, *Against the Grain. A Deep History of the Earliest States*, Yale University Press, 2018. For more details and a vivid description of the stages of the evolution of humanity, read Yuval Harari, *Sapiens. A Brief History of Humankind*, Harper Collins, 2015. Given the analyses in this book/essay, it is very understandable that his second book, goes into the impact of new digital technologies on the humanism and human existence he described in his successful first book.

4   For a clear and concise summary, refer to F. Helbing, *The Automation of Society is Next: How To Survive The Digital Revolution*, CreateSpace Independent Publishing Platform, 2015, p. 3: : 'First: the *Internet* enables global communication between electronic devices. Second, the *World Wide Web* (WWW) has created a network of globally accessible websites, which emerged as a result of the invention of the Hypertext Transfer Protocol (HTTP). Third, the emergence of *social media* platforms such as Facebook, Google+, WhatsApp and Twitter has created social communication networks. Finally, a wide range of previously offline devices such as TV sets, fridges, coffee machines, cameras as well as sensors, smart wearable devices (..) and machines are now connected to the Internet creating the '*Internet of Things' (IoT)* [my italics] or 'Internet of Everything' (IoE).'

5   This **triangle** represents the three main factors in the institutional structure of Western countries in diagram form: **state, market, and civil society**.

I introduced this triangle in a book I published in 2000, entitled *Nieuwe strategieën voor het publieke domein. Maatschappelijk ondernemen in de praktijk* [New strategies for the public domain. Social entrepreneurship in practice] (Samsom, 2000) (in Dutch), based on lectures I gave in the 1990s, in an era when there was ample political focus on and support for privatization of public services, which I addressed in my lectures. I also included and elaborated the triangle that I used in my previous lectures in the resulting book (p. 61). In the debates I hosted, spoke at, and attended at that time, it struck me that virtually everyone there spoke only about the government or the market, as if the political choice that had to be made was only between these two entities. Citizens, whom the democratic state is intended to serve and on whom the state is based in ideological terms, and even organizations founded by citizens or rooted in civil society, such as philanthropic, non-profit, and non-governmental organizations, did not feature in the analyses, considerations, and policy decisions at all. Based on the triangle and this lack of proper insight, I also introduced the concept of '**societal enterprise' (in Dutch: 'maatschappelijke onderneming'**) to capture the **typically Dutch model** where private-sector non-profit organizations borne out of an earlier citizens' initiative assumed an entrepreneurial role or could be driven by their own values in providing public services. Another insight based on the same kind of triangle-based thinking I later found in a book by V. Pestoff entitled

Beyond Market and State. Social Enterprises and Civil Democracy in a Welfare Society, Ashgate Publishers, 1998. Ultimately, much of this triangle-based structure of three major and autonomous components of the macro-order in Western countries can be traced back to the works of Amitai Etzioni, such as *The Active Society* (1968).

One of the uniquely Dutch elements of the public-sector position of my concept of societal enterprises in the Netherlands is that these enterprises are formally and legally recognized as such through concession systems and licensing. As a result, they have to comply with all kinds of requirements, also in terms of governance, and they are restricted in what kinds of public services they are allowed to provide. Still, the official status as a societal enterprise in a specific domain also entitles them to protection by that same government from unfair competition and allows them to use certain public resources. It is a mutual recognition system, often anchored in law, that leads to the creation of private-sector societal enterprises that operate as an extension to the state's role in providing public services. In some cases, they are even included in legislation that regulates and guarantees public services. In the Netherlands, government-subsidized institutions must furthermore meet a range of requirements that come with public services. They must be accessible to the general public, they must cater to all relevant target groups, they cannot discriminate between clients according to their beliefs or missions or values, and they must adhere to national government rules about quality criteria, both in terms of service level and in terms of their governance structures and behavior. And thirdly, their activities often include generating market revenue from other services that are related to the public services they provide, which they offer to citizens with greater spending power. This makes it harder to clearly position this category of organization, meaning that we have to assess each specific organization separately by looking at its form, mission, and position. Some non-profit organizations are full members of civil society and operate based on the same spontaneous and voluntary commitment of and solidarity-based support among citizens, but better organized or with a greater level of professionalism. Others are more like hybrids, while some even have no ties to or affinity whatsoever with civil society, being instead either an extension of the state or functioning entirely as a market player.

Given the historic and civil background of these societal enterprises and their great influence on public services, it was all the more surprising to see a seemingly political and interests-based preference in the Netherlands for the promotion of market and business and disregard for the interests of citizens and civil activity. Although this certainly is due to the close, legal and financial links between state and these societal enterprises as I have outlined. After all, the concepts of citizenship and citizens' initiatives were closely tied to **the Dutch tradition of a strong and proactive civil society**, as analyzed from a Dutch perspective by The Netherlands Institute for Social Research: see P.L. Hupe, *Hybrid Governance. The Impact of the Nonprofit Sector in the Netherlands*, SCP,

2000. This report, in turn, built on global research led by two American-based researchers, Lester Salamon and Helmut Anheier, which I took part in from the Netherlands: 'The Johns Hopkins Comparative Nonprofit Sector Project', which produced a report entitled *Social Origins of Civil Society: Explaining the Nonprofit Sector Cross-Nationally*, Institute for Policy Studies at Johns Hopkins University, 1996. One of the more surprising outcomes concerned the Netherlands, which came out of the research as the country with the largest nonprofit sector in the world, in comparative terms as a percentage of GDP. I was able to explain to the people behind the report that large parts of the Dutch public sector were in fact historically and legally private and operated on a nonprofit basis, and that this had not been decided by politicians who were trying to keep up with the political fashion of the time, but rather that it was borne out of a more than hundred-year-old citizens' initiative in a typically Dutch active and strong civil society. Nowadays, we, the Dutch, often need foreigners to make us aware of the virtues of this tradition. Foreigners such as Russell Shorto, who linked this Dutch background to the typical aspects of 'Dutch Manhattan', as the Dutch exported this idea of a strong civil society to their colony across the pond. His analysis was published as: *The Island at the Center of the World. The Epic Story of Dutch Manhattan and the Forgotten Colony that Shaped America*, Vintage Books, 2005. Shorto also reminds us of this tradition through an analysis from his contemporary American perspective in: *Amsterdam. A History of the World's Most Liberal City*, First Vintage Books, 2014. Ultimately, Shorto even sees a strong connection between the thinking of one of the Netherlands' historic heroes, Erasmus of Rotterdam, 'his brand of Christian humanism...' and a characterization of Dutch society: 'for a society in which strong individuals cooperate with one another to get things done on their own, as opposed to the medieval model that prevailed elsewhere in Europe, in which a nobleman ruled an estate and serfs (p. 38 and 39).'
It is ultimately highly un-Dutch to completely forget about such a successful export!
In analytical terms, the exact names and institutional domains within this triangle are still subject to ongoing debate. The trichotomy could also be characterized as Political, Economic, and Civil, or Public, Private, and Civil. Food for thought.

6   **Swarm behavior** will be used a lot in this book to refer to one of the effects of the new revolution. The core of the concept of swarm behavior is that individual animals of the same species flock together, seeking the safety of the group. At the same time, every individual in the swarm moves based mainly on the distance to other members of the swarm, regardless of whether these are next to, in front of, behind, above, or underneath them. This synchronization is what keeps the swarm together, even when some members of the swarm come under attack or when the swarm has to (suddenly) change course. From the point of view of the individual, this kind of huddling together and seeking the safety

of the group, is rather paradoxical behavior, because it is somewhat counter-intuitive to move in such large groups, while the main danger comes from predators seeking to pick out the weakest individuals. After all, you are, as a big group that predators see as a delicious meal, actually attracting the attention of the predators that you are so afraid of. Still, the individual members join the swarm because they intuitively count on the confusion such a large group can create, more so than an individual on their own, who would be an easier prey (but who would, in turn, find it easier to hide than such a large swarm). This behavior is also prompted by the assumption that collective intelligence in charting the right course or responding adequately in case of attacks is greater than individual intelligence. The continuous synchronization of movements with other members of the swarm explains why the swarm stays together, while the swarm is also capable of extreme deflections to evade certain external threats or avoid obstacles. In swarm behavior, there are therefore three factors at work: a. the intuition to want to be part of a larger group of members of the same species to seek protection and benefit from collective intelligence, while this is, or may at least partly be, contradictory in rational terms, b. to have and use the technical skills to establish and preserve the connection with the group at all time, and c. to continuously monitor the quality of the connection and distance to each other within the swarm. These same three factors explain why more and more people, brought together by modern technology that caters to, stimulates, and accelerates all three factors, are increasingly displaying ever more intrusive swarm behavior, and in increasingly large groups.

7   See Kevin Laland, *Darwin's Unfinished Symphony. How Culture Made the Human Mind*, Princeton University Press, 2017.

8   In his historic overview of strategic thinking, Lawrence Freedman also starts at the Machiavellian intelligence of primates, our biological ancestors: *Strategy. A History*, Oxford University Press, 2013. So, the cooperation techniques that humans could muster were also very useful in their struggle with groups of animals and human competitors. Human cooperation is certainly also an evolutionary advantage in strategy and survival.

9   For a detailed list and insightful analysis, see: Jo Owen, *Myths of Leadership. Banish the Misconceptions and Become a Great Leader*, Kogan Page, 2018.

10   Briefly outlined in Christensen et al., 'What is Disruptive Innovation?', in the December 2015 issue of *Harvard Business Review*. He has also added numerous strategic analyses of the concept, such as about how existing market parties should respond to imminent **disruption** caused by other parties, such as 'Surviving Disruption', *Harvard Business Review*, December 2012. Besides ample criticism of the flimsy scientific basis and meanwhile rather outdated examples (see Jill Lepore, 'The Disruption Machine. What the Gospel of Innovation Gets Wrong,'

in *The New Yorker*, 2014, who refers to Christensen's work as 'handpicked case studies'), my biggest problem with Christensen's definition and recommendations is his narrow view and well-known rather traditional strategy of how new entrants enter a market: new players start to sell cheaper and better products or provide cheaper and better services, entering the lower end of the market, and are therefore not immediately spotted by existing providers, until they fairly unexpectedly push on into the higher segments and end up 'disrupting' the market for the traditional providers. It is clear from this definition that he was familiar with the new platform-based economy, but did not yet foresee that this is a fundamentally different economy with a different strategic balance of forces. This is why the definition of disruption that I am using differs from Christensen's.

11   Data from *The Economist*, May 5th, 2018, *Special report Financial Inclusion*. The title makes it clear that *The Economist* believes that this new technology can lead to better and faster financial services to consumers anywhere in the world who do not have a lot to spend and who are currently not adequately served by or even excluded from existing financial services provided by traditional commercial service providers.

12   Described clearly with an introduction to the three most important visible technological applications in Andrew McAfee and Erik Brynjolfsson, *Machine, Platform, Crowd. Harnessing our Digital Future*, Norton & Company, 2017. They define platforms as follows: '[…] a platform can be defined as a digital environment characterized by near-zero marginal cost of access, reproduction and distribution'.
An even clearer and more concise analysis of the new economy with an explanation of its most important elements, such as platforms, commons, and elimination of traditional market mechanisms through peer-to-peer bartering, comes from Jeremy Rifkin in *The Zero-Marginal Cost Society: The Internet of Things, the Collaborative Commons and the Eclipse of Capitalism*, Saint Martin's Press, 2015. This leads to entirely different strategies in the modern platform economy (a criticism that I briefly touched on in Note 10 on Christensen as the 'inventor' of the term 'disruption'), a good initial summary is provided by Marshall W. Van Alstyne et al. 'Pipelines, Platforms, and the New Rules of Strategy', *Harvard Business Review*, April 2016.

13   For the proper understanding of the triangle, it is necessary to further explain the concept of **civil society**. In doing so, I will draw concisely on my PhD dissertation (De Waal 2014, op. cit.), and in particular 2.1., p 16 et seq. The concept of civil society can be approached from three perspectives:
1. Organizational: Civil society as a separate part and segment of the institutional order, visible in separate organizations, such as volunteering, community work, philanthropy, and nonprofits.
2. Political: The interplay, mutual influencing, and overlap of the three

segments in the administrative and cultural practices in any country, and how the position of citizens and civil organizations is established legally and politically, and, consequently, how it is treated, especially from the perspective of civil society.

3. Values: The underlying set of values on which the institutional order is built, and based on which citizens learn and exercise their citizenship, and especially also how the three segments influence each other in terms of values. For example: politicians who are not happy to see active citizens (because the state supposedly takes good care of you and you can already vote every four years) or market values that are so dominant for a period of time that even voluntary bartering and commitment between citizens are still captured in monetary terms, while they are, in fact, not based on money or commodities in the practices of the civil society.

Needless to say, the third perspective was the primary one in my PhD research, because the core of the research question lay precisely in the area of values and values-driven behavior. This is why I ultimately argued that civil leaders were to be found across the entire spectrum of the private sectors, and within that spectrum also in executive positions, and not only in the institutionally visible and often traditionally defined domain of civil society, such as volunteering and community work. This latter point is actually a 'politically comfortable and safe' definition of citizenship.

A better definition that also marks the tension with respect to the state would be the following: '[…] "civil society" refers to the free public space in which citizens can advance common interests free from state interference', further based on, among others, Arendt, Habermas and Van Gunsteren in Taco Brandsen *et al.*, *Manufacturing Civil Society. Principles, Practices and Effects*, Palgrave Macmillan 2014, p. 27.

I also cite Richard Bellamy (2008) in my thesis, as he provides a very helpful rundown of the basic elements of citizenship: 'First: membership of or belonging to […] a working democracy certainly requires some elements of a common civic culture […] a degree of trust and solidarity among citizens [...]. Second: Rights. Basically, citizenship is the right to have rights. Third: Participation […] Rights involve duties, not least the duty to exercise the political rights to participate […] (p. 22).

My conclusion was therefore 'In sum […],on the one hand, we should not define civil leadership in such a way that it can only be found in civil society. On the other hand, a focus on the organizational level on which these leaders operate should not be biased by the "rational" or "functional" approaches which are dominant in the spheres of market and state' (p. 29). Eventually these conceptual choices explain why I also looked for '**citizenship in boardrooms**', civil leaders with an executive position at larger organizations, for-profit and non-profit.

14 Summarized as follows: 'Outsourcing, offshoring, freelancing, and other aspects of "unbundling the firm" have increased substantially in recent years as digital technologies have improved and diffused' (McAfee *et al.*, *op. cit.*, p. 314).

15 Needless to say, the most venomous criticism of this development of technocratization came from Henry Mintzberg in 'Management is a practice, not a profession', in *Simply Managing. What Managers Do and Can Do Better*, Berrett-Koehler Publishers, 2013 and *Managing*, Berrett-Koehler Publishers, 2009.

16 This analysis of an overly technical, seemingly rational and neutral approach to management was often also made following and as a reflection on the many management scandals of the late 1990s and early 2000s, such as in Cary Cooper (ed.), *Leadership and Management in the 21st century. Business Challenges of the Future*, Oxford University Press, 2005. The contributors to Cary Cooper's book provide the clearest example of such an analysis, which is also in line with my analysis delivered here, in Ken Starkey and Susan Tempest, 'The Business School and Social Capital'. They refer to management at an organization as a community, describing management as the link between the organization and society as a whole.

17 This claim is also substantiated in a review article on the same phenomenon by Gerald Davis, *Can an Economy Survive without Corporations? Technology and Robust Organizational Alternatives*, Academy of Management Perspectives, 2016.

18 One fine example is a nurse-led home care organization in the Netherlands called **Buurtzorg**. This organization has now even gone international: https://www.buurtzorg.com/about-us. In the end, Buurtzorg, which was founded in 2006, has saved my analysis and design of possible models by putting it into practice in their innovative practices and entrepreneurship. What is particularly significant here is that this innovation sprung from the minds of and was developed by care professionals themselves, not by managers and therefore not from a management perspective or interest.

19 This shift in the thinking about optimum organizational forms is partly already ongoing, driven by motives other than technological and strategic ones, such as the pursuit of a more values-driven approach and social responsibility. One fine example, where the evolution of humans and humanity was also explicitly an important driver as I outlined in Note 3, is: Frederick Laloux, *Reinventing Organizations. A Guide to Creating Organizations Inspired by the Next Stage of Human Consciousness*, Nelson Parker, 2014. He bases his organizational design on three building blocks: self-management (as amply referred to above), (inner) wholeness (and therefore not only on rationality or technology), and evolutionary goal

(which in his description is very similar to the aforementioned concept of swarm behavior) (p. 74).

20 Refer to Raffaella Sadun *et al.*, 'Why do we undervalue competent management. Understanding management's value', *Harvard Business Review*, 2017. For a somewhat nostalgic look back that asks 'whatever happened to management?', Mintzberg also goes into the path that management must take to regain its relevance and be taken seriously again, whereby management would supplement the required leadership at organizations, as is also my view, explained in the further paragraphs on leadership: Henry Mintzberg: *Managing, op. cit.*

21 John P. Kotter 'What leaders really do', *Harvard Business Review*, December 2001

22 Particularly refer to the works of Prof. Dr. Frans de Waal for proof of this for competencies such as intelligence, empathy, moral behavior, and many more.

23 This debate started in, among others, Henry Mintzberg, *The Rise and Fall of Strategic Planning*, Prentice Hall, 1994 and Henry Mintzberg et al., *Strategy Safari: a Guided Tour Through the Wilds of Strategic Management*, The Free Press, 1998.

24 A. K. Olson & B.K. Simerson, *Leading with **Strategic Thinking***, Wiley, 2015. They provide a concise outline of the associated strategic competencies that rather reads like a very fitting profile of the goddess Athena in Greek mythology: 'The ability to recognize and take advantage of personal strengths and mitigate personal weaknesses; comfort with and ability to understand complexity; the ability to recognize related concepts and principles; self-confidence and belief in oneself; comfort with ambiguity and uncertainty; a willingness to take risks; the courage of conviction; the willingness to draw conclusions and make decisions; personal assertiveness' (p 6).

25 One quote that echoes my analysis of the unpredictability of life and therefore strategy comes from Carl von Clausewitz: 'The role of chance could never be eliminated in the conduct of war; one of the marks of the great military mind was therefore the recognition that its flux and fog could never be addressed by a rigid set of rules.' (in Elisabeth Samet (ed.), *Leadership. Essential Writings by Our Greatest Thinkers*, Norton & Company, 2015, p. 221.)

26 For a clear link between thinking about connections that is more in tune with today's interconnected times thanks to the Digital Civil Revolution, such as cybernetics and complexity theory, and the impossibility of predicting the future, refer to Nassim Nicholas Taleb, *Antifragile*, and then in particular Book III, 'A Nonpredictive View of the World', Random House, 2012.
One of the most incisive analyses of why the traditional practice of '**forecasting**'

does not work and even less so in today's disruptive times comes from Richard Bookstaber in *The End of Theory: Financial Crisis, The Failure of Economics and the Sweep of Human Interaction*, Princeton University Press, 2017. Bookstaber lists five clear and underestimated phenomena in the quantitative approach to the future. First, he points to the phenomenon of *emergence*, which is the phenomenon that complex patterns can produce new outcomes, as also seen above in my analysis of the impact of 'swarm behavior.' Secondly, he describes *non-ergodicity*, which is the phenomenon that the same pattern does not always produce the same outcome. Thirdly, there is *radical uncertainty*, which means that part of the future is simply unknowable to people, which is in line with my criticism that the future cannot be known rationally, let alone be planned step by step. Fourthly, there is the phenomenon of *computational irreducibility*, which states that no model can be complex enough to cover all possible know-able factors and their effects. And fifthly and lastly, Bookstaber highlights the phenomenon of *reflexivity*, which means that possible outcomes and the associ-ated messages will, in turn, influence behavior that will lead to outcomes that differ from the ones that were initially predicted. This latter point is similar to my point that modern technology leads to an acceleration and reinforcement of information feedback. Eternal, continuous and cumulative, feedback loops can simply not be caught in a single framework. This chimes, of course, with an older argument that says that predictions themselves influence the future and future reflection and behavior, and can therefore be self-fulfilling or self-defeating.

27   See, among others, Humberto Maturana and Francisco Varela, *Autopoeisis and Cognition. The Realization of the Living*, Reidel Publishing Company, 1972. The most fundamental, in my view anyway, book about systems engineering in combination with communication theory is: Anthony Wilden, *System and Structure. Essays in Communication and Exchange*, Tavistock Publications, 1972. Also refer to Melanie Mitchell, *Complexity. A Guided Tour*, Oxford University Press, 2009 and Jamshid Gharajedaghi, *Systems Thinking. Managing Chaos and Complexity: A Platform for Designing Business Architecture*, Elsevier, 2006.

28   To indicate that the same kind of shift can be seen in economics and thinking about the economy, the economist Jean Tirole, who won the Nobel Memorial Prize in Economic Sciences, published an interesting collection of essays with the captivating title: ***Economics for the Common Good***, Princeton University Press, 2017. In these essays (and in the title), Tirole emphasizes that economics must not isolate itself or lock itself up in a strictly market-economic mindset or the false rationality of extensive quantitative research that is based on the fictitious portrayal of humans as homo economicus. After all, this latter concept as the sole characterization of human behavior and motives has already been wiped out by a series of psychological and game theory experiments. Tirole therefore positions economics clearly in the domain of social sciences, which is nothing new for anyone outside the scientific village of economists, but obvi-

ously still an important viewpoint to emphasize. This is again and yet more proof that the insights of Thomas Kuhn into the nature of scientific knowledge, which claim that social cohesion and small-mindedness in scientific circles lead to the dominant paradigm for quite some time and that new scientifically substantiated insights can push that dominant paradigm only aside when the old rulers have lost their positions, see: *The Structure of Scientific Revolutions*, University Chicago Press, 1996 (1962).

29 See note 6. For a highly readable introduction, check Len Fisher, *The Perfect Swarm. The Science of Complexity in Everyday Life*, Basic Books, 2009.

30 A good introduction to this phenomenon in relation to the rise of new technologies and its huge impact on the public sectors and society is (in Dutch): M. Aslander, *Nooit Af. Een nieuwe kijk op de fundamenten van ons leven, werk, school, zorg, overheid en management*, Business Contact, 2017.

31 Further covered and detailed in 'Energiecoöperaties: ambities, handelingsperspectief en interactie met gemeenten'(in Dutch), PBL Netherlands Environmental Assessment Agency, 2014.

32 Marjut Johansson et al., 'Discourse, Context & Media', Researchgate, October 2017, see also Assaf Frances, 'Creating the digital agora', 20 November 2014, www.nesta.org.uk/blog.

33 In his **Rhetoric** (see George Kennedy, ed., *On Rhetoric. A Theory of Civic Discourse*, Oxford University Press, 2007), **Aristotle** distinguishes three core elements: Ethos (a visible and consistent connect between speaker, subject, and primary message), Pathos (an (emotional) appeal to the public to join the thought process and get involved), and Logos (the rational substantiation and reasoning in the argument). In later writings, Aristotle added a fourth element: Kairos, the criterion for rhetoric success at the right place and the right time. This has several elements to it. The first is the timing of the rhetoric when it is delivered, like a speech, linked to the context, and the context as the audience perceives it at that time. Then, as a second element, there is the timing of the design in the speech itself: how is the rhythm of the rhetoric linked to the message and purpose of the speech?

34 Maurice McLeod in *The Guardian*, May 3, 2017.

35 An insightful basic analysis of what is needed for public leadership, albeit set in less disruptive times of the public debate in the still recent past: Paul 't Hart, *Understanding Public Leadership*, Palgrave Macmillan, 2014. For an analysis that ropes in rhetoric and Aristotle, like note 32, read John Uhr's *Prudential*

Public Leadership. Promoting Ethics in Public Policy and Administration, Palgrave Macmillan, 2015.

36 Read *The Economist*, 'Hot under the collar', July 18th 2018, p. 20-21.

37 Taken from Julie Simon *et al.,* 'Digital Democracy. The Tools for Transforming Political Engagement', Nesta Foundation www.nesta.org.uk, January 2017.

38 This is all the more urgent because the number of **democracies** in the world is falling for the first time since WWII. One comparative analysis concludes that there is a correlation between economic wealth and democracy and that non-democracies are doing increasingly well economically, and are therefore not giving 'the people' an incentive to demand greater say and therefore democracy), as well as the cultural clout, i.e. that the cultural dominance of the Western mindset and culture is reducing sharply: see Yascha Mounk and Roberto Foa, 'The End of the Democratic Century' in *Foreign Affairs*, May/June 2018. This can be specified further in the connection between middle class and democracy, which is at the heart of Fukuyama's *The End of History*. Such as Haroon Sheikh: 'The middle class is a large group of people in professions that are not tied to the state or traditional patterns of authority, giving them an impetus to challenge a closed regime.' ('Embedding Technopolis', Boom Amsterdam 2017).
In a recent article (June 16, 2018), *The Economist* adds further lessons in this context, under the ominous title 'How Democracy Dies': 'The main one is that institutions matter. Western democracy promotion had often focused on the quality of elections. In fact, independent judges and noisy journalists are democracy's first line of defense… The second is that the reversals have been driven by opportunistic strongmen rather than the voter's embrace of illiberal democracy. The last, more uncomfortable lesson is that the example set by mature democracies matter' (p. 7). The importance of the free press was recently further underlined in an open letter from over 300 newspapers to President Trump in August 2018.
This international **'undermining' of the constitutional fabric of representative democracy**, added to the technological reinforcement of the need and resources for direct democracy mainly relate to lessons 1 and 3. This consequently leads to huge and fundamental pressure to innovate current legal arrangements and governance practices, in the same way as disruption in the market forced players to innovate. The conclusion we can draw from this is therefore a twofold one. On the hand, there is the rise of non-democracies that are creating wealth for their people and are thus able to ignore calls from the middle classes for greater democracy. On the other hand, there is the emergence of strongmen who can only be stopped by strong institutions in mature democracies. Such strongmen often seize their chance to acquire greater power in immature democracies, sometimes behind a facade of formal democracy to maintain face on the global stage.

This kind of 'undermining' of representative democracy that is seen across the globe, plus the technological reinforcement of the need and resources for direct democracy, which will, in turn, have to lead to a fundamental change in current democracies, mean that democracy currently finds itself in an internationally and culturally fragile predicament as it is about to be disrupted by technology. In addition to the conclusion that democracies need to be mature in their (broadly defined) constitutional structure, the pressing question that arises is whether these democracies have the capacity to adapt and learn to be able to withstand the new technological challenges and to incorporate them into their constitutional structure. Or is this perhaps a case of progress holding us back, where being an advanced democracy actually inhibits us from making further progress: are mature democracies so mature that their rigidity and complacency is causing their demise?

Unfortunately, I currently do not have the impression that many of our professional politicians realize how urgently fundamental innovation of democracy is needed. Instead of the political strategy on the second front specified above (furtherance of the country and democracy), the political strategy on the first front tends to prevail; how do these technologies help us win campaigns and get re-elected?

39 T. Nam, 'Government-Driven Participation and Collective Intelligence', *Information*, 2016.

40 The thing is to study and learn from the first-known true democracy in history, Athenian polis democracy, which dates back around 2,300 years. For clear introductions and critical reflections, read M.I. Finley, *Democracy Ancient and Modern*, Rutgers University Press, 1988 and Paul Woodruff, *First Democracy. The Challenge of an Ancient Idea*, Oxford University Press, 2005.

41 An incisive analysis of what is going on with representative democracy due to the advent of **direct democracy** on the back of new technologies comes from Yascha Mounk in *The People versus Democracy: Why Our Freedom is in Danger and How to Save It*, Harvard University Press, 2018. The only thing is that this analysis also focuses more on the demise of current forms of representative democracy than the subsequent answers to make representative democracy functional again by embracing direct democracy as it is now technologically evoked and culturally expected by 'the people'. This analysis therefore symbolizes the so-called rational and nuanced, semi-scientific analyses that, although critical, subconsciously and implicitly shows a preference for traditional 'professional' politics and not for this direct democracy, as that, in light of their ideological preference, puts too much power in the hands of the people. The ideological gravy of belief in the now well-known form of democracy has seeped through into the deepest consciousness of many people over the past few decades. As far as this is concerned, we had better listen to Paul Woodruff (*op.cit.*): 'If it is

not dangerous, if it does not ask to consider changes that frighten the establishment, it is not about democracy' (p. ix.), something even social scientists have to learn again.

42 An initial explanation of this is available in James Surowiecki's *The Wisdom of Crowds*, Anchor Books, 2005.
For a link between this phenomenon and democracy, there is Paul Woodruff's (*op. cit.*,) concept of **'citizen wisdom,'** which he takes from the core of Athenian democracy that 'the heart of democracy is the idea that ordinary people have the wisdom they need to govern themselves' (p. 145).
Helbing, *op. cit.*, also points to the benefit new technology will have for wisdom, which is that it greatly increases people's freedom to participate and therefore makes the participating group enormously bigger and more diverse. New technology gets entirely new groups involved, which were never reached by traditional information and consultation methods such as town hall meetings, flyering, or newspaper articles: 'diversity wins, not the best' (p. 160). Elbing, *op. cit.*

43 Refer to Emiliana De Blaso and Michele Sorice, *Populism between Direct Democracy and the Technological Myth*, Palgrave Communications, 2018.

44 OECD, *Trust and Public Policy: How Better Governance Can Help Rebuild Public Trust*, Paris, 2017.

45 'Estonia, the Digital Republic', *The NewYorker*, December 2017.

46 '*Regels voor het digitale mensenpark. 'Telen' en 'temmen' van de mens via kiembaanmodificatie en persuasieve technologie*, (in Dutch) Den Haag, Rathenau Institute 2017.

47 For the Netherlands and with lots of Dutch public and political examples, worked out (in Dutch) in Dr. S.P.M. de Waal, 'Transformatie van publiek leiderschap. Disruptieve burgers als uitdaging voor bestuur en politiek', in Gabriel van den Brink (ed.), *Waartoe is Nederland op aarde?*, Boom, 2018. One of the conclusions from this analysis is the following: '*[…] a common mistake made by many political parties is that they are focused more on the state and careers in government than on maintaining close ties with civil society]*' (p. 292) [Translated from the Dutch].

48 Tony Bovaird *et al.*, 'Activating Collective Co-Production of Public Services: Influencing Citizens to Participate in Complex Governance Mechanisms in the UK', *International Review of Administrative Sciences*, Volume 82, 2016.

49 See 'Images Aren't Everything. AI, Radiology and the Future of Work', in *The Economist*, June 9, 2018.

50 Much of the literature on this subject describes the power and influence that co-production gives so-called frontline workers, as well as the breaking down of the outdated supply-side approach of New Public Management. A good early voice in this debate is John Alford with his book *Engaging Public Sector Clients. From Service-Delivery to Co-Production*, Palgrave Macmillan, 2009.

51 *Reclaiming Public Services. How cities and citizens are turning back privatisation*, Transnational Institute and Population Services International, Media Briefing June 2017.

52 Amber Alert is, in fact, a great example of the professional and institutional resistance against citizens' influence. Amber Alert was created at state level in the U.S. in 1996, and went national in 2003. It was introduced in the Netherlands in 2008, even though the mobile technology and practical use needed for it had been available long before that. In many countries, it is, despite its proven effectiveness, still not operational.

53 'Stitch Fix's CEO on selling personal style to the mass market', *Harvard Business Review*, May/June 2018.

54 For an insightful analysis of these new relationships and the power struggle and tensions, refer to Joel Migdal, *State in Society. Studying How States and Societies Transform and Constitute One Another*, Cambridge University Press, 2001, especially Chapter 4: 'An Anthropology of the State: Struggles for Domination'.

55 Rifkin (*op. cit.*, 2014), who, like many others speaks of a third industrial revolution, makes this same link, based also on his analysis of the evident weaknesses in the 'old' economy in comparison to the platform economy, which '[…] is already boosting productivity to the point where the marginal cost of producing many goods and services is nearly zero, making them practically free and shareable on the emerging Collaborative Commons' (p. 13). He then goes on to devote an entire section to the rise of the commons, starting with an article with the brilliant title: 'The Comedy of the Commons' (p. 187 et seq.).

56 *Building People-Centered Enterprises in Latin America and the Caribbean. Cooperative Case Studies*, Cooperatives Europe, 2014.

57 Essential Elinor Ostrom reading includes E. Ostrom, *Governing the Commons: the Evolution of Institutions for Collective Action*, Cambridge University Press, 1990

and Elinor Ostrom *et al.*, *Rules, Games and Common-pool Resources*, University of Michigan Press, 2007.

58   For a historical insight, read Tine de Moor, *The Dilemma of the Commoners. Understanding the Use of Common Pool Resources in Long-Term Perspective*, Cambridge University Press, 2015.

59   Interview in *Woman's Own*, 1987.

60   More about **citizenship values** in Dr. S.P.M. de Waal, *The Value(s) of Civil Leaders*, Eleven, 2014. In this study, the values pattern came from the preparatory work done by Arjo Klamer in 'Waarden doen ertoe in de economie', in P. de Beer and C.J. Schuyt (in Dutch), *Bijdragen aan normen en waarden*, WRR, 2004. He has recently published a book in English that goes into one of the themes that is also addressed in this book along the lines of values analysis, namely how traditional economic thinking has become overly detached from human society: *Doing the Right Thing. A Value Based Economy*, Ubiquity Press, 2017.

61   For an accurate analysis of what is going on here, see: D. Helbing, *op. cit.* He points primarily to the risks when governments use these technologies to gain greater control over their citizens. He rightfully states that we are at a cross-roads: either we maintain the hierarchical model of an all-encompassing and all-knowing government, which based on so-called paternalism, but also political power and bureaucratic organizational mania, monitors its citizens increasingly closely (in which case the technological revolution is not used to overhaul relationships between government and citizens), or we go for an active, self-willed, self-learning, and self-organizing civil society, supported by the government or another form of organized collectivity.

62   Quoted in Jo Owen, *op. cit.*

63   See, among others, Herman van Gunsteren: *A Theory of Citizenship. Organizing Plurality in Contemporary Democracies*, Boulder Westview Press, 1998

64   Rik Peeters in T. Brandsen *et al.*, *Manufacturing Civil Society, op.cit,*, p. 17.

65   Quote from H. van Gunsteren, 'Admission to Citizenship', *Ethics* 98 (4), p. 731-741.

66   There is now quite some literature available on this subject. At the INSEAD business school: N. Craig Smith and Markus Scholz, *Big Investors Call for Company Attention to Social Purpose*; *What Next?*, 2018; interview with Kenneth Frazier van Merck: 'Businesses exist to deliver value to society', *HBR,* 2018; Rodriguez Vila and Bharadwaj: 'Competing on social purpose', *HBR,* 2017.

67 The concept is also explained accurately and substantiated in M. McIntosh *et al.*: *Corporate Citizenship. Successful Strategies for Responsible Companies*, Financial Times Pitman Publishing, 1998. In my book (*op. cit.*, 2000) (in Dutch), I also devote a chapter to corporate social responsibility (CSR), as the umbrella term for these new obligations for commercial enterprises.

68 For an accurate summary of this case, read: 'Facebook and Democracy. The Antisocial Network', *The Economist*, March 24, 2018.

69 Jo Owen, *op. cit.*

70 This is what Sydney Finkelstein et al., in their book *Strategic Leadership*, Oxford University Press, 2009, call 'the managerial mystique': 'the strong human tendency to believe that leaders matter. People seek to have heroes and villains as a way of explaining organizational successes and failures', p. 38.

71 For an engaging methodological outline and a link to Aristotle, see Bent Flyvbjerg *et al.*, *Real Social Science. Applied Phronesis*, Cambridge University Press, 2012. In this book, the authors formulate the same methodological criticism of empirical social sciences as I have offered based on a normative approach to human existence and humanity and what every human activity, including social sciences, contributes to that, as is pinpointed in the description of my academic study on Andragology in my biography. For a good application of the ensuing anthropological methods, refer to R. Rhodes et al. (eds.), *Observing Government Elites. Up Close and Personal*, Palgrave MacMillan, 2007.

72 Burns (in J. Burns, *Leadership*, Harper&Row, 1979, and other works) follows a similar path with his emphasis on transformational leadership (as opposed to transactional leadership), leading to the moral uplifting of these leaders' following, as the intrinsic objective of this kind of leader. Other versions of such visions of leadership always link to a so-called moral compass or a public-service mentality.

73 See, for example, Barbara Kellerman**,** *Bad Leadership. What it is. How it happens. Why it matters*, Harvard Business School Press, 2004 and B. Kellerman and M. Kets de Vries, *Lessons on Leadership by Terror. Finding ZhakaZulu in the Attic,* Edward Elgar, 2005. As an antidote to this one-sided image it is good to mention that Barbara Kellerman also edited and commented on typical examples of Good leadership in 'Leadership. Essential selections on power, authority and influence', McGraw Hill 2010.

74 I have pointed out on several occasions now that there are all kinds of ambiguity, myths, and conceptual confusion with respect to the concept of **Good leader**

and (even more so) Sacred leaders, and therefore with respect to leadership and morality. The debate ranges from the idea that only (morally) Good leaders are true Leaders (Burns) to the idea that only leaders who explicitly and openly take morality into account (and therefore primarily have a 'Good' story) are part of the Good camp. On top of that, there is the rather confusing question of whom to believe, the leader who claims to be moral, his or her followers who claim that their leader is a moral person, or a possible 'objective' observer who claims the leader is a moral person based on his or her Good Works. This is quite the predicament. I find primatology particularly helpful in this respect: 'It is best to learn from biologists, who long ago decided that a focus on the evolutionary level of explanation required them to ignore motivation [...] Thus, even if we explain a certain behavior as based on reciprocity, it is good to realize that reciprocity is not a motivation.' (Paul J. Zak (ed.), *Moral Markets. The Critical Role of Values in the Economy*, Princeton University Press, 2008.)

At the end of the day, it led to me focusing primarily on the publicly visible social result of a civil leader in my doctoral dissertation. Not on the intentions to be Good or the verbal claims that the leader wanted to do Good, but instead on the actually achieved result for society (although this subsequently raises the methodological problem of how to show that the civil leader can indeed be credited for it: the personal connection with what has been achieved and the achieving of the result itself!), in this research this is captured in the concept of 'public value' (see Mark H. Moore: *Creating Public Value: Strategic Management in Government*, Harvard University Press, 1995), but another good concept is 'the 'common good' (which has also been part of the mission of Public SPACE from the start), for example in David Chrislip and Ed O'Malley, *For the Common Good. Redefining Civic Leadership*, KLC Press, 2013.

It is great to see, and entirely in line with the switch in economic thinking that I identified earlier, that many are meanwhile realizing that concepts such as 'public value' and 'the common good' can and must also apply to strategic choices in the world of business. Mark Moore and Sanjeev Khagram capture this realization in the title of a brochure of Harvard Kennedy School: *On Creating Public Value. What Business Might Learn from Government about Strategic Management*. An additional attempt was made by Michael Porter (who happens to be one of the gurus of strategy in the world of business) and Mark Kramer (2007, 2011) who coined the concept of 'shared value': 'the concept rests on the premise that both economic and social progress must be addressed' (S. de Waal, *op.cit.* 2014, p. 94).

75   Jo Owen, *op. cit.*

76   Someone who goes into this in the greatest depth and with the amplest substantiation is Claude Lefort in *Machiavelli in the Making*, Northwestern UP, 2015.

77 An engaging further step away from this misunderstood path of formal rules that are obediently applied to come to leadership (which is in itself a contradiction, as merely following rules is not exactly part of the definitions of leadership) and even (moral) Good leadership and the right strategic choices, can be found in the Dutch report by the Dutch association of non-executive board members in the health care industry entitled 'Mandaat en Moeras. Over het maatschappelijk mandaat als grondbeginsel van intern toezicht in de zorg' (2017)

78 This latter point has always been the argument of Milton Friedman of the Chicago School of Economics, who even went so far as to claim that philanthropic actions or corporate social responsibility are not in the best interest of shareholders, and therefore counterproductive in business. Maximization of profits was always companies' sole duty toward shareholders, who could then do with their share of the profit whatever they wanted, including give it away or fund social initiatives. See, for example, his article 'Rethinking the Social Responsibility of Business. Making Philanthropy Out of Obscenity,' in *Reason*, October 2005. In this article, he most vehemently further illustrates his own arguments by stating the following: 'It would be inconsistent of me to call on corporate executives to refrain from this hypocritical window-dressing because it harms the foundations of a free society. That would be to call on them to exercise a 'social responsibility'!'

79 I have never endorsed this way of thinking. In my book from the year 2000 (*op. cit.*), in which I focus on the importance of entrepreneurship of and for citizens in realizing social goals (leading to the concept of 'societal enterprise'), I devoted a chapter to the importance of corporate social responsibility in the world of business.

80 Arjo Klamer, *op. cit.*, 2017.

81 See, for example, McIntyre A. (1981), *After Virtue: A Study in Moral Theory*, University of Notre Dame Press, 1981. There is ample literature that associates leadership with values and virtues, such as: Al Gini and Ronald M. Green, *10 Virtues of Outstanding Leaders. Leadership & Character*, Wiley-Blackwell, 2013. For a dissenting opinion that shows that it is not all holiness and virtue when pursuing the common good: *The Power of Unreasonable People. How Social Entrepreneurs Create Markets that Change the World*, Harvard Business Press, 2008.

82 I already mentioned **Aristotle**'s lessons in rhetoric and how these are still relevant in modern political analyses, such as in my assessment of the Clinton vs. Trump case. There is also ample reference material available on virtues, character, ethics, and virtues assessments in **practical wisdom**. I will limit myself to a few relevant titles here. About virtues and character: Nancy Sherman, *The Fabric*

of Character. Aristotle's Theory of Virtue, Clarendon Paperbacks, 1989. About phronesis, Aristotle's concept of practical wisdom: Barry Schwartz and Kenneth Sharpe, *Practical Wisdom. The Right Way to Do the Right Thing*, Riverhead Books, 2010. For fascinating and apt descriptions, read Olav Eikeland and Peter Lang, *The Ways of Aristotle. Aristotelian Phroneisis, Aristotelian Philosophy of Dialogue and Action Research*, International Academic Publishers, 2008: 'The call is for ways of thinking, speaking and doing things that enhance the personal mastery of everyday challenges, both individually and collectively, in cognitively, ethically, and politically acceptable and responsible ways' (p. 16); 'The perspective pervading the writings of Aristotle is not how "they" behave or the project of describing 'their' properties […] 'His perspective is throughout how *we* normally do things, or, even more, how *we* do things at our best.'(p. 28) And finally, there is the following concise introduction to Aristotle's writing on philosophy and politics: Alan Ryan, *On Aristotle. Saving Politics from Philosophy*, Liveright Publishing Corporation, 2014.

83 For a fine comparison of Western and Eastern leadership thinking, read: Gregory P. Prastacos et al. (eds.), *Leadership through the Classics. Learning Management and Leadership from Ancient East and West Philosophy*, Springer Verlag, 2012. Confucius is in this respect a bit confusing: on the one hand he put a lot of emphasis on the need of having men of excellent character and virtue (exemplary persons) in leadership roles, while on the other hand he put much emphasis on the rules and rites they needed to know and follow and that, in turn, led to his belief that these virtuous men could only be found in the elite and educated class.

84 For further details and explanation of this values-driven side of government officials, no matter how paradoxical it sometimes is, through the strong emphasis in that context on formal and legal requirements, routines, and principles, read George Frederickson's *The Spirit of Public Administration*, Jossey Bass, 1997.

85 The argument also likened the issue of remuneration to the professional soccer market, which, if you know both markets well as I do, is an argument that does not hold. As a member of the board of professional soccer club FC Utrecht, I'm quite familiar with this market. There really is such a thing as a soccer market, a market of bartering for and actively scouting soccer players. Players are scouted internationally at a young age and players are bought and sold internationally, and not only at the highest levels, whereby the talented youngsters involved actually have to move, often taking their parents with them. Such an international move is sometimes to a country nearby, within Europe, but sometimes also to faraway countries. This is very different from the management industry, where international transfers of the young and talented are initiated and paid for by the young students themselves (or their parents) by enrolling in a business school program or courses in other countries. In the process, these youngsters

incur extensive personal debt to pay their tuition fees. These are proper invest-ments in oneself. Once they are established managers, on the other hand, they are much less likely to make international transfers, and even less so in the form of a self-investment. If they do, it is generally through management develop-ment programs of the corporation where they already hold a management position. This is basically no more than a minor and risk-free investment in the strength and scope of their resume, while for the employer, who pays for it, it is an attempt to improve skills and inspire loyalty to the company.

86 Proof of this came almost at the same time, thanks to PhD research at Erasmus University Rotterdam. Manuel Lokin concluded from his research into remunera-tion of top-level executives that it is pointless to compare their remuneration with that of other executives, and that such comparisons can certainly not be used as the basis on which to establish their remuneration. In fact, he confirms my view that there is no international market for managers at all: Manuel Lokin, *De bezoldiging van bestuurders van beursgenoteerde vennootschappen* [The remuneration of executives of listed companies], Wolters Kluwer, July 25, 2018.

87 One article that paints an accurate picture of this trend, albeit without the disruption-based explanations I am providing in this book, is: Aaron Chatterji and Michael Toffel ,'The new CEO activists. A playbook for polarized political times', *Harvard Business Review,* January / February 2018.

88 The reason for not including the pure government sector in the definition of civil leadership in my dissertation was largely a theoretical one. It is hard to settle on a consistent definition of civil leadership across both the public and the private sector. There was, however, also a practical reason to disregard government, both politics and civil service: the mechanisms for selection and success of leadership are very different in government compared to private-sector environ-ments. As a result, personal motives and considerations, including personal values (which the research focused on), have a very different kind of influence, which is harder to unearth in one single study. On top of that, there is the fact that self-reporting (which the study was partly based on through interviews) will be very different for both groups due to the entirely different kind of public rhetoric training when it comes to motives and values. After all, this also comes with mutually differing forms of accountability and performance assessments. And finally, the study crucially focused on the issue of values, the influence of the governance context from which the leader operates. In a government setting, this influence is really of a very different nature for anyone who is looking to display leadership in a government role, when compared to any kind of private or public services context. Therefore, that particular part of the study focused on a comparison between the impact of values in private-sector governance contexts, i.e. for-profit, non-profit, and informal active citizenship, and not in government-governance context(s).

89 *Great Thinkers*, School of Life Press, 2016.

90 For a broader, more international take on social entrepreneurship, read: Alex
    Nicholls (ed.), *Social Entrepreneurship. New Models of Sustainable Social Change*,
    Oxford University Press, 2008. For further reference, read my early books of 1994
    and 2000, in Dutch, see note 5.

91 A nice new example is the Kialo platform (www.kialo.com), which claims to
    deliver 'noise-free' digital debates. Everyone can submit a topic for debate,
    there is a tool for peer review of the arguments used, and there is an open 'chat'
    feature. This platform publicly taps into the growing suspicion of current social
    media, claiming that they don't want to be like the 'pervasive social media and
    the associated 'noise' caused by algorithms, clutters and the echo chamber
    effect….'. And, there are many more hope-inspiring initiatives, like ParkinsonNet,
    which originated in Holland but is now rapidly rolling out in other countries as
    well. It is a network of professionals who specialize in the symptoms and treat-
    ment of Parkinson's disease. Around 3,000 such professionals have meanwhile
    signed up to the Dutch website, sharing knowledge and insights. This platform
    is also open to patients, who are invited to search this huge network of specialist
    professionals to find the best and most fitting help (www.parkinsonnet.nl).